DEBATING RHETORICAL NARRATOLOGY

THEORY AND INTERPRETATION OF NARRATIVE
James Phelan, Peter J. Rabinowitz, and Katra Byram, Series Editors

DEBATING RHETORICAL NARRATOLOGY

ON THE SYNTHETIC, MIMETIC, AND THEMATIC ASPECTS OF NARRATIVE

Matthew Clark

AND

James Phelan

THE OHIO STATE UNIVERSITY PRESS
COLUMBUS

Copyright © 2020 by The Ohio State University.
All rights reserved.

Library of Congress Cataloging-in-Publication Data is available online at catalog.loc.gov.

Cover design by Martyn Schmoll
Text design by Juliet Williams
Type set in Adobe Minion Pro

*Matthew Clark dedicates this work to his partner,
Reva Marin, and to the memory of Truffles,
a noble dog who filled our lives with love.*

*James Phelan dedicates this work to the loving memory
of his parents, James Joseph Phelan (1923–1974)
and Margaret O'Connell Phelan (1926–2018).*

CONTENTS

Preface An Origin Story and a Description of Our Debate
MATTHEW CLARK AND JAMES PHELAN   ix

INTRODUCTION
            MATTHEW CLARK   1

CHAPTER 1 The Synthetic Aspect
            MATTHEW CLARK   19

CHAPTER 2 The Mimetic Aspect
            MATTHEW CLARK   53

CHAPTER 3 The Thematic Aspect
            MATTHEW CLARK   95

CHAPTER 4 Narrative as Rhetoric and the MTS Model
            JAMES PHELAN   135

CHAPTER 5 The Mimetic, the Synthetic, and the Criterion of
            Correspondence; Or Audiences, the Mimetic Illusion,
            and Ghosts
            JAMES PHELAN   151

CHAPTER 6	The Thematic and the Relation between Comprehensiveness and Correspondence	
	JAMES PHELAN	171
CHAPTER 7	MTS, Fictionality, and Nonfiction: Tobias Wolff's "Old China"	
	JAMES PHELAN	187
CHAPTER 8	"Yes, but..."	
	MATTHEW CLARK	197

Bibliography   215

Index   225

PREFACE

An Origin Story and a Description of Our Debate

THIS BOOK originated in Matthew Clark's engagement with James Phelan's work in rhetorical narratology, especially Phelan's ideas about three components of narrative—and of readerly interest in it: the mimetic, the thematic, and the synthetic (since we contest each other's definitions of these terms, we won't offer definitions here). Matthew found that Jim's ideas were useful but not entirely satisfactory, and as he worked with them, especially in his teaching, he developed his own ideas about the three components. Rather than simply writing a monograph advocating his positions and correcting Jim's, Matthew informed Jim about his work, and then the two of us concocted the plan to conduct the dialogue found in this book. In addition to departing from the usual format of critical combat in which authors write separate tracts proclaiming the superiority of their views, our dialogue, we hoped, could model a friendlier but still deeply serious kind of exchange. Since Jim had, in a sense, gone first in his various proposals about the three components in various publications since he first introduced them in *Reading People, Reading Plots* (1989), we agreed that here Matthew should go first, Jim should respond, and Matthew should offer a final (for now) rejoinder. In this way, each of us would have two turns—though Jim's first turn is outside this book.

In adopting this format, we also hoped to achieve some other benefits: learning from each other ("I hadn't thought of it that way, but you're right"); developing fuller understandings about what's at stake in our ongoing disagreements (What does it mean to be committed to a rhetorical approach?); and above all generating sharper insights into the workings of narrative—and the ways we work on it.

In conducting the dialogue, we decided to hold ourselves accountable to the larger community of narrative theorists by addressing them rather than—or, better, in addition to—each other. Thus, we refer to each other in the third person rather than the second. Our disagreements range from local matters (e.g., how to read particular scenes in Orwell's *1984*) to global ones (Are Matthew's proposals, as he suggests, friendly amendments to Jim's positions, or are they, as Jim suggests, rooted in a fundamentally different conception of narrative?). (At the global level, we preserve the sense of our disagreement by using different abbreviations for our models: for Matthew SMT, and for Jim MTS.) While each of us of course firmly believes that his arguments about the disputed matters are the more convincing ones, those beliefs exist alongside our knowledge that our readers will not all side with one of us—and that many (most?) will have their own views about both local and global issues. Indeed, on some issues, we anticipate that at least some readers will respond by saying, "A pox on both your houses," even as we hope that more readers will say, "Yes, but" and "Yes, and." We welcome this range of responses because they provide opportunities to expand the dialogue and thus further illuminate the workings and effects of both narrative and narrative theory.

Whether the execution of our dialogue is sufficiently effective to generate all the positive effects we aspire to is not for us to say. What we can say is that we have learned from each other—and very much enjoyed the process of learning. We can also express our profound hope that our readers will find both some instruction and some delight in their engagement with our dialogue.

We express our gratitude to two acquisitions editors at the OSU Press, Lindsay Martin, who encouraged us early on to engage in this debate, and Ana Jimenez-Moreno, who guided the results through to publication. We also express deep gratitude to Peter Rabinowitz, Katra Byram, and the external readers for their wise comments that have led us to write a better book. In addition, Matthew sends a shout-out to Brian Richardson and to David Richter for encouragement at different stages of the project, and Jim sends one to Nicolas Potkalitsky and to Drew Sweet for their editorial assistance. We both would like to thank Evan Van Tassell for his work on the index. We are also grateful to the many colleagues and students with whom we've discussed—and debated—the SMT and MTS models over the years.

Finally, in conjunction with The Ohio State University Press, we thank the Faculty of Liberal Arts & Professional Studies, York University, Toronto, Canada, for the financial support it provided to this work.

Matthew Clark and James Phelan

INTRODUCTION

MATTHEW CLARK

I. SYNTHETIC, MIMETIC, THEMATIC

The terms "synthetic," "mimetic," and "thematic"—each with its own long history, reaching back to ancient Greece—were first joined in a narratological model by James Phelan in his *Reading People, Reading Plots* (1989);[1] he has continued to develop this model in his later books, *Narrative as Rhetoric* (1996), *Living to Tell about It* (2005), *Experiencing Fiction* (2007), and *Somebody Telling Somebody Else* (2017), and also in his contributions to the collective volume *Narrative Theory: Core Concepts and Critical Debates* (2012).[2] Phelan's model has established itself in the critical lexicon, and it has been adopted by a number of other scholars.[3] This model has much to recommend it: It usefully distinguishes three kinds of responses and interests a reader may have, it relates these responses and interests to elements of the text or the reading experience, and thus it encourages a sharper and more discriminating critical attention. As it stands, however, it is not without difficulties. A few

---

1. But see Crane 66 for an anticipation of the model.
2. For convenience I will usually use the term "MTS" for Phelan's model. Though this model is at center of this book, I will also examine the work of other scholars, particularly those who work in unnatural, cognitive, and ideological narratology. The MTS model is only part of the larger theory of rhetorical narratology; see section 4 of this chapter.
3. For use of the model in critical and theoretical discussion, see, for example, Heinze, "Violations"; Shen; Gervais; and Falkner.

revisions, intended in the spirit of friendly amendments, can make this model of reading and interpretation more powerful; moreover, the proposed revisions show that the model can accommodate other critical approaches, including unnatural narratology, cognitive narratology, and ideological narratology.

In *Living to Tell about It*, Phelan defines the three terms of the model as follows:

> mimetic/mimesis: Mimetic refers, first, to that component of character directed to its imitation of a possible person. It refers, second, to that component of fictional narrative concerned with imitating the world beyond the fiction, what we typically call "reality." Mimesis refers to the process by which the mimetic effect is produced, the set of conventions, which change over time, by which imitations are judged to be more or less adequate. (215)
>
> thematic: That component of character directed to its representative or ideational function; more generally, that component of a narrative text concerned with making statements, taking ideological positions, teaching readers truths. (219).
>
> synthetic: That component of character directed to its role as artificial construct in the larger construct of the text; more generally, the constructedness of a text as an object. (218)

These components can also be seen in terms of the responses of the reader or audience:

> Responses to the mimetic component involve an audience's interest in the characters as possible people and in the narrative world as like our own. Responses to the thematic component involve an interest in the ideational function of the characters and in the cultural, ideological, philosophical, or ethical issues being addressed by the narrative. Responses to the synthetic component involve an audience's interest in and attention to the characters and to the larger narrative as artificial constructs. (Phelan, *Living* 20)[4]

Below I will offer my revisions of this model, but first it seems appropriate to examine a brief example of the model in action. Phelan offers an analysis of the first three sentences of Mark Twain's *Adventures of Huckleberry Finn*:

---

4. Phelan also notes that readers make interpretive, ethical, and aesthetic judgments about narratives; it is not completely clear if these three kinds of judgments are supposed to align one-to-one with the readers' responses to the three components. See Herman et al. 7 for discussion. Behind these judgments we can perhaps detect the ghost of Kant's three critiques: pure reason, practical reason, and judgment.

> You don't know me without you have read a book by the name of *The Adventures of Tom Sawyer*, but that ain't no matter. That book was made by Mr. Mark Twain, and he told the truth, mainly. There were things which he stretched, but mainly he told the truth. (9)

These three sentences, as Phelan notes, begin to establish Huck's relationship to his audience (or "narratee"); they also characterize Huck as "an unassuming boy" with some concern about truth; and they display Twain's "comic self-awareness." In terms of Phelan's model, "the sentences begin to characterize Huck mimetically as that unassuming boy, thematically as someone concerned with issues of truth and falsehood, and synthetically as a device for Twain's indirect communication to his audience" (Phelan, *Living* 13). A good reading of these sentences thus involves all three components in the model.

Phelan and his collaborator Peter Rabinowitz have more to say about *Huckleberry Finn* in their contribution to the collective volume *Narrative Theory: Core Concepts and Critical Debates* (Herman et al.). Sometimes Phelan and Rabinowitz explicitly use the terms of the model, sometimes not, but I think it is always at least in the background of their discussion.[5] A good example of the model in use can be seen in their discussion of an episode in chapter 21 and the first part of chapter 22 (Herman et al. 116–18). Huck, Jim, and the Duke and the Dauphin stop in a small Arkansas town to put on a show. While Huck is looking over the town, he sees one of the residents, Colonel Sherburn, shoot and kill Boggs, the town drunk, in broad daylight. A lynch mob forms; the Colonel faces them down and delivers a scathing speech deriding their courage, and they slink away.

As Phelan and Rabinowitz argue, the townspeople, who witness the shooting and form the lynch mob, function synthetically when they offer "interpretive and evaluative comments" on Boggs and Sherburn, but they also can be seen in mimetic and thematic terms, as they themselves are characterized and as they represent "the deficient values of shore society" (Herman et al. 116). Sherburn is mimetically characterized as "a proud, imperious, and cruel man," and thematically he represents "another side of those deficient values" (116).

The brazen cruelty of the murder encourages the reader to have some sympathy with the lynch mob, so when Sherburn calls their bluff, the reader, too, is vulnerable to some of his criticism. "In our momentary thematic shock, we do not notice a certain slippage from the mimetic toward the synthetic,"

---

5. See also their discussion of Pap's "reform" (58–59); the setting of the story, especially the Mississippi River (87–91); and the conflict between the synthetic and the mimetic in the Widow Watson's decision to free Jim (113).

since Sherburn's previous characterization is inconsistent with the speech he makes:

> A little reflection reveals that the length and careful logic of Sherburn's speech is not mimetically motivated: rather than being what such a man would say in such a situation . . . it is what Twain needs him to say in order to accomplish his thematic purposes. In a sense Twain has made a sacrifice here, trading his usual concern for mimesis for greater thematic power—but the progression of the scene is so artful that we are likely not to register the sacrifice as we read. (Herman et al. 117)

Huck's primary function in this episode, according to Phelan and Rabinowitz, is synthetic, as a witness and reporter of the incidents. At the end of the episode, however, "Twain moves his mimetic function back into the foreground" (117) as he tells us Huck's reaction to the events. Thematically, Huck's experiences add to the contrast between shore society and Huck's life on the raft with Jim.

The use of the MTS model thus allows us to untangle our complex responses and to understand how each contributes in its own way to our experience of the episode. When all three components are consistent, we probably read well without concern or attention to them. When they are inconsistent, however, our reading stumbles; in such a situation, analysis in terms of the MTS model can be particularly useful. Phelan and Rabinowitz argue, for example, that the last section of *Huckleberry Finn* shows inconsistencies in all three components of the model. Mimetically, the development in Huck's attitudes toward Jim on the river is violated by his treatment of Jim at the Phelpses' farm. This violation is manifested synthetically by the tedium and triviality of Tom's plan to "free" Jim, and also by a restriction in the presentation of Huck's emotional responses to Tom's plan:

> Twain employs restricted narration as Huck reliably reports Tom's speech but refrains from offering any interpretation or evaluation of it. And, as he did in Huck's report about Tom's robber gang in the first chapter, Twain uses the technique to communicate far more than Huck realizes. But here the effects are significantly different: Twain asks his audience to see both the logical absurdity and the ethical deficiencies of Tom's hopes, but the humor here is so broad and—in this context where we've already seen similar absurdities from Tom—so repetitious that the restricted narration weakens rather than strengthens our bond with Huck and consequently with Twain. (Herman et al. 163)

These problems in the mimetic and synthetic components are of course linked to a fundamental problem in the thematic component. The primary ethical concern of the middle of the narrative is a critique of slavery and racism, as shown by Huck's changing attitudes to Jim. The final section of the story, however, is unable to maintain this critique and instead falls back into attitudes Huck should have transcended:

> Twain has signalled to his audience that Huck's decision to go to hell is the climax of his intuitive efforts to define his relation to "sivilization" and its dictates. In the final chapters, however, Twain undermines that climax by showing Huck aiding and abetting Tom's treatment of Jim. (Herman et al. 161)[6]

Conflicts within the mimetic and the thematic components thus are responsible for the discomfort many readers feel about the end of the story.

II. PROBLEMS IN THE MODEL

These brief examples demonstrate the theoretical and practical value of the MTS model. As the model has been formulated, however, it is not without difficulties. The model seems to conflate the mimetic with the realistic and seems to leave nonmimetic narratives as an under-theorized residue. The model also neglects the synthetic elements of realistic narratives, and it tends to restrict the thematic to general meanings consciously intended by the author. Moreover, the three terms of the model are out of balance: Every text is synthetic—Phelan makes a special point that "the synthetic component is always present" (Phelan, *Living* 20)—but some texts are not thematic and some are not mimetic, at least as the terms are defined in the model. The model also suggests that there is some potential conflict between the components; in particular, a narrative that foregrounds the synthetic may do so at the expense of the mimetic (Phelan, *Experiencing* 220; see also Herman et al. 113).[7]

---

    6. In general, "the mimetic component of character may or may not alter over the course of a narrative, but, if it does, the change will typically be tied to the thematic functions of the character and hence to the thematic purposes of the narrative" (115).

    7. Some texts foreground one component, some foreground two, and some foreground all three, so a complete list of narrative types includes mimetic, synthetic, thematic, mimetic–thematic, mimetic–synthetic, thematic–synthetic, and mimetic–thematic–synthetic (Phelan, *Experiencing* 220).

In Phelan's definition, *mimetic* "refers to that component of fictional narrative concerned with imitating the world beyond the fiction, what we typically call 'reality'" (Phelan, *Living* 216).[8] Moreover, "the mimetic component of narrative is responsible for our emotional responses to it, and these responses are a crucial part of the distinctive quality and power of narrative" (Phelan, *Living* 28). It would seem to follow that narratives that foreground the synthetic or thematic at the expense of the mimetic do so at the expense of emotional response—or so the theory would suggest. But the suggestion that emotional response is produced only by mimetic narratives, narratives that imitate reality, is not supported by evidence or experience. The books that charmed Don Quixote were not realistic novels, and Madame Bovary was not carried away by *Madame Bovary*. Many of the greatest and many of the most popular narratives of Western and world literature lie outside what the MTS model defines as mimetic; it is not credible that these have produced no emotional response in readers. In our own time, no book has a more devoted following than *The Lord of the Rings*. If there is a mimetic illusion, there is an equally powerful fantastic illusion.[9]

There seems to be some disjunction here between critical theory and practice. The model, as it is formulated, has a place for realistic narratives, but no place for the nonrealistic, except through negation or absence. Some theorists have developed a category of the "antimimetic" to fill this gap.[10] (Exactly what counts as "antimimetic," however, is not clear. One type might include narratives in which the characters do not seem to be autonomous, a second type might include fantastic narratives, and a third type might include narratives in which the artist's contrivances are foregrounded.) In practice, Phelan and other rhetorical narratologists do discuss "nonmimetic" or unnatural narratives,[11] but some critics have argued that narrative theory tends to privilege "mimetic" or realist narratives:

---

8. The conflation of the mimetic with the realistic is a regular feature of Phelan's discussion of the mimetic: For example, "responses to the mimetic component involve readers' interest in the characters as possible people and in the narrative world as like our own" (Phelan and Rabinowitz in Herman et al. 7).

9. See Pifer, chapter 1 and passim, for an argument that Vladimir Nabokov's "verbal pyrotechnics" do not prevent the creation of engaging characters.

10. Brian Richardson, for example, notes "a realistic tradition, which I will call 'mimetic,' that attempts to provide narrators, characters, events, and settings that more or less resemble those of our quotidian experience," and he argues for a theory of "anti-mimetic" or "unnatural" narratives in opposition to this realistic tradition (Herman et al. 20).

11. See, for example, Phelan's discussion of Toni Morrison's *Beloved* in chapter 2 of Phelan, *Experiencing* 51–78.

Narrative theory has always had a pronounced mimetic bias. Fictional works are largely treated as if they were primarily lifelike reproductions of human beings and human actions and could be analyzed according to real-world notions of consistency, probability, individual and group psychology, and correspondence with accepted beliefs about the world" (Alber, Iversen, Nielsen, and Richardson in Alber et al. 4).[12]

If nonrealist narratives were rare or marginal, this bias could perhaps be excused, but in fact the literary tradition abounds in nonrealist fictions, and any theory that cannot comfortably accommodate *The Divine Comedy, Gulliver's Travels,* and *Ulysses* is seriously deficient. The growth of "unnatural narratology" is in part a response to this perceived deficiency in rhetorical narratology.

The MTS model tends to neglect the synthetic aspects of realist narratives. Although every narrative, according to Phelan, has a synthetic component, in realistic fiction the synthetic component is concealed and the audience has only a "tacit awareness" of it (Phelan, *Living* 20).[13] "Realistic fiction," according to Phelan, "seeks to create the illusion that everything is mimetic and nothing synthetic, or, in other words, that the characters act as they do by their own choice rather than at the behest of the author" (Phelan, *Living* 20). In metafiction, however, the synthetic component is foregrounded and the mimetic "typically recedes into the background" (Phelan, *Experiencing* 6). Richardson, from a different critical standpoint, uses similar terminology to make a similar point:

> Mimetic narratives typically try to conceal their contradictions and appear to resemble non-fictional narratives, while antimimetic narratives flaunt their artificiality and break the ontological boundaries that mimetic works so carefully preserve. (Richardson in Herman et al. 20)

There is general critical agreement that realistic fiction suppresses awareness of the synthetic in order to create something like a mimetic illusion.[14] I

---

12. See also Brian Richardson (Herman et al. 21), and Herman's critique of "mimesis" (Herman et al. 16).

13. Phelan suggests that the synthetic component is covert because it is not available to the "narrative audience," even when it is available to the "authorial audience" (Phelan, *Reading* 4); see below for discussion of these audiences. This argument seems to solve one theoretical problem by invoking another problem.

14. For example, "the creation of realistic fiction depends on the reader's being only momentarily and fleetingly conscious of the artifices and conventions that sustain the illusion" (Gard 144).

certainly grant the power of the mimetic illusion, though I am not prepared to grant the mimetic component sole ownership of the emotional aspect of narrative. I would argue that foregrounding the synthetic can help the narrator express strong emotions in new ways. (See chapter 1 for further discussion of this point.) Moreover, emotional response is not the only form of engagement; the perception of beauty has an independent value. The synthetic aspect is not always well concealed in realistic fiction, and even if it is concealed, it should still be a concern for critics.

An example of not-very-well-concealed synthesis can be found in chapter 16 of *Huckleberry Finn*. In chapter 15, we remember, Huck and Jim are lost in the fog; Huck lies to Jim to make him think it was all a dream, and then reveals that he was lying. Jim leaves angrily, and Huck eventually apologizes: "It was fifteen minutes before I could work myself up to go and humble myself to a nigger; but I done it, and I warn't ever sorry for it afterward, neither. I didn't do him no mean tricks, and I wouldn't done that one if I'd 'a' knowed it would make him feel that way" (Twain 92).

In the next chapter, chapter 6, Huck and Jim think that they are approaching Cairo, the next stage of Jim's escape to freedom. Huck for the first time realizes that he is helping a slave escape:

> Jim said it made him all over trembly and feverish to be so close to freedom. Well, I can tell you it made me all over trembly and feverish, too, to hear him, because I begun to get it through my head that he *was* most free—and who was to blame for it? Why, *me*. (94)

The paragraph continues with an extensive internal debate in which Huck wrestles with his conscience.

Jim continues to talk about his plans for freedom: He will work to save money to buy his wife and two children, and if their master won't sell them he will hire an "ab'litionist" to steal them:

> It most froze me to hear such talk. He wouldn't ever dared to talk such talk in his life before. Just see what a difference it made in him the minute he judged he was about free. It was according to the old saying, "Give a nigger an inch and he'll take an ell." Thinks I, this is what comes of my not thinking. Here was this nigger, which I had as good as helped to run away, coming right out flat-footed and saying he would steal his children—children that belonged to a man I didn't even know; a man that hadn't ever done me no harm. (94–95)

So Huck decides that he will paddle ashore and tell on Jim. He gets into the canoe, pretending that he is going to find out if they are near Cairo. Twain now piles on the irony, as Jim says how much he owes to Huck:

> "Pooty soon I'll be a-shout'n for joy, en I'll say, it's all on accounts o' Huck; I's a free man, en I couldn't ever ben free ef it hadn' ben for Huck; Huck done it. Jim won't ever forget you, Huck; you's de bes' fren' Jim's ever had; en you's de *only* fren' ole Jim's got now." (95)

Huck shoves off and immediately encounters two men with guns in a skiff; they are looking for runaway slaves. They want to see who is on Huck's raft, and Huck finds himself cooking up a lie to protect Jim: His father and mother and sister are on the raft and they are sick. The men are afraid that the family has smallpox, so they leave without inspecting the raft.

> They went off and I got aboard the raft, feeling bad and low, because I knowed very well I had done wrong, and I see it warn't no use for me to try to learn to do right; a body that don't get *started* right when he's little ain't got no show—when the pinch comes there ain't nothing to back him up and keep him to his work, and so he gets beat. Then I thought a minute, and says to myself, hold on; s'pose you'd 'a' done right and give Jim up, would you felt better than you do now? No, says I, I'd feel bad—I'd feel just the same way I do now. (97)

And so on. This is a complex passage of what I think Phelan would call bonding unreliability—that is, Huck holds an ethical position that the reader (one hopes) cannot hold, but in a way that increases the reader's attachment to Huck. This passage is also synthetic, from start to finish, and Twain makes no great effort to conceal the synthetic construction. Huck makes a bad ethical decision, he is immediately tested, and he passes the test. All of the characters—Jim, Huck, and the two men in the skiff—are doing just what Twain needs them to do. Twain doesn't signal the contrivance, but neither does he hide it. Nor does the contrivance reduce the reader's emotional involvement. A sympathetic reader wants Huck to pass the test, even while realizing that the test has been contrived.[15]

---

15. Twain was very concerned about the relationship between the synthetic and the mimetic; the famous passage about learning to read the Mississippi River in chapter 9 of *Life on the Mississippi* can be read as a rhetorical critique of rhetoric.

Similar contrivances can be found in the most scrupulous of writers. In *The Wings of the Dove* (in chapters 15 and 16, toward the end of Book Fifth, and in chapter 17, at the beginning of Book Sixth), Henry James contrives an accidental meeting. Merton Densher has been in the United States; Mrs. Lowder (Kate Croy's Aunt Maude) wants to know if he has returned and wants to know if he and Kate have been communicating, but she can't ask Kate. She asks Milly Theale, who doesn't know.

Shortly thereafter (perhaps the next day, though James is not quite clear on the chronology), Milly decides on a whim to visit the National Gallery, and there she accidentally meets Kate and Densher; he had in fact returned just the day before. Kate had met him at the railway station, where, lost in the crowd, they had a cup of tea together; they had agreed to meet the next morning: "[Kate] had suggested the National Gallery for the morning. . . . They might be seen there, too, but nobody would know them" (220). So they meet at the Gallery because no one they know would go there, and the same morning Milly, on a whim, goes to the Gallery, where she has never been before. Surely James is showing his synthetic hand here, as he moves his characters into the position he needs for the next move of his game.

Perhaps this episode could have been better motivated. James could have figured out a way for both Milly and Kate to have overheard a chance remark about the National Gallery so that each could have had it in mind. Such motivation, however, would not be evidence of lack of contrivance, but of more and perhaps better contrivance. In *Pride and Prejudice,* for instance, Mr. Darcy's second proposal is well motivated: It feels like the inevitable outcome of the three personalities involved—Lady Catherine de Bourgh, Elizabeth, and Darcy—but the motivation is a result of Austen's skill in managing the synthetic component.

The synthetic is everywhere in every narrative. Of course, many readers will prefer being swept away by a story and will pay no attention to how it is made. But the synthetic component is always there, and narrative theory should account for it wherever it is, either foregrounded, as in metafiction, or not, as in some realistic fiction. The MTS model, however, as it has been formulated, makes inadequate theoretical provision for works outside of the realistic tradition or for the synthetic aspect of works within the realistic tradition.

The thematic component in Phelan's definition is "concerned with making statements, taking ideological positions, teaching readers truths" (Phelan, *Living* 219). Making, taking, and teaching all seem to be conscious actions on the part of the author. Authors, no doubt, are often conscious of their themes, but not always, and sometimes the unconscious themes are the most interesting.

The rhetorical analysis of persuasive forms of oratory may properly concentrate on the conscious purpose of the speaker, but a theory of imaginative literature needs to be sensitive to meanings and purposes beyond the conscious awareness of the author and the audience.

III. THE REVISED MODEL

A revision of the MTS model (which I will call the SMT model) can resolve these difficulties. Here is my proposed revision of the model and the reasoning behind it:

Every narrative can be considered from three aspects, the synthetic, the mimetic, and the thematic; these aspects are simultaneous and interdependent. Every text can be seen as synthetic, mimetic, and thematic. Synthetic analysis concerns all kinds of verbal construction, from sentences to whole plots, and also the construction of characters and narrative worlds. Mimetic analysis concerns the representation of characters and worlds constructed in a narrative, realistic or not. Thematic analysis concerns all kinds of meaning imparted by or derived from a text, direct and indirect, intended by the author or not.

1. Phelan says that the three terms denote "components" of narrative. The term "components" seems to suggest things that have some kind of prior existence independent of each other, things that are assembled, in the way, for instance, the various components of a home entertainment center are assembled—as if, for example, the author selects a mimetic component, a thematic component, and a synthetic component and assembles them into a narrative. Moreover, one might choose not to select a particular component—your home entertainment system may not have a turntable, and your narrative may not have a thematic component. I would prefer to say that these terms denote "aspects" of narrative; by "aspect" I mean simply a way of looking or a way of perceiving, so the three aspects are three ways of looking at narrative. In my reformulation of these terms, the synthetic, mimetic, and thematic are simultaneous and interdependent aspects of a unified narrative whole. Every narrative has a synthetic aspect, a mimetic aspect, and a thematic aspect, and any of these can be the topic of analysis and interpretation. Of these three aspects, the synthetic aspect forms, as it were, the base, while the mimetic and the synthetic form the superstructure built on the synthetic base. Each of the three aspects has an independent interest and value, but they are all interconnected and simultaneous.

2. Phelan's definitions of the terms, as quoted above, privilege the application of each term to the study of characterization. Phelan introduced his

model in a book about characters in narrative, and the definitions are taken from another book about character, so this privileging of character is hardly surprising. But as his full definitions indicate, he allows the terms wider application. Character is indeed fundamental to narrative, but so is action, and some narratives have more action than character. Moreover, every narrative happens at some time and in some place; setting is a mimetic representation that is constructed synthetically in the service of thematic meaning. According to the amended definitions, therefore, the synthetic aspect of narrative looks at narrative as construction in general, the mimetic aspect looks at narrative as representation in general, and the thematic aspect looks at narrative as signification in general.

3. As I noted in the previous section, Phelan's definition of the mimetic component tends to restrict it to something like realistic representations. He is of course aware that not all characters in narrative are possible people, and not all narrative worlds are realistic, but these characters and worlds, in his terms, are not mimetic. If mimesis means something like "realism," then I'm not sure we need the term.[16] Moreover, mimesis as realism is not really parallel to the other terms in the triad: It is easy to find narratives that are nonrealistic—that are nonmimetic—but it is harder to find narratives that are nonsynthetic or nonthematic—narratives that are not constructed and have no meaning.

Phelan's definitions seem to create a kind of opposition between the synthetic and the mimetic: Realistic narratives are mimetic, while metafictional narratives are synthetic. This opposition is in some conflict with his statement that all narratives have a synthetic component. The idea of foregrounding may be intended to resolve this conflict—in realistic fiction the mimetic is foregrounded, in metafiction the synthetic is foregrounded—but the idea of foregrounding is in itself problematic. Who does the foregrounding? Sometimes Phelan says that the author does, and sometimes the text. I would argue that the reader can foreground, and any reader at any time can choose to foreground any of the three aspects of a narrative.[17]

---

16. Phelan's usage is consistent with the title of Erich Auerbach's *Mimesis: The Representation of Reality in Western Literature*; see also Doležel x. Brian Richardson takes "mimetic" to mean "realistic," and he calls nonrealistic texts "anti-mimetic" (see Richardson in Herman et al. 235–36). However, the word "mimesis" has had many meanings, not all of which imply realism; compare Falkner 31, who says that mimetic representations are "not to be confused, of course, with their being real or even 'realistic,'" and Ricoeur, who theorizes three kinds of mimesis. I will have more to say about mimesis and realism in chapter 2.

17. As Frank Kermode notes, whenever something in a narrative is put in the foreground, something else is put in the background: "Indeed, it is not uncommon for large parts of a novel to go virtually unread; the less manifest portions of its text (its secrets) remain secret, resisting all but abnormally attentive scrutiny" (84). The whole of Kermode's article is an exemplary study in bringing the background into the foreground.

For all of these reasons, I take mimesis to be all kinds of representation, whether realistic or fantastic. Mimesis includes the representation of characters, but it also includes the representation of the narrative world in general and of events within the narrative world. Moreover, every representation, even the most realistic, is synthetic, that is, artificial, and the artifice of realistic representation needs analysis as much as the representation of the fantastic.

4. The thematic I take to include all kinds of meaning, not just the kinds of meaning expressed in making statements or taking positions or teaching truths. Meaning can be expressed in many ways; it can be explicit or implicit, conscious or unconscious, direct or indirect, transparent or hidden. One of the principal lessons of structuralism properly understood is that structure can convey meaning; one goal of my project is the explication of narrative figures of meaning. Meaning can also be expressed by the relationship of one text to another. Moreover, the meaning of a text is not simply supplied by the author; the reader also creates some of the meaning in the reading experience.

These revisions I intend as friendly amendments to the MTS model, but one might reasonably object that my model is so different from Phelan's that it is really something else altogether. In an earlier version of this book I used three different terms, "construction," "representation," and "signification," precisely to avoid conflict with Phelan's model. In the end, however, I decided to stick with the terms Phelan uses, for several reasons. First, even if I had never come across the MTS model, these terms mean—or can mean—just what I want them to mean. Second, this book in fact derives from and depends on my attempts to use and to teach the MTS model. My misreading, if such it is, is intended with respect. Third, narrative theory already has enough terms, and it doesn't need three more. Fourth, the revision of important terms and systems, the rectification of names, is a regular part of science and scholarship. Of course, the reader may decide that Phelan's original definitions are better than my revisions. The proof of the pudding will be found in the following chapters.

My revisions are intended as a contribution to rhetorical narratology, but I am sympathetic to other schools of narratological theory, particularly unnatural narratology, cognitive narratology, and ideological narratology (which, as I take it, includes feminist narratology, but also the analysis of class, race, religion, and so on). My revision of the MTS model is partly designed to accommodate these other narratologies within the framework of rhetorical narratology.

The following chapters will deal in turn with the synthetic, mimetic, and thematic aspects of narrative. Because the aspects are simultaneous and interdependent, the discussion of any one aspect will often overlap the chapter boundaries. The discussion will include frequent reference to examples, with a continuing attention to a few sample narratives—*Emma* (Jane Austen), *1984* (George Orwell), and the Homeric epics, the *Iliad* and the *Odyssey*.

IV. FURTHER NOTES ON RHETORICAL NARRATOLOGY

The triad of the synthetic, the mimetic, and the thematic is only a part of the larger theory of rhetorical narratology. On several occasions, Phelan has sketched out the fundamental principles of rhetorical narratology, and it seems appropriate here to review these briefly. (I base my discussion mostly on the version presented by Phelan and Rabinowitz in Herman et al. 3–8, since it is their most recent account.) I am generally sympathetic to these principles, and I would consider the model I present at least compatible with rhetorical narratology, but I note here and there a few dissents.

Narrative, according to Phelan and Rabinowitz, is "somebody telling somebody else, on some occasion, and for some purpose, that something happened to someone or something" (Herman et al. 3). They call this a "default" definition, useful insofar as "it captures essential characteristics of most of those works that are widely considered to be narratives in our culture" (Herman et al. 4). This definition makes narrative—both the telling and the hearing of narrative—a human activity, and thus corrects some of the excesses of various kinds of formalism, including structuralism and deconstruction, which sometimes seem to suspend narrative in some disembodied Platonic realm. The reference to narratives of "our culture," however, suggests a serious limitation of rhetorical narratology, both in theory and practice. Narrative theory in general needs to expand its horizons to include more discussion of narratives from other times and other cultures.

This definition of narrative seems to assume that a narrative has a particular author, but some narratives—the Homeric epics, for instance—may be better regarded as the work of a tradition rather than an individual, and all narratives are partly made from previous narratives. Traditional narratives, such as epics and jokes, may be told on specific occasions, but they exist beyond any particular moment; nor, for that matter, is a written narrative bound to a particular occasion. The purpose of telling a joke at a particular moment may be determined by the teller rather than the original author, whose intentions are likely unrecoverable. A director may stage a play for purposes not imagined by the author.

A narrator may have several audiences in mind, audiences with different kinds of knowledge, audiences at various distances in space and time from the original audience. And a narrator may have many purposes—such as making a statement or making a living. Purpose, as Phelan describes it, belongs to the writer, but a reader also has a purpose for reading and an experience of reading, both of which can be considered part of the thematic aspect of narrative. Phelan throughout his work is well aware of the experience of the reader: He titled one of his books *Experiencing Fiction*, his explanations of the three terms of the MTS model include reference to the response of the reader, and his concept of narrative progression also necessarily involves the experience of the reader. His definition of narrative, however, leaves out the reader's purpose.

Following the definition of narrative, Phelan and Rabinowitz present six numbered principles of rhetorical narratology.[18]

1. Narrative is multidimensional and purposive. By "multidimensional," they mean that narration "involves the audience's intellect, emotions, psyche, and values" (Phelan, *Living* 19). Rhetorical narratology is interested not just in the "meaning of narrative but also in the experience of it," not just with "thematic meanings" but also with "affective, ethical, and aesthetic effects" (Herman et al. 3). By "purposive," they mean that "the elements of any narrative . . . are structured in the service of larger ends" (3). This point seems rather general, since purposes and larger ends are virtually without limit. It is also not clear that every narrative has a single larger end, and local purposes can trump the purpose of the work as a whole.

2. The stance of rhetorical narratology is a posteriori rather than a priori; that is, it works by looking at texts and seeing what they do rather than by working from assumptions about what a narrative should do. "In practical terms, this principle means that rhetorical narrative theory does not preselect for analysis particular issues such as gender or cognition or particular kinds of narratives such as those deploying antimimetic elements of story or discourse" (5). In practical terms, this principle can also mean that rhetorical narratology leaves some particular issues or kinds of narratives under-represented or under-theorized.[19]

One goal of my revised model is to open rhetorical narratology more to other approaches.

---

18. This section was drafted before the appearance of Phelan, *Somebody*, which adds three substantive points to the list of principles: "rhetorical theory distinguishes between the ethics of the telling and the ethics of the told"; "Rhetorical theory integrates history in multiple ways," and "The underlying rhetorical situation varies in different kinds of narrative, and it typically varies within individual narratives" (8–10). I am generally sympathetic to these additional principles, which are compatible with the SMT model.

19. See, for example, the various critiques of rhetorical narratology presented by Brian Richardson, David Herman, and Robyn Warhol in Herman et al. part 2.

3. Narratives are structured as a feedback loop "among authorial agency, textual phenomena . . . and reader response" (5). I am not sure that the term "feedback loop" is quite right here. I think the point is simply that (a) authors write (b) texts to be read by (c) readers; that all three of these elements need to be taken into consideration; that any of these elements can be the starting point for analysis: and that a full analysis, wherever it begins, will take all three elements into account (Phelan, *Living* 18).

4. Narrative is structured as progression. The progression of a narrative is "the key means by which an author achieves his or her purposes" (Herman et al. 6). Rhetorical narratology distinguishes textual dynamics, "the internal processes by which narratives move from beginning to middle to ending," from readerly dynamics, the readers' responses to the textual dynamics. The principle that narrative is a progression is a useful corrective to the static analyses favored by some kinds of structuralism, and thus emphasizes the importance of the reader's experience of reading in time.

5. Rhetorical narratology distinguishes a number of different narrative positions.[20] One of the foundational moves of rhetorical narratology was the distinction between the author and the narrator and the positing of the implied author.[21] Further distinctions are possible: One can say that Samuel Clemens is the (flesh-and-blood) author of *Huckleberry Finn*, Mark Twain is the implied author, and Huck himself is the narrator. On the other side of the text, we can distinguish the (flesh-and-blood) reader from various other audiences.[22] The authorial audience is "the hypothetical group for whom the author writes"; this group "shares the knowledge, values, prejudices, fears, and experiences" that the author expects in the audience (Herman et al. 6).[23] The authorial audience is a real person the reader tries to become or a real group the reader tries to join, but the narrative audience exists inside the narrative world; this audience "regards the characters and events as real rather than invented" (Herman et al. 6). The flesh-and-blood reader "pretends" to join this audience.[24] In addition, the narratee is "the intratextual audience specifically

---

20. The origins of this model of audiences can be found in Rabinowitz, "Truth," where the audiences are used to address questions of truth in fiction.

21. In Herman et al., Phelan and Rabinowitz discuss authors and narrators in chapter 2, 29–38, rather than in the introduction along with audiences.

22. On multiple audiences, see Richardson, "The Other."

23. "The authorial audience is the ideal audience that an author implicitly posits in constructing her text, the one which will pick up on all the signals in the appropriate way" (Phelan, *Reading* 5).

24. Phelan argues, for example, that the narrative audience of Browning's "My Last Duchess" does not hear the rhymes (Phelan, *Reading* 5). The same logic would suggest that the narrative audience of Mozart's *Marriage of Figaro* doesn't hear the music.

addressed by the narrator" (Herman et al. 7). One can also identify an "internal narrator" and "internal audience," that is, someone in a story who tells a story and someone who listens.

At a certain point one begins to wonder if this theory has multiplied entities beyond necessity. While I grant the reading experiences described by Phelan and Rabinowitz, this theory seems to turn experiences into entities. I am not at all sure why a reader would want to join, or pretend to join, a narrative audience. When I read the *Odyssey*, does any part of me need to believe in Polyphemos? I am also not sure exactly what determines the authorial audience. Is this the audience that already shares the "knowledge, values, prejudices, fears, and experiences" of the author? Or the audience that can be persuaded to share the author's values, and so on? Phelan grants that "individual readers will find some authorial audiences easier to enter than others," and he "stops short of ever declaring any one reading as definitive and fixed for all time" (Phelan, *Living* 19). Nonetheless, the authorial audience, however it is determined, seems to have some kind of privilege as the locus of some shared experience.

> [Rhetorical reading] assumes that one significant value of reading narrative is the opportunity it offers to encounter other minds—that of the author who has constructed the narrative and those of other readers also interested in shared readings. For these reasons, throughout this book, I will often use the first-person-plural pronoun to refer to the activities of the authorial audience. (Phelan, *Living* 19)

One hopes that critics will resist the temptation to attribute their own personal responses to this "we" of the authorial audience.

6. Audiences respond to three components of narrative: the mimetic, the thematic, and the synthetic. Since the rest of this book is devoted to discussion of these components, or aspects, of narrative, there is no need for further comment here.

CHAPTER 1

The Synthetic Aspect

MATTHEW CLARK

I. THE SYNTHETIC ASPECT AS NARRATIVE INFRASTRUCTURE

Every narrative is synthetic. The synthetic aspect includes style and sentence structure, paragraph construction, chapter divisions, the composition of episodes, and the form of entire plots; it is also the foundation for the fabrication of narrative worlds and the creation of characters in those worlds, or the mimetic aspect, as well as the formation and communication of themes and meaning, the thematic aspect. The synthetic is the infrastructure of narrative; the mimetic and the thematic are superstructures.

Superstructures are not simply reducible to infrastructures. A painting, in a sense, is only paint, but it is also—or it can be—a representation. Paying too much attention to infrastructures can be pointless, inappropriate, or even rude. When the plumbing works, we don't talk about it. Art seems designed to call attention to its own artificiality, but some critics deplore attention to the synthetic for its own sake just as many people deplore puns. As Richard Lanham notes, "The trouble with comedy is that no one will leave it alone. The joke must always be more than a joke. Pleasure is never enough. We must milk it for wisdom" (Lanham 17). The synthetic is the foundation of the mimetic and the thematic, but it also provides a pleasure of its own.

Theoretical discussion has tended to create two parallel dichotomies— "transparent" verbal style tends to be associated with "mimetic" narrative style, while "opaque" verbal style is associated with "synthetic" narrative style.¹ Jane Austen, perhaps, can represent the "transparent" style:

> Emma Woodhouse, handsome, clever, and rich, with a comfortable home and happy disposition, seemed to unite some of the best blessings of existence; and had lived nearly twenty-one years in the world with very little to vex or distress her. (5)

And Samuel Beckett's *How It Is* can represent the overtly synthetic, "opaque" style:

> here then part one how it was before Pim we follow I quote the natural order more or less my life last state last version what remains bits and scraps I hear it my life natural order more or less I learn it I quote a given moment long past vast stretch of time on from there that moment and the following not all a selection natural order vast tract of time. (7)

But Austen's style is hardly transparent, since we are looking at the world she presents through her carefully composed sentences and paragraphs and through her irony, while Beckett, for all his difficulty, presents a complete, if somewhat meager world. (I will support these claims more fully below.)

Historically there has been some resistance to the idea that narrative—or the novel, or the realistic novel—is essentially artificial. The realistic novel is supposed to be simply a transcription of life, and prose, the language of the novel, should be unnoticed and transparent. "The words in prose ought to express the intended meaning and no more; if they attract attention to themselves, it is, in general, a fault" (Coleridge 238). Good prose "allows the writer's meaning to come through with the least possible loss of significance and nuance, as a landscape is seen through a clear window" (Sutherland 77).²

The transparent style is one element of a general realistic project. "Modern fiction's claim to our attention has been that it presents things as they really

---

1. For discussion of "transparency" in the realistic novel, see Shaw, chapter 2. Strictly speaking, no style is truly transparent, and whenever I use the term the reader can silently add scare quotation marks or the qualifier "relatively."

2. Sutherland, however, goes on to qualify this comparison: "We can read page after page of Swift, absorbing the ideas completely and continuously, and scarcely conscious of the author. Scarcely conscious, but never quite unaware of him: Swift still has his own unmistakable voice, and no good prose has the transparency or anonymity of a window-pane" (77). See chapter 2 for discussion of mimesis as a mirror or a camera.

are, that it is truthful to the facts of life on this earth" (Kroeber 118).³ "The creation of realistic fiction depends on the reader's being only momentarily and fleetingly conscious of the artifices and conventions that sustain the illusion" (Gard 144). According to Ian Watt, the style of fiction before the rise of the English novel tended to be opaque, but the realistic novelists wrote in a transparent style: "The previous stylistic tradition for fiction [before Defoe, Richardson, and Fielding] was not primarily concerned with the correspondence of words to things, but rather with the extrinsic beauties which could be bestowed upon description and action by the use of rhetoric" (Watt 30). But Defoe and Richardson aimed for a style that could achieve "immediacy and closeness of the text to what is being described" (Watt 32).⁴ This transparent style is characteristic of the tradition of the realistic novel: "It would appear, then, that the function of language is much more largely referential in the novel than in other literary forms" (Watt 33).⁵

Readers of twentieth- and twenty-first-century fiction can hardly be content with a theory restricted to transparent prose and referential realism, but the recognition of other kinds of narrative—"antimimetic," "unnatural," or "synthetic"—still tends to fall into dichotomies. Brian Richardson (following the Russian Formalist Boris Tomashevsky) divides narrative into two styles: One style seeks to conceal its devices, the other foregrounds them. Richardson suggests that narratives of the first kind, common in the nineteenth century, are more amenable to "mimetic" analysis, while those of the second category, typical of postmodernism, require "synthetic analysis" (Richardson in Herman et al. 236). And according to Phelan, "realistic fiction seeks to create the illusion that everything is mimetic and nothing synthetic . . .; metafiction, on the other hand, foregrounds the synthetic component, making us aware of its own construction" (Phelan, *Living* 20).⁶

---

3. Kroeber leaves the door open to the synthetic: "Insofar as fiction creates 'ideal' worlds these are ideal in the sense of being rearrangements or reorganizations of things as they are, not transmutations of them" (118).

4. But see Harry Shaw's argument that "realistic fiction does not attempt 'transparent representation' based on a more largely referential use of language than one finds in other literary genres" (Shaw 90).

5. Transparency, however, is seen by some as an ideological mask, an attempt to claim an immediate access to reality, an access that in fact is never possible. The style that calls attention to itself is thus more honest than the transparent style. See, for example, Eagleton, *Ideology* 199–200.

6. According to Richardson, rhetorical narratology, as represented by Phelan and Rabinowitz, does not do justice to postmodern or metafictional narratives, in which the synthetic element dominates the mimetic; Phelan and Rabinowitz argue that "antimimetic narrative often depends on the foundation of mimetic fiction to do its work" (Herman et al. 198). One could argue, however, that nonmimetic narrative is historically and logically prior to mimetic narrative, in somewhat the same way that verse is prior to prose.

These theoretical dichotomies fail to do justice to the complexity of verbal and narrative styles and the history of narrative forms. On the one hand, transparent or referential writing was not invented by modern realistic novelists. In ancient Greece the logographer Lysias and the novelist Chariton could write in a relatively transparent style; some of the Icelandic sagas are transparent, and so are the Arthurian stories of Sir Thomas Malory. On the other hand, it is hardly true that once the novel was invented, writers lost interest in style for its own sake. Much writing from the "realistic" period is highly figured, and part of the pleasure of reading these texts lies in the appreciation of the synthetic aspect. Moreover, even relatively transparent prose is synthetic, and the devices of simplicity also deserve attention.

The simple distinction between transparent and opaque styles is too crude to be of much use. Francis-Noël Thomas and Mark Turner present a more complex stylistic analysis: They begin by noting five elements of the "classic" style (truth, presentation, scene, cast, and thought and language) each of which is subdivided, for a total of twenty-three features; they also briefly describe the plain style, the reflexive style, the practical style, the contemplative style, the romantic style, the prophetic style, and the oratorical style. There are as many ways for a narrative to be synthetic as there are kinds of synthetic elements in narrative. As Robyn Warhol notes, "realist novels have been indulging in antimimetic practices for as long as realist novels have been written" (Herman et al. 213).

II. COVERT AND OVERT SYNTHESIS

The distinction between "mimetic" and "synthetic" narratives is based on a few key concepts, expressed by terms such as "mimetic illusion," "concealing," "covert," and "foregrounding." Realistic fiction creates the "mimetic illusion" by "concealing" its synthetic component, which is thus "covert"; metafiction, on the other hand, "foregrounds" the synthetic component.

Phelan uses these terms, for example, in his analysis of Robert Browning's dramatic monologue "My Last Duchess"; here is the opening of the poem:

> That's my last duchess painted on the wall,
> Looking as if she were alive. I call
> That piece a wonder, now: Frà Pandolf's hands
> Worked busily a day, and there she stands.
> Will't please you sit and look at her? I said
> "Frà Pandolf" by design, for never read

> Strangers like you that pictured countenance,
> The depth and passion of its earnest glance,
> But to myself they turned (since none puts by
> The curtain I have drawn for you, but I)
> And seemed as they would ask me, if they durst,
> How such a glance came there; so, not the first
> Are you to turn and ask thus. (Browning 49–50)

"Browning's task," according to Phelan, "is to create the *illusion* that we are not reading a poem but overhearing part of a conversation" (Phelan, *Reading* 5).[7] Thus "the Duke is a character whose mimetic component is overtly emphasized while his synthetic component, though present, remains covert" (5). In addition,

> it may seem odd to argue that the synthetic remains covert when we are reading a poem written in rhymed couplets, but a short thought experiment suggested by Rader will help justify the point. Who is responsible for the rhymes, Browning or the Duke? The fact that we instinctively answer "Browning" indicates the kind of involvement with the Duke we have: we have only his voice but we do not hear *him* rhyming. The synthetic is there but it remains covert. (5)

If, indeed, Browning's task was to create the illusion that we are overhearing a conversation and not reading or listening to a poem, he has done a bad job of it. The rhymes are perhaps muffled by the enjambment, but they are betrayed by the meter, and any attentive reader will see them and hear them.[8]

---

7. Phelan here is following Ralph Rader, "The Dramatic." Rader's point, however, is somewhat different from Phelan's; according to Rader, the rhymes demonstrate "that the poet's presence in the poem is a fundamental aspect of the form, not something we know from outside the poem, but something inseparable from our experience of it" (133). Rader does not ask us to enter a world in which the rhymes aren't there, but to have a complex experience which includes both the Duke, as the fictive speaker, and Browning, as the real poet. The External Reader for this manuscript argues that "just as we see the rhymes but do not fully hear them . . . we understand that the duke is also hiding one intention within another." See McHale for a discussion of the unnatural quality of narrative poetry, with conclusions rather different from Phelan's argument.

8. "It is the very essence of couplets that their chime should be heard, yet here the poet deliberately muffles them. . . . If we assume that the Duke speaks purposefully, we see that the couplets have a very definite function—to give a sense of submerged pattern running, like the Duke's hidden purpose, though the whole" (Rader, "The Dramatic" 139). This important aesthetic effect would not be available to a reader who does not hear the rhymes.

If Browning had really wanted to create this illusion, he should have printed the poem in continuous prose rather than in couplets:

> That's my last duchess painted on the wall, looking as if she were alive. I call that piece a wonder, now: Frà Pandolf's hands worked busily a day, and there she stands. Will't please you sit and look at her? I said "Frà Pandolf" by design, for never read strangers like you that pictured countenance, the depth and passion of its earnest glance, but to myself they turned (since none puts by the curtain I have drawn for you, but I) and seemed as they would ask me, if they durst, how such a glance came there; so, not the first are you to turn and ask thus.

This is closer to conversation, though an attentive reader would eventually catch the rhymes, perhaps at "hands"/"stands," perhaps at "countenance"/"glance," perhaps at "durst"/"first." If Browning was aiming for the illusion of conversation, he should have left the rhymes out altogether. But of course Browning did not write continuous prose without rhymes. He wrote rhymed couplets. Nothing is concealed.[9] The effect of this poem, I would argue, is caused by the tension between the conversational situation and the overt and insistent verse form. Any reader who enters into the "mimetic illusion" and becomes part of the "narrative audience" is just not reading the poem. We should not read poems as if they were prose. Nor should we read prose as if it were prose, that is, as if it were simply mimetic and not also and always synthetic.

Phelan and Richardson agree that there are two main traditions of narrative: Realistic narrative foregrounds the mimetic at the expense of the synthetic, while metafiction foregrounds the synthetic at the expense of the mimetic. Richardson calls for more attention to the synthetic analysis of metafiction, while Phelan argues that rhetorical narratology is open to all kinds of narratives, but neither Richardson nor Phelan gives much attention to the synthetic aspect of the realistic tradition. But even if the synthetic aspect of realistic fiction is relatively covert, it still requires analytical attention. In fact, the covert aspects of a narrative may carry part of the narrative's ideology; bringing the covert into the open is an essential narratological task. (For more on this point, see chapter 3.) Moreover, the synthetic aspect of realistic narrative is not really so covert. Of course, the foregrounding of the synthetic is

---

9. Phelan argues that the rhymed couplets are covert for the narrative audience but heard by the authorial audience. The term "covert" is thus reduced to "covert for the narrative audience." This move, though initially attractive, would suggest that the devices of Joyce's *Ulysses* are covert, because Stephen Daedalus and Leopold Bloom aren't aware of them.

more blatant in metafiction, but an attentive reader can easily see the synthetic devices in realistic fiction.

III. SYNTHETIC STYLE

One important synthetic element in narrative is the construction of sentences—style, more or less. If the prose of realistic fiction were transparent, there would be little to say about its style. But in fact, there is hardly a realistic novelist whose style is even relatively transparent.

Dickens, as critics have often noted, was an intensely rhetorical writer.[10] Consider the beginning of *Little Dorrit*; I have marked the passage to indicate some of the more important synthetic devices:

Thirty years ago, Marseilles lay *burning* in the sun, one day. A *blazing* sun upon a fierce August day was no greater rarity in southern France then, than at any other time, before or since. Everything in Marseilles, and about Marseilles, had **stared** at the fervid sky, and been **stared** at in return, until a **staring** habit had become universal there. Strangers were **stared** out of countenance by [**staring** *white* houses], [**staring** *white* walls], [**staring** *white* streets], [**staring** tracts of arid road], [**staring** hills from which verdure was burnt away]. The only things to be seen not fixedly **staring** and *glaring* were the vines drooping under their load of grapes. These did occasionally *wink* a little, as the hot air barely moved their faint leaves.

There was no wind to make a ripple on the foul water [within] the harbour, or on the beautiful sea [without]. The line of demarcation between the two colours, black and blue, showed the point which the pure sea would not pass; but it lay as quiet as the abominable pool, with which it never mixed. [Boats without awnings were too hot to touch;] [ships blistered at their moorings;] [the stones of the quays had not cooled, night or day, for months.] [Hindoos, Russians, Chinese, Spaniards, Portuguese, Englishmen, Frenchmen, Genoese, Neapolitans, Venetians, Greeks, Turks, descendants from all the builders of Babel], come to trade at Marseilles, sought the *shade* alike—taking refuge in any hiding-place from a sea too intensely blue to be looked at, and a sky of purple, set with one great *flaming* jewel of fire.

The universal **stare** made the eyes ache. Towards the distant line of Italian coast, indeed, it was a little relieved by light clouds of mist, slowly rising

---

10. See in particular Sucksmith passim for discussion of Dickens's rhetoric, and 82–86 for discussion of the opening of *Little Dorrit*.

from the evaporation of the sea, but it softened nowhere else. Far away the **staring** roads, deep in dust, [**stared** from the hill-side], [**stared** from the hollow], [**stared** from the interminable plain]. Far away the dusty vines overhanging wayside cottages, and the monotonous wayside avenues of parched trees without *shade,* drooped beneath the **stare** of earth and sky. [So did the horses with drowsy bells, in long files of carts, creeping slowly towards the interior]; [so did their recumbent drivers, when they were awake, which rarely happened]; [so did the exhausted labourers in the fields]. Everything that lived or grew, was oppressed by the *glare*; except the lizard, passing swiftly over rough stone walls, and the cicala, chirping his dry hot chirp, like a rattle. The very dust was *scorched* brown, and something quivered in the atmosphere as if the air itself were panting.

[Blinds, shutters, curtains, awnings], were all closed and drawn to keep out the **stare**. Grant it but a chink or keyhole, and it shot in like a white-hot arrow. The churches were the freest from it. To come out of the *twilight* of pillars and arches—[dreamily dotted with winking lamps], [dreamily peopled with ugly old shadows piously {dozing}, {spitting}, and {begging}]—was to plunge into a fiery river, and swim for life to the nearest strip of *shade*. So, with people lounging and lying wherever *shade* was, with but little hum of tongues or barking of dogs, with occasional jangling of discordant church bells and rattling of vicious drums, Marseilles, a fact to be strongly smelt and tasted, LAY BROILING IN THE SUN ONE DAY.

IN MARSEILLES THAT DAY there was a villainous PRISON. (39–40)

The most obvious device here is the repetition of the word "stare" and its forms, which I have indicated in bold letters. A traditional rhetorician would call this repetition "palilogia," that is, repetition for vehemence or emphasis.[11] Dickens has made no effort to conceal this device—indeed, palilogia would be hard to conceal. Nor does he conceal the other devices in the passage. One might note, for example, the use of words implying the heat and glare of the sun—"burning," "blazing," "glaring," "flaming," "scorched," "broiling"—as well as the tricolon beginning "Boats without awnings were too hot to touch." The antithetical term "shade" is used three times, and "twilight" should be included in the count. Indeed, the title of the chapter is "Sun and Shade." In

---

11. Other examples of palilogia in *Little Dorrit*: "tick" and its forms five times in five sentences (186); "magnate" eleven times in one long sentence and once more at the beginning of the next sentence (294); "cloud" eight times in three sentences, once more later in the same paragraph, and once again in the following paragraph (484); and "buttoned-up" and its variants eight times in one paragraph (621).

addition to these figures of words, there are figures of phrasing, such as the following five-part crescendo with anaphora:

staring *white* houses
staring *white* walls
staring *white* streets
staring tracts of arid road
staring hills from which verdure was burnt away

And a little later a tricolon crescendo, again with anaphora:

stared from the hill-side
stared from the hollow
stared from the interminable plain.

And we can note other instances of anaphora and tricolon, sometimes used together ("So did . . . so did . . . so did"; "dreamily . . . dreamily," etc.), as well as congeries with asyndeton ("Hindoos, Russians, Chinese, Spaniards, Portuguese, Englishmen, Frenchmen, Genoese, Neapolitans, Venetians, Greeks, Turks, descendants from all the builders of Babel"). And the passage is marked as a unit by ring composition, as the phrasing of the ending echoes the beginning:

THIRTY YEARS AGO, MARSEILLES LAY BURNING IN THE SUN, ONE DAY.
MARSEILLES . . . LAY BROILING IN THE SUN ONE DAY.

And the next paragraph, which begins a new section, starts with a link back to both the beginning and the end of the first section, and then moves on to a new topic:

IN MARSEILLES THAT DAY there was a villainous PRISON.

This passage is overtly synthetic, but it is also a vivid mimetic description (in rhetorical terms, an ekphrasis). The vividness of the mimesis is created by the synthetic devices. In this case there is a real-world referent for the narrative world-making, that is, the French city Marseille (in English sometimes spelled "Marseilles"). But of course every description is selective, and a different description, a different synthesis, would make a different narrative world. This Marseilles is Dickens's synthetic creation. Dickens is asking us to look at Marseilles, but he is equally asking us to look at his language. His world is a world of represented things and representing words. This prose is not transparent.

Perhaps Dickens has allowed himself a little self-indulgence here—and elsewhere—as he is caught up in the pleasure of composing an impressive description without much regard for its function in the novel as a whole. Quite often Dickens seems to get carried away; still in *Little Dorrit*, one might also mention, for example, Flora's wonderful speeches. We should not be surprised to discover that writers like to write. Dickens's rhetoric invites readers who like to read.[12]

Dickens may not be a fair example, he may not count as a strict realist, and therefore he may not serve as the best evidence that realistic writing can be overtly synthetic. George Orwell might be a better test. Orwell writes a transparent style more often than not, but when it suits his purpose, he also writes a more figured and ornate style, even in his last work, *1984*. Here is the opening paragraph:

> It was a bright cold day in April, and the clocks were striking thirteen. Winston Smith, his chin nuzzled into his breast in an effort to escape the vile wind, slipped quickly through the glass doors of Victory Mansions, though not quickly enough to prevent a swirl of gritty dust from entering along with him. (Orwell 3)

Overall, this is good, plain, transparent writing. We don't have to read far in *1984*, however, to find prose that calls attention to itself. During the Two Minutes Hate Winston attended on the morning the story begins, footage of Emmanuel Goldstein, Big Brother's enemy, is shown:

> He was abusing Big Brother, he was denouncing the dictatorship of the Party, he was demanding the immediate conclusion of peace with Eurasia, he was advocating freedom of speech, freedom of the press, freedom of assembly, freedom of thought, he was crying hysterically that the Revolution had been betrayed. (10)

---

12. Dickens's style in general is highly figured; in *Little Dorrit*, for example, there are instances of gradatio (235, 401), congeries (116), anaphora (144, 166, 191, 208, 350–51, etc.), epistrophe (145–46, 357, 361–62, etc.), epistrophe plus polyptoton (166), variatio (270, 284, 695, etc.), synecdoche (294–95), epizeuxis (617, 696, 712, 796, 835, etc.), polysyndeton (518), and so on. Many other passages in Dickens's novels show the kind of rhetorical exuberance and complication found in the opening of *Little Dorrit*.

The insistent repetitions in parallel structure with asyndeton are overtly synthetic.

A somewhat similar construction appears a few pages later, when Winston reacts to the dark-haired girl at the Hate (we will later find out that her name is Julia):

> Better than before, moreover, he realized *why* he hated her. He hated her because she was young and pretty and sexless, because he wanted to go to bed with her and would never do so, because round her sweet supple waist, which seemed to ask you to encircle it with your arm, there was only the odious scarlet sash, aggressive symbol of chastity. (12)

We can note here at least four rhetorical figures: anadiplosis (the repetition of "he hated her" at the end of the first sentence and the beginning of the second); anaphora (the repetition of "because" at the beginnings of the successive clauses); asyndeton (lack of connectives from clause to clause in the second sentence); and polysyndeton (the extra "and" in "young and pretty and sexless").

The next day when Winston is at lunch he hears an announcement from the Ministry of Plenty on the telescreen, filled with claims of impressive production:

> The fabulous statistics continued to pour out of the telescreen. As compared with last year there was more food, more clothes, more houses, more furniture, more cooking pots, more fuel, more ships, more helicopters, more books, more babies—more of everything except disease, crime, and insanity. (41)

Congeries is an appropriate figure for a passage about abundant production of things, even if the claims are obviously false; perhaps the figure helps to reveal the fraud. But an appropriate figure is still a figure, still synthetic, and still overt. Orwell never writes a passage as richly and variously figured as the beginning of *Little Dorrit*; he tends to save his figures for specific moments, often of high emotion, or for specific tasks. He does not, however, always write transparent prose.[13]

Figured prose is not the only kind of synthetic prose. Here is the beginning of E. L. Doctorow's *Ragtime*:

---

13. See further examples of anaphora (35), antistrophe (61), polysyndeton (82), palilogia (87–88).

> In 1902 Father built a house at the crest of the Broadview Avenue hill in New Rochelle, New York. It was a three-story brown shingle with dormers, bay windows, and a screened porch. The family took possession of this stout manse on a sunny day in June and it seemed for some years thereafter that all their days would be warm and fair. The best part of Father's income was derived from the manufacture of flags and buntings and other accoutrements of patriotism, including fireworks. Patriotism was a reliable sentiment in the early 1900's. Teddy Roosevelt was President. The population customarily gathered in great numbers either out of doors for parades, public concerts, fish fries, political picnics, social outings, or indoors in meeting halls, vaudeville theatres, operas, ball-rooms. There seemed to be no entertainment that did not involve great numbers of people. Trains and steamers and trolleys moved them from one place to another. That was the style, that was the way people lived. Women were stouter then. They visited the fleet carrying white parasols. Everyone wore white in summer. Tennis racquets were hefty and the racquet faces elliptical. There was a lot of sexual fainting. There were no Negroes. There were no immigrants. On Sunday afternoon, after dinner, Father and Mother went upstairs and closed the bedroom door. Grandfather fell asleep on the divan in the parlor. (3–4)

And so on; this initial paragraph extends for some three pages—too much to quote here. The whole passage is marvelous, and as it proceeds it develops in unexpected directions. There are a few figures: two short congeries with asyndeton ("parades, public concerts, fish fries, political picnics, social outings" and "meeting halls, vaudeville theatres, operas, ball-rooms"); an instance of polysyndeton ("Trains and steamers and trolleys"); and an example of what ancient rhetoric called "emphasis," that is, implying more than is explicitly said ("On Sunday afternoon, after dinner, Father and Mother went upstairs and closed the bedroom door"). But overall the passage is made of short, plain, uncomplicated sentences, averaging about twelve words, while the sentences in the passage *Little Dorrit* average about twenty-four words.

The sentences from *Little Dorrit* are long, on average, but they are generally not complex; their length comes from addition more than from subordination. The sentences are connected, each one to the next, usually by repeated words or ideas. The sentences from *Ragtime* tend much more to be isolated fragments; it is the reader's job to make the connections, if there are connections to be made ("Patriotism was a reliable sentiment in the early 1900's. Teddy Roosevelt was President." "There was a lot of sexual fainting. There were no Negroes.") This style is no more transparent than the style of *Little Dorrit*. Both styles, then, are overtly synthetic, but in different ways for different ends. Dickens is interested in bringing the reader into a vivid sensory experience of a particular moment, but he does most of the work himself, while the reader watches the performance; Doctorow is interested in drawing a more general picture of a period, and he leaves most of the connections to be made by the reader. Dickens relies on repetition whereas Doctorow prefers juxtaposition.

Style is a way to organize meaning; at a certain point style itself becomes part of meaning. When a style is not transparent—and no style is completely transparent—the style is part of the world that is represented. It is difficult, however, to paraphrase the meaning of a style. Often the meaning of style and of the synthetic aspect in general is the kind of meaning that doesn't easily fit into propositional form. Narrative often works best when its meanings are expressed synthetically, structurally, and we should not expect these meanings to translate easily into direct statements. The world Doctorow represents is a world of fragments, a world in which connections take some effort. Dickens represents a world of sensation; the reader is in danger of sensory overload.

IV. NARRATIVE FIGURES

The study of sentence construction began as early as Aristotle (or even earlier, in the work of the Sanskrit grammarian Panini). Modern scholarship can draw on traditional grammar, linguistics, rhetoric, and stylistics; for example, the discussion of style in the previous section uses the terms now found in standard catalogues of rhetorical figures. But synthesis above the level of the sentence is not so well developed. There is not even a name in common use for this level of synthesis, let alone a catalogue of techniques and devices. In this section I briefly explore some of the techniques of what I propose to call narrative figures. The length and complexity of narrative figures require new kinds of structural analysis. The narrative figures noted in this section include various kinds of repetition, variation, continuity (or the lack of continuity), organization, transition, and juxtaposition. None of these is as yet well defined, and the boundaries between kinds of narrative figures are fuzzy, but precision at this point is less important than an increased attention to the devices and their effects.

Many rhetorical schemes are figures of repetition, and repetition is also important at higher levels of composition. Repetition in narrative figures can involve repeated language, repeated events, repeated narration, or some combination of all three.

Repeated language. The *Iliad* and the *Odyssey,* by the standards of later literature, are extraordinarily repetitive, and the repetitions have been subject to much interpretative controversy. In the nineteenth century, critics known as analysts excised not only repeated lines but even large passages as interpolations from what were judged to be their proper or original places in the epics. Then in the 1920s, Milman Parry showed that the repetitions are inherent in the technique of oral-formulaic composition; but he also suggested that the formulas were mechanical and devoid of meaning. Later scholars argued that the traditional formulas do have meaning, but the meaning itself is traditional.[14]

In book 9 of the *Iliad,* Odysseus, Phoenix, and Ajax come to Achilleus as ambassadors from Agamemnon, to deliver an apology and an offer of recompense. Achilleus welcomes them with the full honors due to visitors; as a part of this hospitality ritual, Achilleus's companion Patroklos roasts the meat and prepares the bread:

Patroklos took the bread and set it out on a table
in fair baskets, while Achilleus served the meats. (Il.9.216–17)

In book 24, Priam, the King of Troy, comes at night to Achilleus to ask for the body of his son Hektor, who had killed Patroklos and had in turn been killed by Achilleus. After Achilleus and Priam converse, and after Achilleus has agreed to return the body of Hektor, he serves Priam a meal with full honors, but Patroklos, of course, is not there to play his part in the ritual, so Automedon acts as his substitute:

Automedon took the bread and set it out on a table
in fair baskets, while Achilleus served the meats. (Il.24.625–26)

The wording of the two passages in Greek is identical, except for the substitution of the name Automedon for Patroklos. The substitution within the formula suggests, without direct statement, the absence of Achilleus's companion, who was killed by Priam's son, Hektor; this repetition is meaningful and moving.

The formulaic repetitions in the Homeric epics are a special case because of their roots in oral composition, but some kind of verbal repetition is com-

---

14. See Parry, which reprints his original papers on formulaic composition. For later work on meaning in formulaic composition, see Whitman; Nagy; Slatkin; and Foley.

mon in later literature,[15] and most other kinds of repetition are likely to involve verbal repetition. The repetition of a word or phrase is usually emphatic and often marks out some thematic element. Near the beginning of *1984*, for example, the narrator tells us the three slogans of the Party: "WAR IS PEACE / FREEDOM IS SLAVERY / IGNORANCE IS STRENGTH" (5). In part 1, the slogans are repeated in exactly the same form three times (12, 19, and 70); in part 2, we find "IGNORANCE IS STRENGTH" (122, 134) and "WAR IS PEACE" (123); and in part 3, "FREEDOM IS SLAVERY" (184), now joined with two other important propositions, "TWO AND TWO MAKE FIVE" (which is itself repeated at 192) and "GOD IS POWER." The synthetic repetition marks these as thematically significant.

Repeated events. Events are not often repeated exactly, and often it is the variation that is important, but often the variation has meaning only because of the repetition. A clear instance of the varied repetition of an event is Mr. Darcy's second proposal to Elizabeth Bennet; the differences between the two proposals and the two answers complete the process of change displayed in the narrative.

In part 1 of *1984*, Winston remembers three failed counterrevolutionaries, Jones, Aaronson, and Rutherford, who had been arrested, rehabilitated, and released; after their release, Winston saw them, now broken and lonely, in the Chestnut Tree Café (51–52). Then, at the very end of the story, after Winston has been arrested and tortured and broken, he is released, and we see him sitting at the Chestnut Tree Café (190–97). Much of the phrasing of the first passage is repeated here. The point, of course, is to draw a comparison between Winston and the old failed counterrevolutionaries; he is literally in their place.

Repeated narration. A single event may be narrated more than once. A very striking example is the death of Snowden in Joseph Heller's *Catch-22*. The narrative returns to this event obsessively; clearly it is one of the key events in the story. It is first mentioned in chapter 4 (35), then again in chapters 5 (50), 17 (165–66, 172), 21 (218), 22, (225–26), 30 (331–32), and 41 (436–40). Each telling adds a little to the description, until the last, in the penultimate chapter of the novel, finally goes into extensive detail. The repetition and gradual revelation is obviously synthetic, and yet the incident is designed to have a compelling emotional impact.

Links. Repetition of a word can be used as a link to provide continuity—not only from sentence to sentence, but also from paragraph to paragraph, from chapter to chapter. The beginning of Joseph Conrad's *The Secret Agent*

---

15. See, for example, Gertrude Stein's "Melanctha," in *Three Lives*, Flann O'Brien's *The Third Policeman*, Samuel Beckett's *How It Is*, or Joseph Heller's *Catch-22*.

uses a number of paragraph links, and then a link from the first chapter to the second. Here are the first three paragraphs, with the links marked in bold:

> Mr Verloc, going out in the morning, left his **shop** nominally in charge of his brother-in-law. It could be done, because there was very little business at any time, and practically none at all before the evening. Mr Verloc cared but little about his ostensible business. And, moreover, his wife was in charge of his brother-in-law.
>
> The **shop** was small, and so was the house. It was one of those grimy brick houses which existed in large quantities before the era of reconstruction dawned upon London. The shop was a square box of a place, with the front glazed in small **panes**. In the daytime the door remained closed; in the evening it stood discreetly but suspiciously ajar.
>
> The **window** contained photographs of more or less undressed dancing girls; nondescript packages in wrappers like patent medicines; closed yellow paper envelopes, very flimsy, and marked two and six in heavy black figures; a few numbers of ancient French comic publications hung across a string as if to dry; a dingy blue china bowl, a casket of black wood, bottles of marking ink, and rubber stamps; a few books with titles hinting at impropriety; a few apparently old copies of obscure newspapers, badly printed, with titles like the Torch, the Gong—rousing titles. And the two gas-jets inside the **panes** were always turned low, either for economy's sake or for the sake of the **customers**. (1)

The links continue: The first sentence of the fourth paragraph links back to the third paragraph with the word "customers." The last sentence of the fourth paragraph and the first sentence of the fifth have the link "bell"; the last sentence of the fifth and the first sentence of the sixth have the link "clattered." There are more or less clear links in several succeeding paragraphs.

The job of this first chapter is to introduce some of the characters—Mr. Verloc, his wife, his wife's mother, and his wife's brother—as well as to describe his disreputable shop and to hint at the mystery about his business. The first sentence of the second chapter then links back to the first chapter as a whole: "Such was the house, the household, and the business Mr Verloc left behind him on his way westward at the hour of half-past ten in the morning." (8)

Paragraph links and chapter links are commonly used, and for the most part they don't attract much notice. They are not so much concealed—there is really no way that they can be concealed; rather, they are sufficiently conventionalized to pass without much notice. Of course, paragraph and chapter breaks often mark a more or less abrupt narrative discontinuity; discontinuity is just as synthetic as continuity. Links provide connection, but connection and continuity are not the same: One can find continuity without a hook, continuity with a hook, discontinuity without a hook, and discontinuity with a hook.[16]

Ring composition. Ring composition occurs when a series of items is repeated in reverse order. A ring can be formed simply when the beginning and the end of a literary unit match, to form an ABA structure, but the pattern of matching can be more elaborate: AB/BA, ABC/CBA, ABCD/DCBA, and so on.[17] Rings can organize small sections or entire plots.

A simple ABA ring can be used to mark the boundaries of a digression, as in the famous scene in book 19 of the *Odyssey* when the nurse Eurykleia washes Odysseus's feet and recognizes his scar: "She came up close and washed her lord, and at once she recognized / that **scar**, which once the boar with his white tusk had inflicted / on him" (Od.19.392–94). The poet then tells at some length just how Odysseus got the scar (Od.19.394–466) and then returns to Eurykleia: "The old woman, holding him in the palms of her hands, recognized / this **scar** as she handled it" (Od.19.467–68). She drops his foot, which has been in suspense for some seventy-five lines. Such digressive rings are very common in later literature.

A more extensive ring is found in book 11 of the *Odyssey*, when Odysseus visits the land of the dead and talks with the shade of his mother. He asks her four questions: (A) How did you die? (B) How is my father? (C) How is my son? (D) How is my wife? His mother then answers these four questions in reverse order (Od.11.170–203).

At a larger level, the beginning and the ending of the *Iliad* form a great ring: At the beginning, an old man, Chryses, comes to the Greek camp to appeal for the return of his child, Chryseis; at the end, an old man, Priam, comes to the Greek camp to appeal for the return of his child, Hektor. The ring can be extended:

A. Chryses's appeal (1.10–42)
B. Conversation between Thetis and Achilles (1.351–427)
C. Conversation between Thetis and Zeus (1.500–530)
D. Gathering of the gods (1.533–611)

---

16. Chapter links are particularly emphatic when they are exact repetitions; see, for example, the link between chapter 9 and chapter 10 in Anthony Trollope's *Framley Parsonage*; this link also crosses the boundary of the third and fourth magazine installments. See also the emphatic chapter links in Toni Morrison's *Jazz*. On links, see Clark, *A Matter of Style* 130–40.

17. For extensive analysis of ring composition, see Douglas. For discussion of ring composition in Homer, see Whitman; Louden.

D. Gathering of the gods (24.32–76)
C. Conversation between Thetis and Zeus (24.100–119)
B. Conversation between Thetis and Achilles (24.126–58)
A. Priam's appeal (24.471–688)

This summary simplifies and omits, but even so the correspondence is a remarkable instance of narrative figuration. The differences are of course as important as the similarities. For example, Chryses's supplication of Agamemnon fails, while Priam's supplication of Achilles succeeds—and this difference indicates an important but unstated meaning of the epic as a whole. Homer, at the beginning of the Western tradition, knew that structure carries meaning.

Ending with the beginning. A simple ring, ABA, can be used to mark the beginning and the ending of a whole story. Often the second A is varied in some way; it can even be the reverse of the beginning.

Henry James's *Roderick Hudson* begins as Rowland Mallet visits his cousin Cecilia in Northampton, Massachusetts; there he meets Roderick Hudson, a young sculptor of great promise but little training, and Mary Garland, his fiancée. Rowland takes Roderick to Europe, and eventually they are joined by Mary. Rowland has fallen in love with Mary, but he is too much a gentleman (or too passive a character) to declare his love. Meanwhile Roderick gradually enters a life of dissipation. Toward the end of the novel, he is killed (or perhaps kills himself) in a mountaineering accident. As the novel ends, Mary is back in Northampton, where Rowland often visits his cousin, but now in hopes of seeing Mary. So the book ends where it began, with a difference.

Ending with the beginning is a very common narrative figure: It is found, for example, in Dickens's *Little Dorrit*, George Eliot's *Silas Marner*, Henry James's *The Wings of the Dove*, Robert Heinlein's *Starman Jones* and *Tunnel in the Sky*, Vladimir Nabokov's *Pnin*, and Ken Kesey's *One Flew over the Cuckoo's Nest*. In each of these, the technique is treated in its own way, and each deserves individual analysis, but they all show the strong impulse toward symmetry and closure in the Western narrative tradition.

Anticipations. At the beginning of Orwell's *1984*, the hero, Winston Smith, attends the Two Minutes Hate at the Ministry of Truth: "Winston was just taking his place in one of the middle rows when two people whom he knew by sight but had never spoken to, came unexpectedly into the room" (8). As it happens, these two people are Julia and O'Brien. Orwell describes both at some length, but then he drops them for a while. Later on they return and become two of the crucial characters in the story. Orwell has introduced them here at the beginning presumably to prepare for their later appearance.

In *Framley Parsonage,* Anthony Trollope uses an anticipation and explicitly marks it. Among those at Mark Robarts's wedding was his younger sister:

> And there was there another and a younger sister of Mark's—who did not officiate at the ceremony, though she was present—and of whom no prediction was made, seeing that she was then only sixteen, but of whom mention is made here, as it will come to pass that my readers will know her hereafter. Her name was Lucy Robarts. (38)

Lucy is next mentioned just one hundred pages later, and then she becomes one of the principal characters of the story.

Juxtaposition. The simplest form of synthetic construction is the juxtaposition of two narrative items, without explicit comment. We have already seen stylistic juxtaposition in Doctorow's *Ragtime* ("There was a lot of sexual fainting. There were no Negroes."), but juxtaposition also occurs at the level of composition. Juxtaposition of some sort is inevitable, but it is not always meaningful; the critical task is to note which instances do have meaning.[18]

A notable instance of juxtaposition is found in *The Hamlet,* the first volume of William Faulkner's Snopes Trilogy, where the episode of Labove's passion for Eula Varner is juxtaposed to the episode of Ike Snopes's passion for a cow. As Edmond Volpe says, "In the descriptions of Eula, her bovine qualities are emphasized; and in the Swinburnian descriptions of the cow, the distinction between female animal and human female is difficult to discern" (Volpe 311).[19]

The technique of juxtaposition can be extended to include parallel plots. William Thackeray's *Vanity Fair,* for instance, is largely structured around parallel plots concerning Amelia Sedley and Becky Sharp; this parallel is clearly established in the first two chapters and continues throughout the novel. Modernist novelists also construct parallel plots, as Mrs. Dalloway and Septimus Smith are the parallel protagonists in Virginia Woolf's *Mrs. Dalloway.* Woolf has to go to some work to establish the parallel, since the two characters are only tangentially connected. In *The Wild Palms,* William Faulkner takes the principle to its extreme: The book is composed of alternating chapters of two evidently unconnected stories, one titled "Wild Palms" and the other titled

---

18. Juxtaposition is by no means a modern discovery; Thucydides, for example, in his History of the Peloponnesian War, juxtaposes the Melian Dialogue at the end of book 5 and the failed Athenian expedition to Sicily at the beginning of book 6 (see Connor 158). The implication is that Athenian arrogance led to disaster.

19. The famous passage at the Agricultural Fair in *Madame Bovary* (part 2, chapter 8) is somewhat more complicated, since the two scenes are not only juxtaposed but also interwoven.

"The Old Man." Each of these can be read independently, and they have been published separately, but when Faulkner published them in alternating chapters, he must have intended the reader to make something of the arrangement.[20] The parallels in *Mrs. Dalloway* and *The Wild Palms* perhaps seem artificial—that is, synthetic—but really they are no more a matter of artifice than the parallel between Amelia and Becky, which is, after all, a synthetic invention in itself; Thackeray simply adds the artifice of a constructed relationship between Amelia and Becky to justify the artifice of the parallelism.

Character sets. Some narratives concentrate on a single principal character, others on two, or three, or perhaps a few more. These sets are not random; most storytellers have a very good sense of how many principals are needed and how many extras, but some authors are more economical than others. Sets can be formed in various ways. The character set of *The Return of the Native* (Clym Yeobright > Eustacia Vye > Damon Wildeve > Thomasin Yeobright > Diggory Venn) forms a chain somewhat like the character set of *The Great Gatsby* (Jay Gatsby > Daisy Buchanan > Tom Buchanan > Myrtle Wilson > George Wilson), though Nick Carraway complicates the comparison. Other narratives are organized in patterns of contrasting characters or relationships, as in *Pride and Prejudice* there is a set of contrasting couples and marriages (Elizabeth Bennet + Mr. Darcy, Jane Bennet + Charles Bingley, Lydia Bennet + George Wickham, Charlotte Lucas + Mr. Collins).[21]

Architecture. The larger shape of a narrative, its architecture, is also synthetic. The shape of Dante's *Divine Comedy* models his view of the Christian afterlife in three parts; each part is thirty-three cantos long, and with one canto of prologue, the whole is exactly one hundred cantos. J. R. R. Tolkien's *The Lord of the Rings* also has a tripartite construction: There are three volumes (*The Fellowship of the Ring*, *The Two Towers*, and *The Return of the King*), and each volume is divided into two parts; each of these parts ends at a turning point of the story. Part of the pleasure of reading this story is provided by the sense of an order that controls the events of this imagined world.

Anthony Burgess's *A Clockwork Orange* is justly famous for its verbal invention, but it is also remarkable for its architecture.[22] The story is another narrative in three parts. Each of these parts has seven chapters: Part 1 takes the story up to the arrest of the protagonist, Alex; part 2 tells about his time

---

20. The version with the two novels in alternating sections was first published in 1939 with the title *The Wild Palms*. Faulkner 1948, also titled *The Wild Palms*, omits *The Old Man* and *The Old Man* was published as one of three short novels in Faulkner 1961.

21. For more on character sets and narrative geometries, see Clark, *Narrative*.

22. Peter Rabinowitz points out that the three parts can be seen as exposition, development, and recapitulation in sonata form.

in prison and the psychological treatment he receives there; part 3 begins as he is released from prison.[23] The plot is organized around a number of crucial repetitions. The first sentence of the book ("What's it going to be then, eh?") is repeated several times in quick succession (twice on 5 and once more on 6). It is then the first sentence of part 2 (85), and it is repeated four more times (86, 87, 88, and 94). It is also the first sentence of part 3 (147), and it is repeated twice more (148 and 150). It is the first line of chapter 7 of part 3 (200), and it is repeated once more (201).[24]

In addition to these verbal repetitions, part 3 recapitulates important events of part 1. The first element to be recapitulated is Alex's return home (36 and 151). This repetition is plausible, and perhaps it would not attract the reader's attention as synthetic, but the other repetitions are more marked. Immediately after his return home, Alex goes to the record store he had frequented in part 1 (47 and 156). Immediately after that, he goes to the milk bar where we first met him (3 and 158). Immediately after that, he goes to the library and happens across the very man he assaulted in chapter 1 of part 1 (7 and 161). And immediately after that, he encounters Billyboy, the policeman who had arrested him in chapter 6 of part 1—and most surprisingly, the policeman's partner turns out to be Alex's old gang mate, Dim (72 and 166). Billyboy and Dim take Alex out to the country, work him over, and leave him lying in a field. When he recovers consciousness, he makes his way to a nearby house, which turns out to be the very house where Alex had committed the brutal rape in chapter 2 of part 1 (23 and 170). This quick series of repetitions lacks all plausibility, but plausibility has nothing to do with Burgess's intent.

The final chapter begins with an exact repetition of the first line of the first chapter, and it continues with nearly exact repetition of the words and situation of the first chapter, as Alex is sitting in the milk bar with a new gang. But as the chapter continues, the reader sees that Alex is changing. As he is getting older, he is losing his interest in random violence; instead he is developing a desire for domestic life, with a wife and children.

Thematically, the story insists on the importance of free will: People can choose good only if they are able to choose evil. On the other hand, the final chapter suggests that bad boys simply grow up; if so, we do not so much choose good as grow into it. Burgess clearly was deeply concerned with the ideas he presents, but he paid great attention to the construction of the narrative, the synthetic aspect.

---

23. The first US publication of *A Clockwork Orange* (1962) had only six chapters in part 3. The omission of the final chapter destroyed the symmetry of the architecture and changed the theme of the story; see Burgess's introduction to the 1986 reprint.

24. Note also the repetition of the title within the text on 25, 141, and 172.

V. THE SYNTHETIC ASPECT OF *EMMA*

There is no novel, I suppose, more central to the "realistic" or "mimetic" narrative tradition than Jane Austen's *Emma*. *Emma* is also a masterpiece of narrative synthesis, and its synthetic quality does not detract from the mimetic or thematic aspects. Some of the synthetic devices are obvious on first reading; others become clear only on second or later readings. None of them, however, seem particularly covert.

Jane Austen's style has often been praised.[25] As Robyn Warhol notes, Austen "has always received credit for the beautiful symmetry of her periodic sentences" (Herman et al. 166); "Austen's voice," Warhol says, is "a distinctive blend of ironic hyperbole, orderly syntax, parallel phrasing, free indirect discourse, and periodic sentences" (40). Kroeber praises Austen's style with a qualification: "I yield to no one in my admiration for Jane Austen's skill as a writer, but I feel that an impressive feature of her skill is her ability never to become a mere stylist—meaning rather than manner is invariably her primary focus" (Kroeber 175). Norman Page argues that "style is a component of exceptional importance in Jane Austen's work" (2), that "the 'triumph' of the novels is to a large extent a triumph of style" (9), and that Austen was "an innovator . . . notably in prose syntax and narrative modes" (9). If Austen's style were truly transparent, if it were covert, it would not have received this kind of attention. I will not present here a comprehensive account of Austen's style, but a few examples will help to show the importance of the synthetic aspect in *Emma*.[26]

It is easy to find well-turned sentences in *Emma*. (Strictly speaking, Austen writes few periods, at least in the Ciceronian manner of periodic construction, but writers on English style often use a less formal concept of the period, depending more on symmetry than on suspension of meaning.) Austen is fond of parallel structure, antithesis, and tricolon. In volume 3, chapter 5, Emma is assuring Mr. Knightley that Frank Churchill and Jane Fairfax feel nothing for each other: "She spoke with a confidence which staggered, and a satisfaction which silenced, Mr. Knightley" (242). And in the following chapter, when Mr. Weston indicates to Emma his good impression of Mrs. Elton, "Emma denied none of it aloud, and agreed to none of it in private" (244).

In chapter 15 of volume 2, Emma hears that Jane Fairfax has been spending time with Mrs. Elton: "Emma's only surprize was that Jane Fairfax should

---

25. I have particularly benefited from discussions of Austen's style in Babb; Page; and Stokes. For a recent appreciation of style in *Emma*, see Davidson.

26. Previous critics have discussed at length Austen's use of irony and free indirect discourse in *Emma*, so I will not repeat that discussion here.

accept those attentions and tolerate Mrs. Elton as she seemed to do. She heard of her **walking** with the Eltons, **sitting** with the Eltons, **spending a day** with the Eltons!" (196). A little later, in chapter 17 of volume 2, during a dinner party at Hartfield, Mrs. Elton is talking with Jane Fairfax, who is looking for a position as a governess. Mrs. Elton insists that Jane "must be and shall be **delightfully**, **honourably** and **comfortably** settled" (208); Jane replies, "You may well class the **delight**, the **honour**, and the **comfort** of such a situation together.... [T]hey are pretty sure to be equal" (208). Here tricolon is combined with polyptoton, as the words in question change from adverbs to nouns. On the following page, Mr. Weston comes in late to the party after a long day; Mr. John Knightley (Emma's brother-in-law) is astonished to see him come when he could have stayed home: "*A man who had been in motion since eight o'clock in the morning,* **and might now have been still,** *who had been long talking,* **and might now have been silent,** *who had been in more than one crowd,* and **might have been alone!**" (209). Here each member of the tricolon is itself divided.

A somewhat longer passage from a few chapters earlier, chapter 14 of volume 2, shows a number of typical devices of Austen's style. Mrs. Elton has just arrived in Highbury for the first time: "Mrs. Elton was first seen at church; but though devotion might be interrupted, curiosity could not be satisfied by a bride in a pew, and it must be left for the visits in form which were then to be paid, to settle whether she were very pretty indeed, or only rather pretty, or not pretty at all" (185). We note the parallel construction ("devotion might be interrupted / curiosity could not be satisfied") followed by an elegant tricolon decrescendo ("very pretty / rather pretty / not pretty at all").

A few days later, Emma takes Harriet on a formal visit to the Eltons and gets to know Mrs. Elton a little better:

She did not really like her. She would not be in a hurry to find fault, but she suspected that there was no elegance—ease but not elegance.—She was almost sure that for a young woman, a stranger, a bride, there was too much ease. Her person was rather good; her face not unpretty; but neither feature, nor air, nor voice, nor manner, were elegant. Emma thought at least it would turn out so.

As for Mr. Elton, his manners did not appear—but no, she would not permit a hasty or a witty word from herself about his manners. It was an awkward ceremony at any time to be receiving wedding-visits, and a man had to be all grace to acquit himself well through it. The woman was better off; she might have the assistance of fine clothes, and the privilege of bashfulness, but the man had only his good sense to depend on; and when she considered how peculiarly unlucky poor Mr. Elton was in being in the same room at once with the woman he had just married, the woman he had wanted to marry, and the woman whom he had been expected to marry, she must allow him to have the right to look as little wise, and to be as much affectedly, and as little really easy as could be. (186)

Much here deserves comment. First we might note the repetitions of "elegant," a key word that runs through the whole book (here it is opposed to "ease" and, at the end of the second paragraph, "easy"). There are several tricolons, including the quite striking "the woman . . . / the woman . . . / the woman." "Not unpretty" is a good litotes; there is parallel structure in "the assistance of fine clothes, and the privilege of bashfulness"; and the whole is an excellent example of free indirect discourse, particularly marked by the aposiopesis, the sudden break in the discourse, at the beginning of the second paragraph.[27]

Aposiopesis occurs at some key moments in the novel. In chapter 15 of volume 1, Mr. Elton proposes to Emma, who rejects him; she tells him she had thought he was attracted to Harriet, and he replies, in part, "I wish her extremely well: and no doubt, there are men who might not object to— Everybody had their level" (94). Here he cannot bring himself to say explicitly that Harriet is illegitimate. Then, in chapter 11 of volume 2, Frank Churchill is on the verge of telling Emma that he is engaged to Jane, but Emma misunderstands and thinks that he is about to propose to her:

"In short," said he, "perhaps, Miss Woodhouse—I think you can hardly be quite without suspicion"—

He looked at her, as if wanting to read her thoughts. She hardly knew what to say. It seemed like the fore-runner of something absolutely serious, which she did not wish. (180)

These instances of aposiopesis are part of a larger pattern of misunderstandings and failed communications. When Harriet tells Emma that she is in love with Mr. Knightley, Emma understands her to mean Frank Churchill, because neither provides an antecedent for her pronouns.

One of the most common features of Austen's style is simple conjunction of clauses, as in the first two paragraphs of the novel:

---

27. Free indirect discourse is of course created synthetically, but it also functions mimetically, as a representation of consciousness.

> Emma Woodhouse, handsome, clever, and rich, with a comfortable home and happy disposition, seemed to unite some of the best blessings of existence; **and** had lived nearly twenty-one years in the world with very little to distress or vex her.
>
> She was the youngest of the two daughters of a most affectionate, indulgent father, **and** had, in consequence of her sister's marriage, been mistress of his house from a very early period. Her mother had died too long ago for her to have more than an indistinct remembrance of her caresses, **and** her place had been supplied by an excellent woman as governess, who had fallen little short of a mother in affection. (5)

The first clause in any of these sentences could well stand on its own:

> Emma Woodhouse, handsome, clever, and rich, with a comfortable home and happy disposition, seemed to unite some of the best blessings of existence. . . . She was the youngest of the two daughters of a most affectionate, indulgent father. . . . Her mother had died too long ago for her to have more than an indistinct remembrance of her caresses.

The effect, of course, is much inferior. Not only is information missing, but the rhythm is wrong: if the missing clauses were added as independent structures, the information would be there, but we would miss the flow and continuity of Austen's style:

> Emma Woodhouse, handsome, clever, and rich, with a comfortable home and happy disposition, seemed to unite some of the best blessings of existence. She had lived nearly twenty-one years in the world with very little to distress or vex her.
>
> She was the youngest of the two daughters of a most affectionate, indulgent father. In consequence of her sister's marriage, she had been mistress of his house from a very early period. Her mother had died too long ago for her to have more than an indistinct remembrance of her caresses. Her place had been supplied by an excellent woman as governess, who had fallen little short of a mother in affection.

A second example shows a slightly different situation. This passage comes in chapter 2 of volume 1, as Austen is giving some background about Mr. Weston: "He had made his fortune, bought his house, and obtained his wife; **and** was beginning a new period of existence with every probability of greater happiness than in any yet passed through" (13). Here the tricolon of the beginning of the sentence is not allowed to stand on its own, as the continuation softens the effect of the figure.

Austen's habit of conjunction tends to lengthen the rhythm—the rhythm of sound and also the rhythm of information—and it can reduce the insistent formality of tricolon or parallel structure. Because Austen's figures are often augmented by little additions, they never seem to force the meaning to fit the figure. Sometimes (not always) Austen also avoids isocolon (that is, an equal number of words or syllables in the parts of a figure). For instance, when Mr. Elton takes Emma's drawing of Harriet to London to be framed, Emma tells Harriet that Mr. Elton will have the drawing with him all the time: "It is his companion all this evening, his solace, his delight. It opens his designs to his family, it introduces you among them, it diffuses through the party those pleasantest feelings of our nature, eager curiosity and warm prepossession" (41). Here there are two tricolons ("companion"/"solace"/"delight"; "opens"/"in troduces"/"diffuses") and a doublet ("eager curiosity" / "warm prepossession"), but none shows isocolon.

Austen's relaxed additive style, when she uses it, allows her to cover a lot of ground within a single sentence. In the following, Mr. Weston has arrived late at Emma's dinner party because he had business to attend to elsewhere, and Mr. John Knightley is surprised that he has come at all when he could have stayed away:

> Mr. Weston meanwhile, perfectly unsuspicious of the indignation he was exciting, happy and cheerful as usual, and with all the right of being principal talker, which a day spent any where from home confers, was making himself agreeable among the rest; and having satisfied the inquires of his wife as to his dinner, convincing her that none of all her careful directions to the servant had been forgotten, and spread abroad what public news he had heard, was proceeding to a family communication, which, though principally addressed to Mrs. Weston, he had not the smallest doubt of being highly interesting to every body in the room. (209)

Here the main syntax of the sentence can be reduced to its essentials: "Mr. Weston meanwhile . . . was making himself agreeable among the rest; and . . . was proceeding to a family communication." Everything else is subordinate.

Austen's style combines ease and elegance: The elegance comes from figured symmetry, the ease from variation and addition. Compare, for example, the beginning of Anne Brontë's *Agnes Grey*, which shows a much more formal syntax.

Austen is very good at individualizing each character's manner of speech. For our purposes, it is sufficient to note Mr. Elton's habit of saying "Exactly so," Mrs. Elton's habit of self-reference and self-contradiction, and of course Miss Bates's habit of fragmentary and irrational association. Miss Bates's manner of talking becomes a key element in the plot when Emma insults her during the Box Hill outing and earns Mr. Knightley's rebuke.[28]

The chatter of a group is represented as a series of fragments not attributed to any particular individual, as in the party at Donwell Abbey, when "strawberries, and only strawberries, could now be thought or spoken of":[29]

"The best fruit in England—every body's favorite—always wholesome.—These the finest beds and finest sorts.—Delightful to gather for one's self—the only way of really enjoying them.—Morning decidedly the best time—never tired—every sort good—hautboy infinitely superior—no comparison—the others hardly eatable—hautboys very scarcer—Chili preferred—white wood finest flavour of all—price of strawberries in London." (247)

And so on. This passage certainly counts as overt synthetic construction.[30]

Austen uses both paragraph and chapter links. Harriet Smith was introduced in chapter 3 of volume 1; chapter 4 begins, "**Harriet Smith's** intimacy at Hartfield was soon a settled thing" (20). There is then a link to the second paragraph of the chapter, which begins, "**Harriet** was certainly not clever." This paragraph develops a contrast between Mrs. Weston and Harriet, and ends, "**Harriet** would be loved as one to whom she could be **useful**. For Mrs. Weston there was nothing to be done; for Harriet every thing," and the next paragraph begins, "Her first attempts at **usefulness** . . . ." This paragraph ends, "Harriet had no penetration. She had been satisfied to hear and believe just what **Mrs. Goddard** chose to tell her; and looked no further," and the next paragraph begins, "**Mrs. Goddard**, and the teachers, and the girls, and the affairs of the school in general . . ."

---

28. Style in dialogue is ordinarily linked to the portrayal of personality. Mrs. Elton's obtuse and insistent officiousness is synthetic in its construction but mimetic in its effect, and so for the other characters. For discussion of dialogue in *Emma* and in particular the styles of Emma and Mr. Knightley, see Babb.

29. Some critics attribute this whole passage to Mrs. Elton, but the narrator's comment at the end ("Such, for half an hour, was the conversation") suggests that it represents general discussion.

30. See also the representation of Frank's monologue when he first meets Emma in volume 2, chapter 5 (133).

The ending of chapter 2 of volume 1 ("There was a strange rumor in Highbury of all the little Perrys being seen with a slice of Mrs. Weston's wedding-cake in their hand: but **Mr. Woodhouse** would never believe it") links to the beginning of chapter 3 ("**Mr. Woodhouse** was fond of society in his own way" [15]), and the ending of chapter 3 ("The happiness of **Miss Smith** was quite equal to her [Emma's] intentions" [19]) links to the beginning of chapter 4 ("**Harriet Smith's** intimacy at Hartfield was soon a settled thing" [20]). Chapter 2 of volume 2 ends, "Emma could not forgive her," and chapter 3 begins with exactly the same words (117).

Once the reader starts to look for these links, they are easy to find, though of course they are not used everywhere; sometimes Austen makes an abrupt transition from one chapter to the next. A very interesting structure is found in chapters 4, 5, and 6 of volume 1. In chapter 4, Harriet reveals her attraction to Robert Martin, but Emma discourages her; she wants Harriet to marry Mr. Elton. Chapter 4 ends, "**The girl** who could be gratified by a Robert Martin's riding about the country to get walnuts for her, might very well be conquered by **Mr. Elton's** admiration" (27). Chapter 5 begins with an abrupt change of characters, time, setting, and form: "'I do not know what your opinion may be, Mrs. Weston,' said Mr. Knightley, 'of this great intimacy between Emma and Harriet Smith, but I think it is a bad thing'" (27). And the rest of the chapter is taken up with dialogue between these two characters. Chapter 6 then begins, "Emma could not feel a doubt of having given **Harriet's** fancy a proper direction and raised the gratitude of her young vanity to a very good purpose, for she found her decidedly more sensible than before of **Mr. Elton's** being a remarkably handsome man" (31). The beginning of chapter 6 thus follows smoothly from the end of chapter 4. Chapter 5 is something of an intrusion, but the intrusion makes a point: Mr. Knightley's disquiet puts Emma's actions in a completely different light, and the reader is prepared for the argument between Emma and Mr. Knightley in chapter 8, after Harriet, at Emma's direction, has turned down Mr. Martin's proposal. The structure here is elegant, including the transitions from chapter 4 to chapter 5 to chapter 6. This kind of structural elegance is part of the beauty of Austen's writing, which we see in her manner of composition as well as in her style.

It is not my intention to give a complete account of the synthetic aspect of *Emma*, so I will pass over Austen's construction of paragraphs and chapters, except to say that in general her chapters are designed to perform one or two specific narrative tasks, but composed in a variety of forms in order to avoid any feeling of monotony.

Chapters are grouped into blocks that form the major movements of the plot, though the episodic construction is somewhat blurred by anticipations, gradual transitions, and overlapping, as well as by variations in the lapse of time. Austen's episodes are more like strands in a braid than like beads on a string.[31] As Babb notes, "Jane Austen interlocks these movements beautifully, the new situation and its characters always beginning to claim our attention before the old movement is quite finished" (176).

Emma (somewhat like the *Divine Comedy*, *The Lord of the Rings*, and *A Clockwork Orange*) can be divided into three major episodes, which might be called "Emma's first mistake," "Emma's second mistake," and "Emma's third mistake." The beginning of each episode roughly coincides with the beginning of one of the original volumes, but in a sense all three episodes end only at the end of the whole story.[32]

The first volume is mostly taken up with Emma's first mistake; the major characters in this episode are Emma herself, her friend Harriet Smith, Harriet's suitor Robert Martin, and Mr. Elton, but other elements of the story are subtly introduced as well. Chapter 1 begins by getting Emma's governess, Miss Taylor, married off to Mr. Weston; Emma credits herself as the matchmaker, and when her father urges her to make no more matches, she replies, "Only one more, papa; only for Mr. Elton. Poor Mr. Elton! You like Mr. Elton, papa,—I must look about for a wife for him" (11). Chapter 2 gives an account of Mr. Weston; one point here is to mention, in anticipation, Mr. Weston's son, Frank Churchill, though he is quickly dropped—kept in reserve for the second episode.

Chapter 3 introduces Harriet Smith to Emma and to the reader. Chapter 4 begins, "Harriet Smith's intimacy at Hartfield was soon a settled thing. Quick and decided in her ways, Emma lost no time in inviting, encouraging, and telling her to come very often" (20). Emma learns that Harriet is in danger of marrying Robert Martin, but "Mr. Elton was the very person fixed on by Emma for driving the young farmer out of Harriet's head" (26). Emma's plans go all wrong, and in chapter 15 Mr. Elton proposes to Emma instead of to Harriet, and she rejects him indignantly. In chapter 16 she reflects on her mistakes and resolves to be more careful for the future. In chapter 17 Mr. Elton leaves Highbury and goes to Bath for an indefinite stay, and Emma finally talks with Harriet about what has happened. Harriet's story will continue as a counterpoint to Emma's story until the end of the novel; her eventual marriage to

---

31. The elegance of Austen's architecture has often been noticed; W. J. Harvey, for instance, praises the plot of *Emma*: "There is a humble but valid aesthetic pleasure to be derived from the sheer ingenuity of the plot, from the scrupulousness with which Jane Austen seeds her clues and the neatness with which she bundles up her complicated harvest" (Harvey 233).

32. The tripartite structure of *Emma* is noticed by Duffy and Shannon, but neither takes full account of the importance of the volume divisions.

Robert Martin would count as a (partial) example of the ring structure ending with the beginning.

With Mr. Elton's departure, the first episode is suspended for the time being, but the volume continues with one more chapter, which is mostly concerned with Frank Churchill's failure to visit his father and stepmother. Frank, of course, will be an important character in the rest of the novel. Then the first chapter of volume 2 brings Jane Fairfax on stage. (She was previously mentioned, in an anticipation, in chapter 10 of volume 1.) These two chapters, straddling the break between the volumes, begin the second episode, Emma's second mistake: Emma thinks that Jane is romantically involved with a married man (Mr. Dixon, the husband of her former friend Miss Campbell) and that she herself is the object of Frank's romantic attentions. Eventually the reader will find out that Frank and Jane have been secretly engaged; Austen has to maintain the secret while subtly preparing the reader for the revelation of their relationship.

Volume 2 begins: "Emma and Harriet had been walking together one morning, and, in Emma's opinion, been talking enough of Mr. Elton for that day" (107). Here Austen is also telling the reader, "enough of Mr. Elton"—at least for the time being. He will, of course, return. Emma decides that she and Harriet will visit Mrs. Bates and her daughter Miss Bates, Jane's grandmother and aunt; Emma, who doesn't much like Jane, remarks "that as well as she could calculate, they were just now quite safe from any letter from Jane Fairfax" (107). But she is wrong; she learns that Jane has sent a letter saying that she will be coming for a visit: "Highbury, instead of welcoming that perfect novelty which had been so long promised it—Mr. Frank Churchill—must put up for the present with Jane Fairfax" (115). Thus Frank and Jane are first coupled in an exclusive disjunction—either Frank or Jane but not both. Later in the chapter, however, Emma learns that Jane has met Frank, though Jane's answers to Emma's questions suggest that she hardly knows him.

Frank himself does arrive shortly thereafter, in chapter 5 of volume 2; he and his father go to Hartfield to visit Emma and her father, and in the course of discussion he mentions that he is already acquainted with Jane Fairfax. Emma remarks that Jane is a very elegant young woman; Frank agrees, "but with so quiet a 'Yes,' as inclined her almost to doubt his real concurrence" (135). After his visit to Hartfield, he goes to visit the Bateses; the next day (in chapter 6), he reports to Emma that he had stayed longer than he wished and that Jane did not look well. His comments also lead her to suggest an illicit attachment between Jane and Mr. Dixon. Frank is hesitant to agree, but he defers to Emma's superior knowledge of Jane (141). Emma also begins to suspect that Frank fancies her (143, 147, 148, etc.). Finally in chapter 8, Frank and

Jane are in the same place at the same time, at the party given by the Coles, but Frank pays more attention to Emma than to Jane. He sings duets with both, but he dances with Emma, and he tells her as they are leaving that he is just as happy that the party ended early: "I must have asked Miss Fairfax, and her languid dancing would not have agreed with me after your's [sic]" (159). Frank continues to flirt with Emma throughout volume 2, and Emma is convinced that he is at least a little in love with her.

There is much more to be said about Austen's management of this episode,[33] but even this brief summary shows the care Austen takes in managing the flow of information. Frank is first mentioned by himself, and then Jane by herself; then they are coupled, but in a disjunction; then each suggests to Emma that they are barely acquainted; then Frank reports negatively on his first visit to the Bateses; then Emma imagines that Jane is attached to Mr. Dixon and that Frank is attached to her; and so on. As the episode continues, there are many clues to the truth, clues that only Mr. Knightley seems to notice. At what moment any particular reader recognizes the truth about Frank and Jane it is impossible to say, but we can say when Emma recognizes it: not until she is told, in chapter 10 of volume 3.

The third episode—Emma's third mistake—begins more or less at the beginning of volume 3. In chapter 1, Frank returns and seems not to be so much in love with Emma, to her relief; he is now freed up for further duties. The ball finally takes place in chapter 2. In chapter 3, Harriet encounters the gypsies and is rescued by Frank. At this point Emma gets the idea that Frank should marry Harriet:

> Such an adventure as this,—a fine young man and a lovely young woman thrown together in such a way, could hardly fail of suggesting certain ideas to the coldest heart and the steadiest brain. So Emma thought, at least. Could a linguist, could a grammarian, could even a mathematician have seen what she did, have witnessed their appearance together, and heard their history of it, without feeling that circumstances had been at work to make them peculiarly interesting to each other?—How much more must an imaginist, like herself, be on fire with speculation and foresight!—especially with such a groundwork of anticipation as her mind had already made. (230)

---

33. For instance, the coincidence of Frank's haircut and the gift of the piano, or the party at Box Hill, or Mr. Knightley's rather negative view of Frank, and innumerable small touches that will likely be noticed only on second or later reading.

Then in chapter 4, Harriet confesses to Emma that she is in love—she means with Mr. Knightley, but Emma misunderstands and assumes that she means with Frank.

The resolution of the three plot lines is cleverly managed. In chapter 9, Mrs. Churchill, Frank's adoptive mother, dies. Emma hopes that he will now feel free to marry Harriet (268). In chapter 10, Frank writes to Mr. and Mrs. Weston with the news that he and Jane have long been secretly engaged. Mr. and Mrs. Weston fear that Emma is in love with Frank and that she will be disappointed, but when they tell her the news, she assures them that she was never in love with Frank.

Emma fears, in turn, that Harriet will be disappointed. Harriet hears the news from Mr. Weston and goes to tell Emma. Emma is surprised at Harriet's composure, but then Harriet explains that she was not love with Frank, but with Mr. Knightley, and she has hopes that Mr. Knightley returns her affections.

> Emma's eyes were instantly withdrawn; and she sat silently meditating, in a fixed attitude, for a few minutes. A few minutes were sufficient for making her acquainted with her own heart. A mind like her's [sic], once opening to suspicion, made rapid progress. She touched—she admitted—she acknowledged the whole truth. Why was it so much worse that Harriet should be in love with Mr. Knightley, than with Frank Churchill? Why was the evil so dreadfully increased by Harriet's having some hope of a return? It darted through her, with the speed of an arrow, that Mr. Knightley must marry no one but herself![34] (281)

Mr. Knightley is in London, so Emma has to remain in distress for a while, but in chapter 11 Mr. Knightley comes to visit. Each is in love with the other, but each fears that the other is in love with someone else. The clarification comes in slow stages, for the characters and for the reader. First, Emma assures Mr. Knightley that she was never in love with Frank. When Mr. Knightley begins to make his declaration, Emma assumes that he is going to tell her that he is in love with Harriet. But Mr. Knightley declares that he loves her, and soon all is well.

Only one plot line remains to be resolved. In chapter 18, we learn that Harriet is to be married to Robert Martin, her first suitor; thus Emma's first mistake is repaired, and the end returns to the beginning.

---

34. Once again we note Austen's figured style, here in perhaps the turning point of the narrative: anadiplosis, tricolon, and erotesis.

These marriage plots require four men and four women, in a complex network. Emma intends that Harriet marry Mr. Elton, but Mr. Elton proposes to Emma and eventually marries Miss Hawkins, whom we know then as Mrs. Elton. Frank flirts with Emma, and Mr. and Mrs. Weston hope that they will marry; Emma, however, intends that Harriet marry Frank, but he has been engaged to Jane all along and eventually marries her. Mrs. Weston imagines that Mr. Knightley favors Jane, and Harriet falls in love with him, but he and Emma marry. And Robert Martin wants to marry Harriet at the beginning of the story, and at the end, he does. We can see that each man—except for Robert Martin—is involved, really or in imagination, with three women (Mr. Elton: Harriet, Emma, Miss Hawkins; Frank: Emma, Harriet, Jane; Mr. Knightley: Jane, Harriet, Emma). Both Emma and Harriet are involved, again really or in imagination, with all three of these men, and finally Harriet marries the fourth, Robert Martin.

Furthermore, Emma is implicitly or explicitly thrown into comparison with each of the other women. Emma is clever, but Jane is in many ways more accomplished; Mr. Knightley, however, faults her for her lack of openness. Both Emma and Mrs. Elton are bossy and both desire the first place in Highbury, but Mrs. Elton's officiousness makes Emma's faults seem trivial. Harriet in a way is the anti-Emma. She is poor, illegitimate, and ignorant. Emma is attractive to all the men (except Robert Martin); Harriet is attractive to none of them (except Robert Martin). When Emma feels remorse after the embarrassment with Mr. Elton, she compares herself to Harriet, and she is "really for the first time convinced that Harriet was the superior creature of the two—and that to resemble her would be more for her own welfare and happiness than all genius or intelligence could do," but "it was rather too late in the day to set about being simple-minded and ignorant" (100).

For the most part, Austen does not foreground her synthetic devices the way they might be foregrounded in a postmodern self-conscious narrative, but neither, for the most part, does she hide them. There is, however, one great exception to this rule. The story hinges on a mystery—the mystery of the secret engagement of Frank and Jane. Austen manages to give just enough hints so that the reader will not feel she has cheated, but not enough to give the game away too quickly. In a sense these hints are covert—only on first reading. The experience, and therefore the meaning, of *Emma* changes from first reading to second reading, partly because what was perhaps covert on first reading becomes overt on later readings.[35] Moreover, many minor points

---

35. Burrows comments that "the business of distinguishing, moment by moment" Frank's real motives "makes part of one's pleasure as a reader—or presumably, a re-reader" (86).

that are easily passed over on first reading become significant on later readings. For example, Emma's third mistake and its resolution are anticipated early on in the story. In volume 1, chapter 5, Mr. Knightley tells Mrs. Weston, "I would very much like to see Emma in love, and in some doubts of a return" (30), and of course later on she is in love with him and in doubt of a return. In volume 1, chapter 8, during an argument about Harriet, Emma tells Mr. Knightley, "Were you, yourself, ever to marry, she is the very woman for you" (47), and of course, that is what later on she fears.

A full interpretation of *Emma* would require examination of many other aspects of the story as well as its historical and social context. My goal here, however, has not been an interpretation in the usual sense, but an exploration of the synthetic aspect of the narrative. *Emma* is a realistic novel—in Phelan's terms, a mimetic narrative. It is also synthetic, and many of the synthetic devices are quite overt—and those that are covert, or that are not foregrounded, can be noticed with a little attention.

In this chapter I have touched on a variety of synthetic devices, including features of style and compositional devices, such as links, anticipations, repetitions, ending with the beginning, architecture, and character sets, in order to show that the synthetic aspect of narrative is important not just in postmodern or "anti-realistic" fictions, but throughout the tradition of Western literature. The synthetic aspect of narrative provides its own kind of pleasure, and in addition, synthetic devices contribute to the mimetic and thematic aspect, as the following chapters will demonstrate.

CHAPTER 2

The Mimetic Aspect

MATTHEW CLARK

IN CHAPTER 1, I argued that the synthetic aspect is important for all narratives, including texts central to the realistic tradition of narrative; even when the synthetic aspect is not obvious or foregrounded, it is still important and worthy of critical attention. This chapter turns to the mimetic aspect. Mimesis is a complex term with many meanings. Each of these meanings has its proper place and function, but they should be kept distinct where they are distinct, and any theory that uses the term should make it clear which meaning is intended. The SMT model develops a broad concept of mimesis, including realism but also including all kinds of representation in narrative. Mimesis in the SMT model is compatible with unnatural narratives as well as with narratives in the realistic tradition.[1]

In the MTS model, the mimetic component is "that component of character directed to its imitation of a possible person," and it is also "that component of fictional narrative concerned with imitating the world beyond the fiction, what we typically call 'reality.'" Mimesis is produced by "conventions, which change over time," and "imitations are judged to be more or less adequate" in terms of these conventions (Phelan, *Living* 215). "Responses to the

---

1. The word "mimesis" is sometimes left untranslated, as in Phelan's definition; it can also be translated as "imitation" or "representation" or "reenactment." The literature on mimesis is large; I have consulted Potolsky; Pam Morris; Melberg; Golden; Goodman; Boyd; Gombrich; and Adams.

mimetic component involve an audience's interest in the characters as possible people and in the narrative world as like our own" (Phelan, *Living* 20). Mimesis in the MTS model thus seems to be closely bound to some version of realism. Moreover, "realistic fiction seeks to create the illusion that everything is mimetic and nothing synthetic, or, in other words, that the characters act as they do by their own choice rather than at the behest of the author" (Phelan, *Living* 20). Many narratives, however, are concerned with characters and worlds that are not part of "what we typically call 'reality'" or "a world like our own." The MTS model has no theoretical account of fantastic narratives, which foreground the unrealistic or the impossible, or "unnatural" narratives, which foreground their fictionality.[2] By contrast, the SMT model defines the mimetic as world-building in general, including the realistic, the fantastic, and the unnatural, and also their complex interrelationships. The following discussion begins with a brief general account of mimesis and continues with examination of particular aspects of world-building.

I. VARIETIES OF PICTORIAL MIMESIS

A simple instance of one kind of mimesis might be a painting of an object. Here the object is the original and the painting is the copy. Many ideas of mimesis imply an original and a copy in some relation, but some kinds of mimesis may not require an original and may not be a copy.

Some aesthetic theories privilege "realistic" pictorial representations, the more realistic the better. In Plato's *Republic*, Socrates ironically argues that anything and everything could be represented by someone who just carries a mirror around (*Republic* 596d). According to this model, the best painting aspires to be a mirror. (I will say more about mimesis as a mirror in the next section.) Pliny the Elder (in his *Natural History*, book 25, chapter 24) told the story of a contest between two painters, Zeuxis and Parrhasius. Zeuxis's painting of grapes was so realistic that birds came down to eat them. But when Zeuxis tried to pull aside the curtain covering Parrhasius's painting, he discovered that the curtain itself was the painting. Zeuxis said, "I have deceived the birds, but Parrhasius has deceived Zeuxis." In practice, however, illusionism has usually been a secondary virtue, if that. People want enough visual

---

2. For discussion of antimimetic or unnatural narrative, see, for example, Alber et al.; Richardson, *Unnatural Voices*; and Alber and Heinze. The terms "antimimetic" and "nonmimetic" are not originally part of the MTS model, but Phelan and Rabinowitz adopt the terms, for example, in Herman et al. 198.

information to know what (if anything) is being represented, but beyond that requirement, conventions and fashions vary greatly.

Plato's objection to visual mimesis (and to mimesis in general) is famous.[3] An object in our world—his example is a bed—is itself only an imperfect imitation of the Platonic form of the bed; the painting of a bed is thus only an imperfect imitation of an imperfect imitation. Mimesis is a double falling away from what is real. The philosopher will strive to perceive the forms themselves; physical objects are a distraction from the real, paintings of objects even more so (*Republic* 597a–c).

Plato's objection can be partly countered—a painting could attempt to represent the forms directly, bypassing the intermediate stage of the physical object. One can imagine that a geometer's diagram of a circle could be closer to the form of a circle than any naturally formed circular object.

For some, including Aristotle, who do not credit Plato's forms, mimesis can be the representation of universals. Universals are types, but they exist only in particulars, not in Platonic forms. Red, for instance, is a universal, but it exists only in red objects.[4] The business of the artist, however, "is to examine, not the individual, but the species; to remark general properties and large appearances. He does not number the streaks of the tulip" (Samuel Johnson, *History* 28). If mimesis is the representation of a universal, it is not quite the copy of an original, at least not the way that the mimesis of the forms would be, since a universal is not an original.

A painting can also be the copy of another painting. Artists commonly learn by copying paintings, and there are many famous paintings that are versions of earlier paintings. Some theorists would argue that every work of art is in some sense a copy of other works.

An imitation can also be composite rather than specific. The Greek painter Zeuxis, whom we have already met, is supposed to have been commissioned to paint a portrait of Helen of Troy. There was no one woman he could use as a model, so he gathered a group of women and composed his painting by copying what was most beautiful in each. Such a painting is not an imitation of a

---

3. Golden (following Robinson) argues that Plato recognized the value of mimesis as a cognitive counterpart to dialectic: The "instruments of dialectic" are "*elenchus*, syllogism, *epagoge*, and *diairesis*," while the "techniques of mimesis" are "analogies, examples, and images including myths" (47). The myths in Plato's dialogues (such as the Myth of Er in book 10 of the *Republic*) are mimetic rather than dialectic, though in Phelan's terms they would be antimimetic, since they are not realistic.

4. Phelan's argument that a character becomes thematic when it is representative is, I think, a version of mimesis as the representation of a universal. Emma Woodhouse is representative of a young English woman as a type, but there is no Platonic form of a young English woman.

particular original, and certainly not an imitation of Helen of Troy herself, but the imitation of parts of various originals. A composite such as Zeuxis's portrait is an example of representation as "nature perfected," but the same process could be used to represent "nature imperfected," if the painter copies what is worst in each model, or even of "nature impossible," if the painter combines features from different species, as in the painting of a centaur, or from different perspectives, as in a drawing by Escher. A painting of this composite form does not have to be realistic as a whole, even if each of its parts is realistic.

The original of such a composite does not exist as an object in the world, but as a conception in the mind of the artist—more or less what we today might call an "idea." And if mental phenomena can be imitated, then the original could be an emotion; an "abstract" painting represents the artist's feelings. If what is imitated is something within the artist, then mimetic theories can fade into expressive theories.

At this point we have identified eight kinds of pictorial mimesis: (1) the imitation of a physical object; (2) the imitation of a physical object, which is in turn an imitation of the Platonic form of that object; (3) the direct and unmediated imitation of the Platonic form; (4) the imitation of a type or universal; (5) the imitation of a previous imitation; (6) the representation of a composite of features from various physical objects; (7) the representation of an idea in the mind of the artist; and (8) the representation of the feelings of the artist. All of these have been claimed as varieties of visual mimesis.

II. DESCRIPTIVE MIMESIS

Pictorial mimesis has often been used as a model for mimesis in general. Plato moves quickly from his discussion of mimesis as a mirror and as two steps away from the truth to a similar discussion of poetic mimesis:

> So shall we classify all poets, from Homer onwards, as representers of images of goodness (and of everything else which occurs in their poetry) and claim that they don't have any contact with the truth? The facts are as we said a short while ago: a painter creates an illusory shoemaker, when not only does he not understand anything about shoemaking, but his audience doesn't either. . . . And I should think we'll say the same goes for a poet as well. (*Republic* 600e–601a)

Stendhal claimed in *Le Rouge et le Noir* that "a novel is a mirror walking along a main road" ("un roman est un miroir qui se promène sur une grande route"):

Stendhal 241). The narrator of George Eliot's *Adam Bede* also figures narration as reflection: "With a single drop of ink for a mirror, the Egyptian sorcerer undertakes to reveal to any chance comer far-reaching visions of the past. This is what I undertake to do for you, reader" (Eliot 7). Later the narrator shows some doubt about the fidelity of the image.[5]

Plato uses the analogy of the mirror as a part of his general attack on literature, while Stendhal and Eliot use it as a defense, but in any case the analogy is not without problems. Many of the points explored in the previous section translate reasonably well from pictorial mimesis to poetic mimesis, but qualification is necessary: For example, we should distinguish the description of an object or a location from the narrative of an action. This section will very briefly examine an example of description, and the following section will consider the mimesis of action.

A painting and a verbal description may represent the same object, but the manner of representation is essentially different. The painting of a red apple can be red, while a verbal apple can only be described as red. Words lack the ability to imitate colors with colors or shapes with shapes; they do, however, have the ability to imitate time with time or sequence with sequence.[6]

Every instance of verbally descriptive mimesis is unique, but an example will demonstrate a few points. In book 7 of the *Odyssey,* Odysseus has arrived at the land of the Phaiakians; he has met Nausikaä, who has given him clothing; and he has followed her to the city. In the following passage he is looking at the garden of King Alkinoös:

> On the outside of the courtyard near the doors is a great orchard,
> four measures big, and a fence is driven on both sides,
> and there his great flourishing fruit trees grow,
> pear trees and pomegranate trees and apple trees bearing fine fruit,
> and sweet fig trees and flourishing olives.
> The fruit of these never perishes nor fails,
> in winter time and summer, all the year, but always
> the blowing West Wind starts some and ripens others.
> Pear matures on pear, apple upon apple,

---

5. In a more modern figure, the narrator of Christopher Isherwood's *Goodbye to Berlin* says, "I am a camera with its shutter open, quite passive, recording, not thinking" (13). On the other hand, "art finds her own perfection within and not outside of her self. She is not to be judged by any external standard of resemblance. She is a veil rather than a mirror" (Oscar Wilde, in Adams 680).

6. The standard reference for this topic is Gotthold Lessing's *Laocoon: An Essay on the Limits of Painting and Poetry,* but the discussion goes back at least to Dio Chrysostom in the first century; see Hunter for a discussion of Dio's *Olympic Oration.*

> grape cluster on grape cluster, fig upon fig.
> There a fruitful vineyard grew,
> some of it, warm on level ground,
> is baked in the sun, but elsewhere they gather grapes
> and others they trample. In front of these, unripe grapes
> have cast off their flowers while others are becoming dark.
> And there well-ordered herbs beside the furthest row
> grow, of all kinds, all year they gleam brightly.
> And in it two springs disperse, one through all
> the orchard, one on the other side flows under the courtyard threshold
> towards the lofty house, where townspeople draw water.
> Such are the glorious gifts of the gods at the house of Alkinoös.
> (Od.7.112–32; my translation)

This description is the poetic equivalent of pictorial mimesis, and yet it is very unlike any picture one might draw of the orchard. Compared to a picture, it is massively underspecified, at least in visual terms. The sizes of the fence and the trees are only vaguely suggested. There is very little color in the description; presumably the narrator expects the audience to fill in the colors according to their own knowledge of the colors of pears, pomegranates, apples, figs, and grapes.

This description is not in itself narrative. It lacks the kind of time sequence and sense of causation that narrative demands. And yet time is an essential feature of the description, or rather the defeat of time and the defeat of the seasons. Evidently the seasons do follow their regular course, but the fruits of the orchard are not affected; they grow all year long, and all the stages are present at once: flowers, young grapes, ripening and fully ripened grapes, grapes drying in the sun, grapes being trampled out to make the wine—all these coexist. This is nature perfected. It also must count as an unnatural description, since this is a garden that could never be, at least in our world.

Although this description is not narrative, it is part of a narrative. It is focalized as the experience of Odysseus, and it becomes a part of his story. It is also part of a sequence of actions in an episode, beginning when Odysseus arrives at the land of the Phaiakians and ending when he leaves. This is the final episode of his travels, and it functions as a sort of transition as he moves from the world of marvels back to the ordinary world of mortals.

Most narratives include some description, but the amount and kind of description in narrative varies greatly. It is well known, for example, that Balzac's novels are rich in extensive detailed descriptions; *Eugenie Grandet* begins with several pages describing the town where the story takes place. Jane Austen, on the other hand, describes objects and locations only rarely and only for a direct narrative point.[7] The following passage from *Emma* takes place during an outing to Donwell Abbey to pick strawberries. The adjoining property is the Abbey-Mill Farm, the home of Robert Martin, Harriet's disappointed suitor.

> It was a sweet view—sweet to the eye and the mind. English verdure, English culture, English comfort, seen under a sun bright, without being oppressive.
> In this walk Emma and Mr. Weston found all the others assembled; and towards this view she immediately perceived Mr. Knightley and Harriet distinct from the rest, quietly leading the way. Mr. Knightley and Harriet!—It was an odd tête-à-tête, but she was glad to see it.—There had been a time when he would have scorned her as a companion, and turned from her with little ceremony. Now they seemed in pleasant conversation. There had been a time also when Emma would have been sorry to see Harriet in a spot so favorable for the Abbey-Mill Farm; but now she feared it not. It might be safely viewed with all its appendages of prosperity and beauty, its rich pastures, spreading flocks, orchard in blossom, and light column of smoke ascending. (249)

This description, like Homer's description of the garden of Alkinoös, is embedded in narrative. The description is focalized through Emma's perspective, but Emma's perspective is, as usual, wrong. On the one hand, this little tête-à-tête will encourage Harriet to believe that Mr. Knightley fancies her. On the other hand, Robert Martin is by no means out of the picture, and at the end of the book he will marry Harriet. The description is important because it contributes to the entanglements of the personalities.

The description itself is sketched with the lightest of strokes. We are given only English verdure, English culture, English comfort, and a bright sun, then rich pastures, spreading flocks, a blossoming orchard, and a light column of smoke. Any reader trying to visualize this scene would have to fill in most of the picture.

This description, meager as it is, has occasioned some comment. J. F. Burrows notes, "Presumably all novels contain inadvertent slips; and *Emma* is not flawless. Jane Austen's family were quick to notice that the orchard of the

---

7. "In Austen's fiction, places are virtually only names. Hartfield, Randalls, Donwell Abbey, Miss Bates' house, the Crown—the names signify social distinctions and relations but are void of concrete physical specification" (Kroeber 159). There are exceptions: The physical setting of the Crown, for example, is in fact discussed at some length. But as a general characterization, Kroeber's comment is accurate.

Abbey-Mill Farm blossoms in mid-summer" (Burrows 84). John Wiltshire notes that the column of smoke "is also oddly unseasonal," but he then offers a defense of the passage:

> Perhaps "mistake" is too simple an explanation for the effect: what is being presented here is not a place but an idyll, the fantasy of the pastoral paradise. There is an enthusiasm that seeks to represent Donwell and its estate, not as just admirable and august, but as having everything—strawberries at their peak of ripeness, sunshine, "spreading flocks," "ample gardens washed by a stream," prosperous farmland, and the domestic hearth: a rich constellation of all that desire encompasses. (Wiltshire 74)

Homer's garden of Alkinoös and Austen's Abbey-Mill Farm are thus close literary cousins. Wiltshire's defense of this passage, which probably will not persuade everyone, depends on allowing the representation of impossibilities even in realistic fiction.

Verbal mimesis can also represent objects that could not be represented in a painting, such as objects that are characterized by negativity, which has no pictorial counterpart. In the following passage from Flann O'Brien's *The Third Policeman*, the narrator and one of the policemen have entered a region that is supposed to be eternity. The policeman comes to a cabinet that has two openings, one above the other. The policeman presses some keys and turns a knob:

> At once there was a rumbling noise as if thousands of full biscuit boxes were falling down a stairs. I felt that these falling things would come out of the chute at any moment. And so they did, appearing for a few seconds in the air and then disappearing down the black hole below. But what can I say about them? In colour they were not white or black and certainly not an intermediate colour; they were far from dark and anything but bright. But strange to say it was not their unprecedented hue that took most of my attention. They had another quality that made me watch them wild-eyed, dry-throated and with no breathing. I can make no attempt to describe this quality. It took me hours of thought long afterwards to realize why these articles were astonishing. *They lacked an essential property of all known objects.* I cannot call it shape or configuration since shapelessness is not what I refer to at all. I can only say that these objects, not one of which resembles the other, were of no known dimensions. They were not square or rectangular or circular or simply irregularly shaped nor could it be said that their endless variety was due to dimensional dissimilarities. Simply their appearance, if even that word is

not inadmissible, was not understood by the eye and was in any event indescribable. That is enough to say. (O'Brien 116–117)

O'Brien is pushing the limits of mimesis by representing the unrepresentable.

III. NARRATIVE MIMESIS

Narrative mimesis, like pictorial or descriptive mimesis, can represent the real and the imagined, the possible and the impossible, the universal or the particular, but unlike pictorial mimesis and descriptive mimesis, which primarily represent objects in space, narrative mimesis represents action in time according to principles of cause and effect. (Animation and live-action movies combine visual mimesis with the mimesis of time and action; they are more like drama than like painting.)

Action, according to Aristotle, is the essence of poetic mimesis.[8] Whereas Plato's model of mimesis is a mirror, Aristotle's model is drama as the imitation of action: Thus, "in tragedy it is action that is imitated," and "tragedy is a representation, not of men, but of action" (*Poetics* 1450a). Of course, characters are necessary in narrative, since it is characters who act, but plot remains the most important element of tragic mimesis.[9] Action is not simply a temporal sequence, but also a sequence of cause and effect: The beginning, middle, and end of a plot are defined by their causal relationships (*Poetics* 1450b). The understanding of causation is part of the cognitive aspect of narrative mimesis.

Drama in ancient Greece was action in another sense as well. Poetry on the page was almost unknown. What we think of as literature was almost always performed, either in the acting of a drama or in the recitation of an epic. It is clear (for example, from Plato's *Ion*) that epic recitations were vigorously active. A play represents an action and the actors imitate the actions of the characters as they perform. Here, in fact, is one of Plato's objections to mimetic drama: A good man is debased when he imitates the words or the

---

8. Aristotle's concept of mimesis included various forms of poetry and also music (*Poetics* 1447a), but in the *Poetics*, the center of his discussion of mimesis is tragic drama. He mentions visual representations (*eikones*) and allows spectacle as an element of drama, but for the most part he leaves these out of the discussion.

9. It is not my intention to take sides in the debate about action versus character. It seems clear that some narratives emphasize character, some emphasize action, and some seek a balance.

actions of a bad man (*Republic* 395d–396c). Thus mimesis can be the imitation of an action and it can be the action of imitation.

The original of a Greek tragedy could be the myth which the tragedy represents. Tragedy in this sense is a kind of reenactment of events that are supposed to have taken place in the past.[10] A few tragedies represented historical events rather than myths; the only extant example is Aeschylus's *Persians*, which is in no way historically accurate and was not intended to be so. Nor did the Greek dramatists feel bound to follow previous versions of the myths. There is some reason to believe, for instance, that Euripides was the first poet to have Medea kill her own children; in earlier versions most likely the children were killed by the citizens of Corinth. Tragic mimesis did not exclude invention.

Tragedy was not realistic in our usual sense of the word. Women's roles were played by men, the actors and chorus wore masks, the dialogue was composed in complex meters and some of it was sung while the chorus and actors danced. In the MTS model, Greek tragedy would have to be called antimimetic and overtly synthetic, and yet it is Aristotle's model of mimesis.

Mimesis for Aristotle is primarily cognitive. Representations are a source of pleasure because they provide information: "Learning is pleasant not just to philosophers but also to others in a similar way. . . . This is the reason that they enjoy looking at representations (*eikonas*), because as it happens that those observing learn (*manthanein*) and reason out (*syllogizesthai*) what each thing is, for example that this thing is that thing" (*Poetics* 1448b). The poet's job is not the representation of "what has actually happened, but the kinds of things that might happen"; thus poetry is more philosophical than history, because "poetry is concerned with universal truths" while "history treats of particular facts" (*Poetics* 1451a–b).[11]

Aristotle also recognizes the emotional aspect of tragedy: "Tragedy is the representation . . . of incidents that awaken fear and pity" (*Poetics* 1452a), and "the plot should be so ordered that even without seeing it performed anyone merely hearing what is afoot will shudder with fear and pity as a result of what is happening" (*Poetics* 1453b). According to Leon Golden, "tragic *mimesis* leads us from an encounter of some particular pitiable or fearful event to the

---

10. A ritual such as Passover or Communion is even more explicitly a reenactment. The Platonic dialogues are presented as mimetic reenactments, though there is no certainty that any of the conversations presented actually occurred, and some surely are Plato's invention.

11. Compare Dangerfield 393: "Social history, like history itself, is a combination of taste, imagination, science, and scholarship; it reconciles incompatibles, it balances probabilities, and at last attains the reality of fiction, which is the highest reality of all."

philosophical comprehension of the universal nature of pity and fear in the human creature" (Golden 25–26).

The presentation of actions then brings about *katharsis* (*Poetics* 1449b). *Katharsis* is often understood as a kind of purging of emotion, as if emotion were a disease, to be cured by the discharge of contamination, or a religious pollution, to be cleansed by purification; both of these ideas would be supported by the Greek text. But Golden argues, in my opinion persuasively, that *katharsis* is primarily cognitive; he understands *katharsis* as "intellectual clarification" rather than "moral purification or medical purgation" (Golden 26).[12] Thus the structure of a drama, organized according to principles of causality, leads to the intellectual clarification of pity and fear through the philosophic understanding of universals.

Mimesis, in Aristotle's account, is not limited to realism. As he notes, "it is quite likely that many things should happen contrary to likelihood" (*Poetics* 1456a) and "it is probable enough that things should happen contrary to probability" (*Poetics* 1461b). Furthermore, "probable impossibilities are to be preferred to improbable possibilities" (*Poetics* 1460a). Impossibilities can be justified for the sake of poetic effect, as an attempt to improve on reality, or because of tradition (*Poetics* 1461b).

IV. MIMESIS AS WORLD-BUILDING

A narrative theory that ties mimesis to the imitation of reality leaves out a large and important body of narratives. The realistic bias of much narrative theory has received some criticism. Brian Richardson notes "a significant and unusual gap" in most narrative theory: "a sustained neglect of anti-mimetic narratives" and "an absence of comprehensive theoretical formulations capable of encompassing these works" (Herman et al. 21). David Herman argues, in effect, that the concept of mimesis favored by Phelan and Rabinowitz is caught on the horns of a dilemma:

> On the one hand, if mimesis is defined narrowly as imitation or reproduction, the very concept becomes untenable—since there can be no direct representation of the world, no bare encounter with reality, without mediating

---

12. "Tragic *katharsis* is, first and foremost, a learning experience about the cause, nature, and effect of pity and fear," and "we must first process intellectually the flow of data from the drama whose carefully structured beginning, middle, and end is linking by dramatic and psychological necessity and probability" (Golden 31).

world-models. On the other hand, if mimesis is defined as part of a family of strategies for deploying world-models, then the concept cannot do the work my co-authors [Phelan and Rabinowitz] try to get it to do—for example, when they set mimesis up as a standard or touchstone against which "anti-mimetic" stories, or the "synthetic" and "thematic" dimensions of narrative, can be measured. (Herman in Herman et al. 16)

Phelan and Rabinowitz argue, however, that rhetorical narratology seeks an approach "sufficiently flexible to respond to narrative in all its variety, whether it be mimetic, non-mimetic, or anti-mimetic" (Herman et al. 190). An understanding of mimesis as world-building provides the flexibility Phelan and Rabinowitz desire. On this understanding, all narratives are mimetic, since all narratives represent a world and characters within that world, but varieties of mimesis differ. Some narratives do attempt to represent a world more or less like what we typically call reality—though there are many kinds of realistic representation, and they should not be conflated. Other narratives attempt to represent worlds that are not like reality, fantastic worlds—though again, there are many kinds of fantasy. And some narratives, "unnatural narratives," foreground the fictiveness of the representation—and again, there are various kinds of unnatural narratives.[13]

Under this understanding, mimesis includes all kinds of narrative world-making: for example, the representation of setting, including time and place; objects; social structures; characters and their actions, thoughts, and forms of consciousness. The definition of mimesis as world-building links mimesis to theories of cognitive narratology and possible world theory.[14] The worlds of narrative are made of representations, and these representations are made of language. Language represents, but it does not paint pictures; nor can language be a mirror or a camera. At best, the representations in a narrative provide hints that must be filled out by the imagination of the reader.[15]

---

13. The critical terminology in this area is somewhat confused; I use "realistic," "fantastic," and "unnatural" as broad general terms, while trying to avoid "antimimetic" or "nonmimetic," which are not compatible with the broad view of mimesis offered here.

14. See, for example, Pavel; Ryan; Ronen; Doležel; and Herman, *Story Logic*. Note that Ronen's and Doležel's definition of "possible" (noncontradictory) is different from Phelan's (realistic).

15. See, Doležel 169–84 on gaps and saturation.

V. THE MIMETIC ILLUSION

Part of Phelan's conception of mimesis is the effect he calls the mimetic illusion:[16] "Realistic fiction seeks to create the illusion that everything is mimetic and nothing synthetic, or, in other words, that the characters act as they do by their own choice rather than at the behest of the author" (Phelan, *Living* 20). Furthermore, our "interest in the mimetic component" depends on our "participation in the narrative audience, which takes the events in a fiction as history and the characters as real people" (Herman et al. 115). "To participate in the illusion is to enter . . . the narrative audience; to remain covertly aware of the synthetic is to enter . . . the authorial audience" (Phelan, *Reading* 5); the authorial audience has a "double consciousness" of the mimetic and synthetic, while the narrative audience has only the single consciousness of the characters and actions as real.[17]

We have seen the idea of mimesis as illusion before, for instance, in the story of Zeuxis and Parrhasius, where illusion amounts to deception. The idea of mimesis as deception is not restricted to visual mimesis: "The function of dramatic art both tragic and comic was in the opinion of a large body of neoclassicists and in their own phrase, to delude the audience into a belief in the reality of the action represented upon the stage" (Green 128). The unities of time and place were justified "if the audience was to *believe* that it was actually present at the time and place of representation, and . . . if this belief were shattered, theatrical illusion vanished" (Green 206).

Many scholars, however, do not accept the idea of mimesis as deception. According to Samuel Johnson, "It is false, that any representation is mistaken for reality; that any dramatick fable in its materiality was ever credible, or, for a single moment, was ever credited. . . . Imitations produce pain or pleasure, not because they are mistaken for realities, but because they bring realities to mind" (Samuel Johnson, "Preface" 26–28). Morris applies this principle to realistic novels: "Realistic novels do not seek to trick their readers by 'illusion'; they seek to give them pleasure from the recognition of verisimilitude" (Pam Morris 119). And Kroeber says quite specifically, "Jane Austen's fiction never pretends to be anything but fiction" (125).

---

16. The mimetic illusion is probably to be distinguished from such experiences as "reading absorption" and "reading trance"; for these, see Nell, chapter 10.

17. Phelan is certainly not alone in his description of the mimetic illusion; compare, for example, Gard 144: "The creation of realistic fiction depends on the reader's being only momentarily and fleetingly conscious of the artifices and conventions that sustain the illusion." The mimetic illusion is not universally admired: See, for example, Potolsky 85–86 on Brecht's "alienation effect."

Phelan's concept of the mimetic illusion divides the flesh-and-blood reader into two parts, one of which (the authorial audience) knows that the fiction is a fiction, and one of which (the narrative audience) believes that the fiction is history; thus the flesh-and-blood reader is only half deluded.

The narrative audience is a purely theoretical entity. Its justification presumably is to account for the emotional engagement the reader feels for realistic fiction: "The mimetic component of narrative is responsible for our emotional responses to it, and these responses are a crucial part of the distinctive quality and power of narrative" (Phelan, *Living* 28). There is no reason to believe, however, that in order to have an emotional response to a narrative the reader needs to be deceived into false belief, and there is no reason to suppose that readers have no emotional response to nonrealistic narratives.[18]

Even if one grants the existence of a narrative audience, it does not distinguish "mimetic" narratives from "nonmimetic" or "antimimetic" narratives. If the narrative audience stands within the story, it can also stand within a nonrealistic story. If the narrative audience of *Emma* can believe in Emma, then the narrative audience of *Dracula* can believe in Dracula. The same principle applies even to more difficult cases; the narrative audience of Samuel Beckett's *How It Is* would presumably believe in the reality of the characters, including the narrator and Pim:

> here then part one how it was before Pim we follow I quote the natural order more or less my life last state last version what remains bits and scraps I hear it my life natural order more or less I learn it I quote a given moment long past vast stretch of time on from there that moment and following not all a selection natural order vast tracts of time. (7)

In such a narrative there is a great distance between the world of the narrative and the world of the flesh-and-blood reader; it is this distance that makes the reading experience "unnatural," not the absence of a narrative audience or the mimetic illusion as Phelan has defined it.

The heroine of J. M. Coetzee's *Foe*, Susan Barton, late in the novel begins to question her own existence; she has been writing and telling her story of shipwreck and survival to Mr. Foe (who represents the real person Daniel Defoe), but now she falls into perplexity:

---

18. Basset discusses the "epic illusion" produced by the *Iliad* and the *Odyssey*. See also Power for discussion of "transportation" in Homeric epic, and discussion of relevant ancient Greek vocabulary, including the verb "thelgein" ("to enchant") and the noun "kêlêthmos" ("spell").

"In the beginning I thought I would tell you the story of the island and, being done with that, return to my former life. But now all my life grows to be story and there is nothing of my own left to me.... But now I am full of doubt. Nothing is left to me but doubt. I am doubt itself. Who is speaking me? Am I a phantom too? To what order do I belong? And you: who are you?" (133)

And Foe replies to her:

"But if you cannot rid yourself of your doubts, I have something to say that may be of comfort. Let us confront our worst fear, which is that we have all of us been called into the world from a different order (which we have now forgotten) by a conjurer unknown to us.... Then I ask nevertheless: Have we thereby lost our freedom? Are you, for one, any less mistress of your life? Do we not of necessity become puppets in a story whose end is invisible to us, and towards which we are marched like condemned felons?" (135)

Coetzee, like some other modern writers, has taken advantage of the fictiveness of fiction to ask questions that in fact have application to our own lives and speculations.[19] Who are we? Are we called into our world from a different order—Plato would have it so—and are we masters and mistresses of our own lives? Do we have free will, or are we puppets marching toward an unknown end? These are questions we can all ask of ourselves and our lives and world. This unnatural narrative leads to a very natural emotional response.

VI. PLAUSIBILITY AND REALISM

Phelan ties the mimetic illusion to notions of plausibility or possibility and to notions of reality. Mimetic fiction specifically creates "the illusion of a plausible person" (Phelan, *Reading* 11). The mimetic component is "that component of fictional narrative concerned with imitating the world beyond the fiction, what we typically call 'reality'" (Phelan, *Living* 215).

The association of mimesis with plausibility and reality is problematic, for a variety of reasons. Many narratives are not plausible or realistic, some critics

---

19. Many other "postmodern" fictions self-consciously foreground the fictionality of the text; Vladimir Nabokov's *Invitation to a Beheading* and *Bend Sinister* are good examples. The technique also can be found in popular art, especially in comic strips: The cartoonist Stephen Pastis is a frequent character in his strip *Pearls Before Swine*.

argue that realism is ideologically coercive, and it is by no means clear what counts as plausible or real.

Phelan notes the difficulty of determining plausibility and decides "to err on the side of generosity" (Phelan, *Reading* 12)—but generosity on what standard? Is plausibility to be judged externally ("I don't like *The Lord of the Rings* because I don't believe in wizards and hobbits and magic rings") or internally ("I don't like the end of *Huckleberry Finn* because I don't believe the Huck we have come to know earlier in the book would treat Jim that way")? In the second half of the *Odyssey*, Odysseus tells a series of lies about his travels, the so-called Cretan tales, which are plausible but false, while the story he tells the Phaiakians is implausible but true. In fantasy, too much realism is unrealistic.

As Harry Shaw notes, "the term 'realism' resists the status of the purely descriptive: it always tends to attract epistemological and moral claims" (6). I am happy to pass by the deeper philosophic questions about the nature of reality, but realism belongs to literature as well as to philosophy. Philosophy may seek the truth about reality; literature presents a range of responses, a range of realities.

At the very beginning of Dickens's *The Mystery of Edwin Drood*, the reader is presented with a puzzle of realism:

> An ancient English Cathedral town? How can the ancient English Cathedral town be here! The well-known massive grey square tower of its old Cathedral? How can that be here! There is no spike of rusty iron in the air, between the eye and it, from any point of the real prospect. What IS the spike that intervenes, and who has set it up? Maybe, it is set up by the Sultan's order for the impaling of a horde of Turkish robbers, one by one. It is so, for cymbals clash, and the Sultan goes by to his palace in the long procession. Ten thousand scimitars flash in the sunlight, and thrice ten thousand dancing girls strew flowers. Then, follow white elephants caparisoned in countless gorgeous colors, and infinite in number and attendants. Still, the Cathedral tower rises in the background, where it cannot be, and still no writhing figure is on the grim spike. Stay! Is the spike so low a thing as the rusty spike on the top of a post on an old bedstead that has tumbled all awry? Some vague period of drowsy laughter must be devoted to the consideration of this possibility.
>
> Shaking from head to foot, the man whose scattered consciousness has thus fantastically pieced itself together, at length rises, supports his trembling frame upon his arms, and looks around. (37)

The reader quickly discovers that this description represents an opium dream. Is it fantastic, as the narrator says, or is it a realistic depiction of a disordered mind? Does the narrative itself question the boundaries of the real? Nor do we need to go to opium dreams to pose these questions about narrative realism. Dickens's description of Marseilles quoted in chapter 1 is no dream, but neither it is simply realistic; the point of the passage is an impression rather than a transcription of "what we typically call 'reality.'"

Narrative realism is manifested in various registers. Realism can imply an attention to the world of objects, the furniture of reality; it can also imply a restriction to realistic or plausible actions; it can imply realism of characterization; it can imply attention to the reality of social relationships; and it can imply a realistic attitude to history. These are not always mutually compatible: As we see in the novels of Henry James, a highly developed attention to the interiority of characterization tends to remove a story from social or historical realism.

Realism is not universally admired. Some critics argue that realism is ideologically coercive; by claiming to represent things-as-they-are, realism tends to perpetuate things-as-they-are: "Realism supposedly attempts to make the world of the bourgeoisie seem 'natural' and 'full,' thereby giving its vision of reality a peremptory power over our imaginations" (Shaw 9).[20]

The range of representation in narrative is enormous; the MTS model tends to reduce that range to a dichotomy of the "mimetic" or realistic and the "antimimetic." Even within realism there is a range of representation, and the dividing line between the realistic and the nonrealistic is not easily drawn. My proposed revision to the model takes mimesis as all sorts of representation; it is then the task of further analysis to distinguish among the various ways representation can occur.

VII. TIME AND SPACE

Narrative mimesis requires action, and action requires time and space in which to occur. Newtonian time and space are undifferentiated voids in which material things exist and processes occur, but narrative time and space have quality and vary from story to story. In general the story itself creates the time

---

20. As Shaw notes, "realism can be viewed positively either because it is totalistic or because it is not, or negatively either because it is totalistic or because it is not" (13).

and the space in which it occurs; the representation of time and space is a synthetic creation.[21]

Some aspects of the representation of time and space in narrative have been well studied, and there is no point here in detailed recapitulation of previous work;[22] it is enough to note some of the topics, such as order, duration (the ratio of the time telling to the time told), frequency, analepsis (flashback), prolepsis (flash forward), repetition, and iteration; path, container, portal, and access (including ideas of public and private space). All of these elements, and others, are used in particular narratives to create particular narrative worlds.

The events of the *Iliad* take place over a relatively restricted period of time; although the Trojan War lasted ten years, the epic takes a little over fifty days in total, and most of the action is concentrated into just nine days. By and large, time is divided naturally, by the rising and setting of the sun. The events of the *Odyssey* take about forty days, from the time of the first council of the gods to the final resolution, but again, the principal events take nine days. Both epics are organized to drive toward a climatic moment, but both epics also include references to time outside the time of the story itself. Some scholars believe that books 2 and 3 of the *Iliad* were originally composed to narrate events from the beginning of the war, where they would make more sense; the composer of our *Iliad* then borrowed these for his own story. In books 8 to 13 of the *Odyssey*, Odysseus tells the story of his travels beginning from the end of the war, ten years earlier. Vergil borrowed the idea of a retrospective narration by the hero in books 2 and 3 of the *Aeneid*, and a retrospect, often in the second chapter, becomes a standard device in later European narrative.

Although the action of the *Iliad* is concentrated, the poem has a deep sense of time. The characters are very aware of the past and the future: They often mention the great heroes of their past, such as Herakles or Meleager; both Helen and Achilles worry about the way people in the future will think of them; and the narrator is very aware that he is telling a story about events of long ago. No one in the story has time to age, but the story indicates the span of human life through the ages of the characters, from the baby Astyanax to the aged characters Priam and Nestor.

The time span of many narratives is only roughly indicated—a few days, a few months, a few years—but the time narrated is never just a convenience

---

21. For a recent discussion of time and space in narrative in rather different terms, see Gomel.

22. See, for example, Bridgeman in Herman, *Cambridge Companion*; also, among others, Bal; Rimmon-Kenan; and Genette. See also Bachelard for a philosophical account of the meaning of space. For discussion of unnatural time and space, see Heinze, "Whirligig"; and Alber, "Unnatural Spaces."

of narration; it is always a part of the meaning of the story. Many narratives in the Western tradition have the kind of concentrated time found in the *Iliad* and *Odyssey*. Some short stories represent a short time, but others cover quite a long period, though the climax is usually concentrated. Some longer narratives—novels, roughly speaking—are extremely concentrated. Examples of books that take one day or less include *Under the Volcano* (Malcolm Lowry), *Ulysses* (James Joyce), *Mrs. Dalloway* (Virginia Woolf), *One Day in the Life of Ivan Denisovich* (Alexander Solzhenitsyn), and *Seize the Day* (Saul Bellow); typically a narrative so concentrated will employ flashbacks.

Emma takes just one year from start to finish, and the elapse of time is marked with some care.[23] The story begins in October, with the marriage of Miss Taylor and Mr. Weston, and it ends the following October, with the marriage of Emma and Mr. Knightley. In between, the months and the seasons are tracked with special attention to the weather. At times the weather influences the action: the snowy night of the party at the Westons (79–92), the rain shower that brings Harriet and Mr. Martin together in Ford's shop (122–23), the heat and the sun during the strawberry picking at Donwell (246–52). The weather at the moment of crisis, when Mr. Knightley proposes to Emma, is particularly worthy of note: The night before the proposal was gloomy, cold, and stormy: "Nothing of July appeared but in the trees and shrubs, which the wind was despoiling" (290). The following morning started much the same, "but in the afternoon it cleared; the wind changed into a softer quarter; the clouds were carried off; the sun appeared; it was summer again" (291–92), and the change of weather is shortly followed by the proposal. The rhythm of the year, the seasons, and the weather are all part of the world Austen creates.

Many other stories cover an extended period of time, sometimes from birth to maturity, especially marked by marriage (Dickens's *Great Expectations*), or sometimes death; some cover more than a generation (Thomas Mann's *Buddenbrooks*, Gabriel Gárcia Marquez's *One Hundred Years of Solitude*).[24] All of these various ways of creating the time of a story are based on the human meaning of time: a day of crisis, the rhythm of the seasons, the important moments in a life, the rhythm of an entire life, the passing of time from one generation to the next. Narrative time can be rooted in history or it

---

23. Although the time of the novel is compressed, the span of life is suggested by the birth of the Westons' child and the death of Mrs. Churchill. Other one-year books include *Framley Parsonage* (Anthony Trollope), *The Return of the Native* (Thomas Hardy), and *The Romantic Comedians* (Ellen Glasgow).

24. For a good discussion of time in the "dramatic novel" and in the "chronicle," see Muir.

can float in a mythic once-upon-a-time.[25] As usual, the synthetic, the mimetic, and the thematic are simultaneous.

The *Iliad* and the *Odyssey* deal with space in very different ways. The *Iliad* mostly takes place within a fairly confined space, between Troy and the beach where the Greek ships are moored, with the battlefield between. Certainly other spaces exist—other cities sacked by the Achaeans, for instance, and of course the Achaean cities detailed in the Catalogue of Ships—but the story itself never ventures outside its narrow confines. The *Odyssey*, however, ranges over a large geography, particularly in the first half of the story, though Odysseus almost always remembers that he is heading home; the second half of the story concentrates the action in Ithaca. Space comes in many varieties. Space in *Pride and Prejudice* is different from space in *Emma*; space in *The Return of the Native* is different from space in *Tess of the D'Urbervilles*. Space can be centered, diffused, or polarized; confined or expansive; friendly or hostile. Space, like time, is represented as human space with human meaning.[26]

Science fiction has been much interested in the representation of time and space. Time travel has been a frequent theme, sometimes simply as a device to move a character into another time frame or historical period, as in Jack Finney's *Time and Again* and *From Time to Time*, but sometimes it is used more substantively as a way to explore various paradoxes. The major character of Robert Heinlein's great story "All You Zombies," for example, is his own mother and father and son and daughter; in fact, all of the characters in the story are the same person along different time streams. In *The Door into Summer*, Heinlein uses a little time travel to justify a little pederasty. In *Time for the Stars*, Heinlein, again, uses relativistic time to have his twin characters age at different rates. A number of science fiction writers have explored "future history" in a systematic way; Heinlein is a pioneer in this genre, but other noteworthy examples are Isaac Asimov's Foundation series and the many stories of Cordwainer Smith, which extend time into the far-distant future.

Space travel is of course a staple element in science fiction, but many science fiction stories have difficulty dealing with the enormity of space, which extends beyond what is humanly meaningful. Space ships are often little more than modernized sailing ships, and many battles in space are totally implausible. Faster-than-light engines or hyperspace are invoked to solve the prob-

---

25. Shaw argues that there is a close connection between historical narrative and realism. It is certainly true that many mythic narratives (such as the *Mahabharata*) and many postmodern narratives (such as Beckett's *How It Is*) lack a grounding in historical time, but many nonrealistic romances (such as Dumas's *The Count of Monte Cristo* or Orczy's *The Scarlet Pimpernel*) depend on historical setting.

26. See Clark, *Narrative* for a discussion of the "locative self" in narrative.

lem of the great distances of space, but some writers have taken advantage of galactic distances to create new and different kinds of worlds: Larry Nivens's *Ringworld,* for instance, creates a world shaped like an enormous ribbon circling a distant star. Philip José Farmer is perhaps the most prolific maker of worlds, not only in his Riverworld series, but also in the series called The World of Tiers, which represents many different worlds with wildly different characteristics.

Nor is the creation of strange worlds limited to science fiction. The world (perhaps the underworld) of Samuel Beckett's *How It Is* consists mostly of mud and slime. The time of the story is divided into three parts. In part 1, the narrator seems to be all alone as he crawls through the mud; his only possessions are a sack with a cord, some tins, and a tin opener. Now and again the narrator gives us glimpses of another world, another life, "life in the light," available in images that are perhaps memories:

> life in the light first image some creature or other I watched him after my fashion from afar thought my spy-glass side-long in mirrors through windows at night first image. (9)

> I look to me about sixteen and to crown all glorious weather egg-blue sky and scamper of little clouds I have my back turned to me and the girl too whom I hold who holds me by the hand the arse I have. (29)

In part 2 the narrator, whose name may be Bom, meets a second character, Pim, whom the narrator torments in various ways as they lie in the mud and slime:

> first lesson theme song I dig my nails into his armpit right hand right pit he cries I withdraw them thump with fist on skull his face sinks in the mud his cries cease end of first lesson. (62)

In the third part, the narrator develops a complex theory of his world. He supposes that this world is inhabited by perhaps by a hundred thousand people, perhaps a million, perhaps only four, crawling through the mud, perhaps in an enormous circle. At times, the first person torments the second and the third torments the fourth; then these couples part for a time, and next the second person torments the third and the fourth torments the first—and so on, depending on the number of inhabitants. Thus in the time before the story begins, there was a time when the narrator was tormented, as in part 2 he torments Pim:

> two there were two of us his hand on my arse someone had come Bom Bem one syllable m at the end all that matters Bem had come to cleave to me see later Pim and me I had come to cleave to Pim the same thing except that me Pim Bem me Bem left me south. (109)

What initially seem to be names, Pim and Bom, may designate roles, so that the person tormenting is Bom or Bem and the person tormented is Pim, but the roles keep switching:

> and that linked thus bodily together each one of us is at the same time Bom and Pim tormenter and tormented pedant and dunce wooer and wooed speechless and reafflicted with speech in the dark the mud nothing to emend there. (140)

In addition, there may be a character, or perhaps two characters, named Kram and Krim, a witness and a scribe. All of this is explained in some detail in some of the least obscure writing in the book.

Late in the story, the narrator supposes that another world may be possible, a world "merciful enough to shelter such frolics where no one ever abandons anyone and no one ever waits for anyone and never two bodies touch" (143). But then a page later, the whole construction is thrown into question: "all these calculations yes explanations yes the whole story from beginning to end yes completely false yes" (144). The reader is left with no certainty.

By Phelan's definition, *How It Is* is hardly mimetic. Beckett's text insistently foregrounds the verbal synthetic, with a web of sentence fragments, repetitions, antitheses, contradictions, links, and so on, and the world depicted is far from "what we typically call reality." But the reader who stays at the level of the verbal synthetic will miss the point of the story; moreover, in the terms I am proposing, the story is mimetic, because it builds a world, synthetically, and the world of the story is essential to the meaning of the story. This meaning, the thematic aspect, is available only through interpretation of the world represented in the narrative, the mimetic aspect. The world of *How It Is* is not much like our world, but it is no more different than the world of Dante's *Inferno*, to which it probably refers.

As a general rule, narrative time and space are not simply there, an empty and featureless background; they must themselves be represented, they can be represented variously, and the varieties of time and space have meaning. The artificiality of time and space in science fiction worlds is easy to see, but the worlds created in realistic fiction are also artificial, even when they are reasonably congruent with our own world. And even fantastic worlds are often intended as a kind of commentary on what might be called the "real" world.

VIII. OBJECTS

Harry Shaw asks, "Why do realist novels contain so many objects?" (44). Part of the answer is that many do not. Moreover, objects are not an exclusive feature of realism; nonrealistic narratives can also be well furnished. Realism and detail are not the same. For the most part, the detailed descriptions in most narratives are not referential, in the usual sense of the term. Most of the places and objects and people described exist only in the mind of the author. Narrative representation is mostly pseudo-reference.

Huckleberry Finn is full of objects. In the first chapter, we read about a dinner bell, new clothes, food, the Bible, snuff, a spelling book, a piece of candle, a table, the stars, leaves rustling, an owl, a whippowill, a dog, the wind, a spider, a lock of hair, a horseshoe, a window, and a shed. Every chapter has a similar catalogue of objects. Objects are essential in the narrative of Huck's escape from the cabin where he has been confined by Pap. In chapter 6 Pap returns to the cabin from town with supplies:

> The old man made me go to the skiff and fetch the things he had got. There was a fifty-pound sack of corn meal, and a side of bacon, ammunition, and a four-gallon jug of whisky, and an old book and two newspapers for wadding, besides some tow. (33)

All of these are instrumental in the actual escape. In chapter 7, when Pap is away again, Huck makes his escape:

> I took the sack of corn meal and took it to where the canoe was hid, and shoved the vines and branches apart and put it in; then I done the same with the side of bacon; then the whisky jug. I took all the coffee and sugar there was, and all the ammunition: I took the wadding; I took the bucket and gourd; took a dipper and a tin cup, and my old saw and two blankets, and the skillet and the coffee-pot. I took fish-lines and matches and other things—everything that was worth a cent. I cleaned out the place. [He then shoots a wild pig].
>
> I took the axe and smashed in the door. I beat it and hacked it considerable a-doing it. I fetched the pig in, and took him back nearly to the table and hacked into his throat with the ax, and laid him down on the ground to bleed. . . . Well, next I took an old sack and put a lot of big rocks in it—all I could drag—and I started from the pig and dragged it to the door and through the woods down to the river and dumped it in, and down it sunk, out of sight. You could easy see that something had been dragged over the ground. . . .

> Well, last I pulled out some of my hair, and blooded the ax good, and stuck it on the back side, and slung the ax in the corner. Then I took up the pig and held him to my breast with the jacket (so he couldn't drip) till I got a good piece below the house and then dumped him into the river. (40–41)

Then he took the sack of meal and used it to make a trail off to a nearby lake; he dropped Pap's whetstone there as well. This is all very elaborate and chock full of things used to create the impression that Huck has been killed and dumped in the river. The objects are essential to the effect, both as tools to create the false appearance and also as supplies Huck will need as he travels down the river. In general, objects appear because they are used or experienced. They are functional, but only functional, without much psychological import. But Huck also notes objects imbued with superstitious awe, such as Jim's five-cent piece.

Jane Austen is also a realist, but her use of objects is very different from Twain's. It has often been noted that her books are barely furnished. In the first chapter of *Emma*, a number of objects are mentioned—Emma's house itself, the lawn and the shrubberies, a carriage and horses and a stable, a backgammon table, shoes, and umbrellas—but they are only mentioned in conversation, and none are actually used during the scene, except for the backgammon table, which is put aside as soon as Mr. Knightley comes to call.

When Austen introduces a specific object, it is usually more than a thing to be used. Objects matter because of the way they fit into social interactions or because of their psychological import. In volume 1, chapter 4, Harriet tells Emma that Robert Martin had gone out of his way to bring her some walnuts. The nuts are important not in themselves, but in their symbolic meaning. Chapter 6 begins the story of Emma's sketch of Harriet; this plays a major role in Emma's misunderstanding of Mr. Elton's intentions. In chapter 9 Emma and Harriet make their riddle book, which also plays a role in Mr. Elton's ambiguous courtship. In chapter 10 Emma deliberately breaks her shoelace so that Mr. Elton can talk in private with Harriet. In volume 2, chapter 9, Frank Churchill fixes the rivet in Mrs. Bates's spectacles as an excuse to spend more time with Jane Fairfax. A number of objects are gifts: Robert Martin's gift of walnuts to Harriet; Emma's gift of a quarter hog to the Bateses (volume 2, chapter 3); Mr. Knightley's gift of apples to the Bateses (volume 3, chapter 9); Emma's gift of arrowroot to Jane Fairfax (volume 3, chapter 9), which Jane refuses; and of course Frank's surreptitious gift of the piano to Jane Fairfax (volume 2, chapter 8), which is the topic of much discussion and speculation. The gifts in *Emma* are particularly interesting, because they are part of a highly elaborated social system of duties and obligations and status.[27]

Among the most interesting objects in *Emma* are the court plaister and pencil end that Harriet saved as mementoes of Mr. Elton. Harriet has kept them since volume 1, when Emma led her to believe that Mr. Elton was courting her, until volume 3, chapter 4, when she finally summons up the determination to have done with her sentimental regrets. A large part of the effect of this little scene is the humble nature of the mementoes. An important part of some varieties of realism is the inclusion of the ordinary. Erich Auerbach argued that this inclusion is a significant difference between classical and Christian literature, and this pathetic touch in *Emma* certainly seems to support his argument.[28]

Classical literature is not, however, devoid of objects, nor of humble objects, nor of noble objects placed in humble situations.[29] Homer's use of objects is in some ways like Austen's. Objects are signs of honor and status (though there is no money in Homer). Gifts are fundamental tools in social interactions. Specific objects in the epics often have some kind of symbolic value. The Homeric epics include heroic objects, such as weapons and armor, but also ordinary objects, such as food, laundry, footstools, and pigsties. When Odysseus in disguise first approaches his home, he is recognized only by his old dog, who is lying neglected on a dung heap; the dog sees him, wags his tail weakly, and dies (*Odyssey* xvii.290–327). In book 6 of the *Iliad*, as Hektor is going toward the battlefield, he meets his wife Andromache and his son Astyanax, who is frightened when he sees Hektor's helmet:

> Hektor held out his arms to his baby,
> who shrank back to his fair-girdled nurse's bosom
> screaming, and frightened at the sight of his own father,
> terrified as he saw the bronze and the crest with its horse-hair,
> nodding dreadfully, as he thought, from the peak of the helmet.
> (Il.VI.466–70; my translation)

Hektor's courage is all that stands between Astyanax and death at the hands of the Greeks, and yet the child is terrified by the heroic object that stands for battles and blood.

---

27. For discussion of the social meaning of gifts and the importance of consumer products in *Emma*, see Byrne, chapter 5. On money in Austen, see Copeland.
28. See Auerbach, particularly the epilogue.
29. For discussion of objects in Homer, see Griffin, chapter 2.

Objects are not limited to realistic effects in realistic narratives. Many fantasy or science fiction stories need to establish their own worlds through objects. Here, for example, is a passage from the beginning of George MacDonald's fantasy novel *Phantastes*. The hero of the story has just turned twenty-one, and on his birthday he has been visited by his grandmother, who happens to be a fairy. She tells him that the next day he will find the way to Fairy Land. The next morning, when he awakes, he finds that the world is strangely transformed: His wash basin was overflowing like a spring; a stream of water was flowing over the carpet, down the length of the room; and the carpet had turned into a field of grass and flowers, which bent and swayed with the motion of the current.

> My dressing table was an old-fashioned piece of furniture of black oak, with drawers all down the front. These were elaborately carved in foliage, of which ivy formed the chief part. The nearer end of this table remained just as it had been, but on the further end a singular change had commenced. I happened to fix my eye on a little cluster of ivy leaves. The first of these was evidently the work of the carver; the next looked curious; the third was unmistakably ivy; and just beyond it a tendril of clematis had twined itself about the gilt handle of one of the drawers. Hearing next a slight motion above me, I looked up, and saw that the branches and leaves designed upon the curtains of my bed were slightly in motion. Not knowing what change might follow next, I thought it high time to get up; and, springing from the bed, my bare feet alighted upon a cool green sward; and though I dressed all in haste, I found myself completing my toilet under the boughs of a great tree, whose top waved in the golden stream of the sunrise with many glittering interchanging lights, and with shadows of leaf and branch gliding over leaf and branch, as the cool morning wind swung it to and fro, like a sinking sea wave. (19–20)

The manufactured objects in this passage are themselves mimetic—the carpet imitates grass and flowers; the carvings on the dressing table imitate ivy—but then the imitations are transformed into the natural things they are imitating; mimesis becomes reality, or at least the reality of fantasy. MacDonald has outdone Parrhasius.

IX. ACTION

Actions in narrative extend from the smallest motions to the shape of the plot as a whole. However large or small, actions usually, perhaps always, leave something for the reader to fill in. At the very beginning of *Emma*, Miss Taylor, Emma's governess and companion, has just married Mr. Weston, much to the distress of Emma's father, who dislikes change of any sort. Emma tries to console him with the reminder that Mr. and Mrs. Weston live nearby and that they will see them often.

> Emma spared no exertions to maintain this happier flow of ideas, and hoped, by the help of backgammon, to get her father tolerably through the evening, and be attacked by no regrets but her own. The backgammon-table was placed; but a visitor immediately afterwards walked in and made it unnecessary. (8)

The reader has to know what backgammon is (this is the kind of detail that an editor a few centuries from now might have to footnote). Austen doesn't tell us what a backgammon table looks like, nor where in the room it was set up. Nor do we know who did the setting: Is this something Emma could do, or was a servant called in to move the table, a servant whose existence is hidden in a deleted agent phrase? Probably the latter, but evidently the point is not supposed to be important. When a visitor arrives (it turns out to be Mr. Knightley), does he just walk in or is he announced? This point also is unimportant. In a play or a film, however, many of these details would have to be filled in. Narrative depends on the reader's ability to fill in the gaps or to disregard them.

No one, I suppose, would say that Austen's novels are action-packed. There are, to be sure, memorable actions in *Emma*, such as Mr. Elton's proposal or Emma's unkind remark to Mrs. Bates. Often, however, Austen places the moments of greatest action somewhat offstage. Jane Fairfax's story could well have been the plot of an interesting novel, but probably not a novel by Austen. The obstacle in the way of the final marriage of Emma and Mr. Knightley is their lack of self-knowledge, and the action is organized to bring them to the awareness they need: Emma must fear that Mr. Knightley is in love with Harriet, while Mr. Knightley must fear that Emma is in love with Frank. Early on in the story, Mr. Knightley says, "I should like to see Emma in love, and in some doubt of a return; it would do her good" (30). He is right, but the comment applies to him as well. Both Emma and Mr. Knightley come to know their desires only when their desires are threatened. In addition to this major trajectory of the story, Austen includes the stories of Jane Fairfax and Frank Churchill, as well as the story of Harriet and Robert Martin, and she throws in Mr. and Mrs. Elton, Emma's father, and so on, to create a network of characters and actions.

Plot has been somewhat de-emphasized in some varieties of fiction (in so-called serious fiction at least since the days of Henry James) and also in academic criticism, where characterization and theme have been at the center of attention.[30] Readers of popular fiction, however, have retained an interest in plot. Plot has its own value and importance as an element of narrative, and it should not be neglected by theorists.

In what sense are narrative actions, including plots, mimetic? They are not generally copies of some specific original action. But we have seen above that mimesis does not have to fit the form of an original and a copy. They are imitations of general actions, which readers understand as frames and scripts, or perhaps of archetypes, in a broad sense of the term, such as the archetypes of life and death, meeting and marriage, departure and return, lack and fulfillment.[31] There is pleasure, to be sure, from recognizing that a story belongs to an archetype, but greater pleasure in seeing how an archetype is manifest in some particular story.

X. CHARACTERS

Characters are at the center of Phelan's concept of mimesis. The mimetic component is "that component of character directed to its imitation of a possible person," and "responses to the mimetic component involve an audience's interest in the characters as possible people and in the narrative world as like our own" (Phelan, *Living* 20). Phelan is primarily interested in realistic characters, but there are many unrealistic characters in narrative, and a theory of narrative should be able to account for these as well.

Characters, whether nonfictional or fictional, are represented by the accumulation of traits, as well as by actions. The representation of a nonfictional character is referential—that is, it claims to refer to a real human being. The representation of a fictional character is pseudo-referential—that is, it has (more or less) the same form as the representation of a nonfictional character, but without external reference. The description of a fictional character is synthetic, as is the character; a real person is not synthetic, but the description of a real person is synthetic. We can compare, for example, A. J. P. Taylor's refer-

---

30. See, for example, Lowe ix: "'Plot' is an unloved word in narrative theory: no longer quite the four-letter vulgarity it was to critics a generation or two ago, but still not much used in polite conversation." See also Clark, "The Concept," for a discussion of the meaning of the plot of the *Iliad*.

31. See Clark, *A Matter of Style*, on general narrative plot forms. Recent work in narrative theory has largely neglected plot grammars, though they were important at earlier stages of narrative analysis, roughly from Propp to Pavel. I have argued elsewhere that a way forward is the examination of narrative micro-grammars (Clark, "The Cognitive Turn").

ential representation of Bismark to Henry James's nonreferential representation of Christopher Newman, the hero of *The American*.³²

James's novel begins with an extended description of the hero of the story, at a particular time and place: "On a brilliant day in May, in the year 1868, a gentleman was reclining at his ease on the great circular divan which at that period occupied the centre of the Salon Carré, in the Museum of the Louvre" (17). James now gives a more particularized portrait of Newman at this moment: He was sitting in the softest spot of the divan, his head was thrown back and his legs were stretched out, he had taken off his hat, and he was serenely enjoying his posture. He was warm and weary: "And yet he was evidently not a man to whom fatigue was familiar" (17). Looking at paintings, however, was a new kind of effort for him. His physiognomy indicates that he was shrewd and capable. An observer with an eye for national types would have identified him easily as an American—a fine American, but also a fine man. "He appeared to possess that kind of health and strength which, when found in perfection, are the most impressive—the physical capital which the owner does nothing to 'keep up'" (18). He did not exercise. "His usual attitude and carriage were of a rather relaxed and lounging kind, but when, under a special inspiration, he straightened himself, he looked like a grenadier on parade" (18). He did not smoke. He had a well-formed head, brown hair, a brown complexion, a bold nose, a clear, cold grey eye, an abundant moustache (18).

> He had the flat jaw and sinewy neck which are frequent in the American type; but the traces of national origin are a matter of expression even more than of feature, and it was in this respect that our friend's countenance was supremely eloquent. The discriminating observer we have been supposing might, however, have perfectly measured its expressiveness, and yet been at a loss to describe it. (18)

His countenance had vagueness without vacuity, blankness without simplicity; his eye blended innocence with experience.

> It was full of contradictory suggestions; and though it was by no means the glowing orb of a hero of romance, you could find in it almost anything you looked for. Frigid and yet friendly, frank yet cautious, shrewd yet credulous, positive yet sceptical, confident yet shy, extremely intelligent and extremely

---

32. Here I concentrate on fully developed "novelistic" characters, but narratives also include "flat" characters, such as Mr. Woodhouse in *Emma;* characters in short stories usually have just enough particularity to make the point of the story.

good-humoured, there was something vaguely defiant in its concessions, and something profoundly reassuring in its reserve. . . . Decision, salubrity, jocosity, prosperity, seem to hover within his call; he is evidently a practical man, but the idea, in his case, has undefined and mysterious boundaries, which invite the imagination to bestir itself on his behalf. (18–19)

This description is a list of traits and actions, invented and organized by the writer. The physical description is lavish, and yet it fails to give a complete picture; some interpretations would be ruled out, but two different painters could paint two different portraits equally faithful to the details given. The psychological details also fail to give a single portrait; the antitheses, in particular, provide an excess of information. When Newman is placed in some situation, which side of the antithesis will determine his behavior? Will he be frigid or will he be friendly? Shrewd or credulous? Confident or shy?

This description can be compared to A. J. P. Taylor's initial description in his biography *Bismark*. This description of a real person is also synthetic. Taylor begins by noting the time and place of Bismark's birth, which set the historical and social context of his life, and he gives a brief description of Bismark's parents.[33] He then begins to characterize Bismark himself as the child of his parents: "He was the clever, sophisticated son of a clever sophisticated mother, masquerading all his life as his heavy, earthy father" (Taylor 9).

Taylor continues with physical description: "He was a big man, made bigger by his persistence in eating and drinking too much. He walked stiffly, with the upright carriage of a hereditary officer. Yet he had a small, fine head; the delicate hands of an artist; and when he spoke, his voice, which one would have expected to be deep and powerful, was thin and reedy" (9). Taylor seems (here and elsewhere) to particularly note contradictory or inconsistent qualities: Conflict creates interest.

After a bit more physical description, Taylor moves on to psychology:

Despite his Junker mien, he had the sensitivity of a woman, incredibly quick in responding to the moods of another, or even in anticipating them. His conversational charm could bewitch tsars, queens and revolutionary leaders. Yet his great strokes of policy came after long solitary brooding, not after discussion with others. . . . He felt himself always out of place, solitary and a stranger to his surroundings. . . . He spent the twenty-eight years of supreme power announcing his wish to relinquish it; yet no man has left office with

---

33. James does not say anything about Newman's parents, but of course there are many novels that do begin with an ancestry. James puts the reader immediately into a narrative situation, while Taylor's description is abstract, but it is easy to find works of history and biography that begin with an initial narrative situation.

such ill grace or fought so unscrupulously to recover it. He despised writers and literary men; yet only Luther and Goethe rank with him as masters of German prose. . . . He found happiness only in his family. . . . Yet he ruined the happiness of his adored elder son for the sake of a private feud, and thought nothing of spending a long holiday away from his wife in the company of a pretty girl. . . . He claimed sometimes to serve the king of Prussia, sometimes Germany, sometimes God. All these were cloaks for his own will; and he turned against them ruthlessly when they did not serve his purpose. . . . The young Junker had no vision that he would unify Germany on the basis of universal suffrage; and the maker of three wars did not expect to end as the great buttress of European peace. (9–10)

This description is referential, and it depends on external sources, such as portraits and descriptions of Bismark by those who knew him. But the description is also a synthetic literary construction. The traits are roughly organized in three major categories, which come more or less in sequence; first, physical description; second, psychological characterization; and third, an account of his relationships with other people. In addition, the traits are often organized antithetically, as were the traits in James's description of Newman; the grammatical markers here include the words "yet," "actually," "despite," and "but." One could perhaps argue that the antitheses are referential, that they existed in Bismark and are simply noted by Taylor, but an examination of Taylor's other writing (such as the beginning of his history of the Hapsburgs) shows that Taylor tends to think in antitheses. Perhaps a different biographer, with a different cast of mind, would have produced a different kind of description.

These two descriptions are in some ways very similar—though not, of course, exactly alike. Both descriptions are fundamentally lists of traits and actions. Both are marked by antithesis. And both put the character within a type—Newman is an American, Bismark is a Junker—but both also play the character against the type.

Bismark, of course, was a real person, and therefore he was more than a list of his traits and actions—or perhaps not, depending on one's idea of what makes a person. But even if there is in a real person some ineffable surplus of subjectivity, the description of a person can only be a description of traits and actions. Newman, as a fictional character, is entirely synthetic, and he has no existence beyond whatever is given by his creator. The difference, however, is not so much internal to the descriptions, but external—we know that Bismark was a real person and that Newman was not. A reader lacking this external knowledge, however, would be hard pressed to say exactly what makes the one description fiction and the other nonfiction.

As we examine the books as a whole, however, we may see that the two descriptions function somewhat differently. Taylor's initial description of Bismark serves as the background for the biography; we understand and interpret the following account of Bismark's political decisions and actions against this description. In a sense, Bismark springs fully formed from Taylor's description. James's description of Newman, however, leaves a residue of indeterminacy that is not resolved until the end of the novel, when he makes his final choice not to reveal his secret knowledge; we understand and interpret Newman's character against this final action.[34]

James's description of Newman is not referential, simply because there never was a real person to which the description refers, but the description takes the form of a referential description, such as Taylor's description of the real person Bismark. There is nothing strange in this relationship between reference and pseudo-reference: It is made possible by general features of language, which linguists identify as displacement and prevarication—that is, we can speak about things that aren't present, and we can lie; these features and the additional features of abstraction, elaboration, and imagination allow for the creation of characters that are not only fictional but also fantastic.[35]

Unrealistic characters probably outnumber realistic characters—depending, of course, on what counts as realistic. Do we count among the realistic Aeschylus's Clytemnestra, Sophocles's Antigone, or Euripides's Medea? Is Gilgamesh realistic? Dracula? James Bond? Robinson Crusoe? Edmond Dantes (the Count of Monte Cristo)? Sir Peter Blakeney (the Scarlet Pimpernel)? Sir Galahad? Parzival? Gandalf? Pantagruel? Captain Ahab? What about the animal characters in Aesop's fables? The various gods in Greek or Hindu myth? Or, for that matter, Jesus? Perhaps these are not to be judged as more or less realistic, but as more or less convincing.

Science fiction has explored various kinds of abnormal or unnatural characters, including people with psychic powers, but also various nonhuman characters: humanoids, apes, other kinds of mammalians, avians, reptilians, arthropods, cephalopods, worms, living planets, and beings made of pure energy. It is an interesting critical question how far any of these are convincing aliens rather than people wearing funny suits.

---

34. Compare, for example, Trollope's comment on his presentation of Mark Roberts, the hero of *Framley Parsonage*: "But little has been said, personally, as to our hero himself, and perhaps it may not be necessary to say much. Let us hope that by degrees he may come forth upon the canvas, showing to the beholder the nature of the man inwardly and outwardly" (Trollope 37).

35. See Hockett for a discussion of these features of language.

Science fiction has also taken the opportunity to examine what it is to be human. The following passage comes from C. S. Lewis's *Out of the Silent Planet*. The hero, Ransom, has been kidnapped by the two villains of the story, Weston and Devine, and taken to Mars (Malacandra). Once on Mars, he manages to escape from his captors and spends some months with the various sentient Martian species: the sorns, roughly humanoid, but very tall and thin, "spindly and flimsy things, twice or three times the height of a man," their faces "thin and unnaturally long, with long, drooping noses and drooping mouths of half-spectral, half idiotic solemnity" (Lewis 45); the hrossa, "six or seven feet high and too thin for its height," with "a coat of thick black hair . . . very short legs with webbed feet, a broad beaver-like or fish-like tail, strong fore-limbs with webbed claws or fingers" (55); pfifltriggs, "tapir-headed, frog-bodied animals"; and eldil, invisible to human eyes but audible to human ears (71).

After some months among these various Malacandrians, Ransom travels to be presented to Oyarsa, an eldil who is the presiding intelligence of the planet. While he is speaking with Oyarsa, he sees a procession approach:

> As the procession drew nearer Ransom saw that the foremost *hrossa* were supporting three long and narrow burdens. They carried them on their heads, four *hrossa* to each. After them came a number of others armed with harpoons and apparently guarding two creatures which he did not recognize. The light was behind them as they entered between the two farthest monoliths. They were much shorter than any animal he had yet seen on Malacandra, and he gathered that they were bipeds, though the lower limbs were so thick and sausage-like that he hesitated to call them legs. The bodies were a little narrower at the top than at the bottom so as to be very slightly pear-shaped, and the heads were neither round like those of *hrossa* or long like those of *sorns*, but almost square. They stumped along on narrow, heavy-looking feet which they seemed to press into the ground with unnecessary violence. And now their faces were becoming visible as masses of lumped and puckered flesh of variegated colour fringed in some bristly, dark substance. . . . Suddenly, with an indescribable change of feeling, he realized that he was looking at men. The two prisoners were Weston and Devine and he, for one privileged moment, had seen the human form with almost Malacandrian eyes. (125)

Here the human is seen from the perspective of the alien and the natural is seen as unnatural. Realistic mimesis has been turned on its head.

XI. THE MIMETIC ASPECT OF *1984*

This section examines the mimetic aspect of George Orwell's *1984*, particularly mimesis as world-making, and more particularly the interweaving of time, place, and objects in Orwell's world.[36] As usual, the mimetic is closely tied to the synthetic and the thematic, and it will not be possible to keep the three aspects completely separate. I will have more to say about the thematic aspect of *1984* in chapter 3.

The world of *Emma* was essentially the world of its original audience, more or less, and therefore Austen could leave a good deal of world-making to the reader, but Orwell could not depend on his readers to have familiarity with the world he imagines and constructs. According to Orwell, *1984* "is in a sense a fantasy but in the form of a naturalistic novel." I think he means that the narrative has the kind of detail and specificity found in a naturalistic novel; the manner of presentation, however, is quite different.[37] Phelan notes "a tension of unequal knowledge between author and authorial audience: he and his narrator surrogate know all about this world but plunge us into the narrative without orienting us" (Phelan, *Reading* 29). Writers of speculative fiction have developed a number of techniques for dealing with this tension: Some science fiction novels begin with invented encyclopedia articles giving narrative background (Isaac Asimov's *Foundation* novels, for instance); some begin with what in the trade is called an "information dump," in which one character tells another character what the reader needs to know (as in Robert Heinlein's *Methuselah's Children*); but others, like *1984*, feed the information bit by bit ("incluing") and trust that the reader will have the ability and patience to put it all together.

The title of *1984* tells the reader that time is important. For the original reader in 1949, the time of the story was the future, but the near future: An original reader who was thirty in 1949 could well expect to live long enough to see if Orwell was a prophet or a fabulist. But perhaps the title was a slight transposition of 1948, the year the novel was written; the world of the novel

---

36. Phelan, *Reading* 28–43 has an extensive discussion of mimetic characterization in *1984*, but with less attention to mimesis as world-building. I have also consulted Gertrude Clark Whittal; Mulvihill; Howe; Roger Fowler, *Language*; Calder; and Gleason, Goldsmith, and Nussbaum.

37. The quotation, from a letter of May 31, 1948, to F. J. Warburg, is often cited; see Phelan, *Reading* 34. Orwell was by no means the first to write naturalistic fantasy; one could mention, for example, Jules Verne, H. G. Wells, Aldous Huxley, and Olaf Stapledon, as well as a number of American science fiction writers. Orwell was directly influenced by Yevgeny Zamyatin's *We*, published in English in 1924. It is also instructive to compare *1984* to Robert Heinlein's *Revolt in 2100*, first published, in a shorter version, under the title "If This Goes On—," in 1939.

then would be an interpretation of its own time. Irving Howe notes that "the unfuture of Oceania had some pretty keen resemblances to the immediate past of England. . . . He [Orwell] knew . . . that to make credible the part of his book which would spiral into the extraordinary, he had first to provide it with a strong foundation of the ordinary."[38]

Although the title simply asserts a date, the reader may be surprised to learn (on page 7) that Winston Smith, the main character in the story, doesn't actually know the date for certain. Does the reader know more than the hero? Or is the assertion of the title really false assurance? Is everything about this world similarly open to question?

The first paragraph of the story continues the emphasis on time, introduces the main character, and adds some physical detail:

> It was a bright cold day in April, and the clocks were striking thirteen. Winston Smith, his chin nuzzled into his breast in an effort to escape the vile wind, slipped quickly through the glass doors of Victory Mansions, though not quickly enough to prevent a swirl of gritty dust from entering along with him. (3)

Our earlier investigations of narrative mimesis have taught us to be aware of the seasons and the weather. The story begins in April; Orwell is probably alluding to other Aprils in English literature.[39] On this April day, the weather itself is hostile, and Winston's attempts to protect himself are futile. The clock is striking thirteen, or, as we would probably say, it is one o'clock in the afternoon. I will return to the clock in a moment; for now it is enough to say that here Orwell introduces a detail that distances the narrative world from the world of the original audience.[40]

The second paragraph of the story continues to construct the narrative world: "The hallway smelt of boiled cabbage and old rug mats." Many writers never mention smells; some mention the good smell of a meal or a cozy fire; but bad smells are rare in literature and worthy of notice. The bad smell at the beginning of *1984* is only one manifestation of the general tone of disgust with the world of the story.[41] Of course, the world of objects in *1984* is in decay and disrepair, but the story conveys a deeper quality of sensory malaise. In the second chapter of part 1, Winston's neighbor Mrs. Parsons asks him to unclog

---

38. Howe, 4–5. See also Meyers 79; and Donaghue 60.
39. See Miller 22–23.
40. On the first paragraph of the novel, the month, and the clock, see Crick 98.
41. On Orwell's use of "sordid realism," see Roger Fowler, *Language* 195–99.

her sink. Orwell takes the opportunity to give a general picture of the conditions of life in Victory Mansions:

> These amateur repair jobs were an almost daily irritation. Victory Mansions were old flats, built in 1930 or thereabouts, and were falling to pieces. The plaster flaked constantly from ceilings and walls, the pipes burst in every hard frost, the roof leaked whenever there was snow, the heating system was usually running at half steam when it was not closed down altogether from motives of economy. . . . The kitchen sink was full nearly to the brim with filthy greenish water which smelt worse than ever of cabbage. . . . Winston let out the water and disgustedly removed the clot of human hair that had blocked up the pipe. (15)

The narrator's own emotion is evident. Nor is this a unique moment. Winston himself has a varicose ulcer on his leg; we read about this in the second paragraph of the book and many times thereafter. The gin he drinks before starting his diary "gave off a sickly, oily smell" (5). The food in the canteen is barely edible and the canteen itself is filthy: On the table where Winston has his lunch, "someone had left a pool of stew, a filthy liquid that had the appearance of vomit" (35).

> [Winston] meditated resentfully on the physical texture of life. Had it always been like this? Had food always tasted like this? He looked around the canteen. A low-ceilinged, crowded room, its walls grimy from the contact of innumerable bodies: battered metal tables and chairs, placed so close together that you sat with elbows touching, bent spoons, dented trays, coarse white mugs; all surfaces greasy, grime in every crack; and a sourish, composite smell of bad gin and bad coffee and metallic stew and dirty clothes. Always in your stomach and in your skin there was a sort of protest, a feeling that you had been cheated of something that you had a right to. It was true that he had no memories of anything greatly different. In any time that he could accurately remember, there had never been quite enough to eat, one had never had socks or underclothes that were not full of holes, furniture had always been battered and rickety, rooms underheated, Tube trains crowded, houses falling to pieces, bread dark-colored, tea a rarity, coffee filthy tasting, cigarettes insufficient—nothing cheap and plentiful except synthetic gin. (41)

Even the people are disgusting: "Nearly everyone was ugly. . . . It was curious how the beetlelike type proliferated in the ministries: little dumpy men, growing stout very early in life, with short legs, swift scuttling movements, and fat inscrutable faces with very small eyes" (41). "Sexual intercourse was to be looked on as a slightly disgusting minor operation like having an enema" (45). Winston's wife had been unresponsive, and his experience with a prostitute is repellent (44–47). Of course, things are different with Julia.

The most notorious elements of the world of the novel are Big Brother, the telescreens, and the unending war. Big Brother is introduced in the second paragraph, just after the smell of boiled cabbage and old rug mats: A poster tacked to the wall of the hallway depicted "an enormous face, more than a meter wide: the face of a man about forty-five, with a heavy black mustache and ruggedly handsome features. . . . On each landing, opposite the lift shaft, the poster with the enormous face gazed from the wall" (3). Again the narrator leaves much unexplained, much for the readers to figure out as they continue.[42]

The telescreen is introduced in the third paragraph. Here the narrator provides an explanation needed by the authorial audience but not by the narrative audience: "The voice came from an oblong metal plaque like a dulled mirror which formed part of the surface of the right-hand wall. . . . The instrument (the telescreen, it was called) could be dimmed but there was no way of shutting it off completely" (3). The placement of the telescreen leaves an alcove in the living room outside of the range of surveillance, and therefore Winston can write in his diary unobserved. As the narrator says, "For some reason the telescreen in the living room was in an unusual position" (3). The reason is clear: The narrator needs both universal surveillance and also a tiny exception, so that Winston can write in his diary. The mimetic aspect here is determined by the thematic requirements of the story.

The world of *1984* is a world at war. Britain has become Airstrip One, just a part of Oceania, no longer an independent nation. There are two other powers, Eurasia and Eastasia; sometimes Oceania is allied with Eurasia against Eastasia, sometimes with Eastasia against Eurasia. Shifts in alliance are sudden, without rationale, and change is never acknowledged; a shift in alliance can occur even in the middle of a political demonstration (120). The war is used as justification for repression.

The present world of the story is thus a world of poverty and filth, war, unremitting surveillance and repression. This present is contrasted with the past and the future, both of which are important mimetic and thematic elements of the story.

---

42. As critics have noted, Big Brother looks somewhat like Joseph Stalin, while the dissident Emmanuel Goldstein looks like Leon Trotsky.

The narrative past, the original reader's present, is implicitly called to mind by comparison whenever the narrative present is unnatural or unreal. Even in the first sentence there is a clash between two times, and two ways of measuring time: "It was a bright cold day in April, and the clocks were striking thirteen" (3). There is no reason in nature that clocks should start over after twelve—military time, after all, works on a twenty-four hour clock—but for an ordinary person in 1949, the hour thirteen was a little strange, and perhaps it seemed unnatural. This oddity is the readers' first clue that the world of the story will be different, and this way of telling time is inevitably, if illogically, associated with the ugliness, filth, and surveillance that dominate the world of this story.[43]

Clock time is significant later on in the story as well. The room where Winston and Julia carry on their affair has a clock with a twelve-hour face (65, 91). This clock returns the characters to the past, to a world before time changed: "The room was a world, a pocket of the past where extinct animals could walk" (100). The clock is part of a larger nostalgia, a romantic conservatism characteristic of the story. But Julia is a child of the revolution, and to her the twelve-hour clock is absurd (97).

Another passage similarly romanticizes imperial measure, when an old prole tries to buy a pint of beer; the barman has only liters and half liters: "A 'alf liter ain't enough. It don't satisfy. And a 'ole liter's too much. It starts my bladder running" (60). Thus imperial measure is justified by physiology. Winton's notebook and pen are also part of this romantic conservatism:

> It was a particularly beautiful book. Its smooth creamy paper, a little yellowed by age, was of a kind that had not been manufactured for at least forty years past.... Winston fitted a nib into the penholder and sucked it to get the grease off. The pen was an archaic instrument, seldom used even for signatures, and he had procured one, furtively and with some difficulty, simply because of a feeling that the beautiful creamy paper deserved to be written on with a real nib instead of being scratched with an ink pen. (6–7)

Charrington's shop is a repository of romantic conservatism—and it is also a trap. Everything positive in Orwell's vision lies in the past or in relics of the past, not in the present and not even in the future.

---

43. There are several other references to the twenty-four-hour clock: "It was the lonely hour of fifteen" (52; see also 20, 79, 96, 121, 190, 195). Naturalization of cultural facts is, of course, an important element of ideological thought; on the one hand, the story opposes ideology, but on the other, it forms its own ideology.

Another refuge from the miseries of the present is provided by the English countryside, where Winston and Julia have their first tryst; the countryside is described as an idyllic place, a place of lanes and streams and wildflowers and dappled shade (79ff.). In a sense, the countryside is like the world of the paperweight, a piece of the past hermetically sealed. Winston had dreamed about this place before he ever saw it: "The landscape that he was looking at [in his dream] recurred so often in his dreams that he was never fully certain whether or not he had seen it in the real world. In his waking thoughts he called it the Golden Country" (22). When he meets Julia in the country, he calls it "the Golden Country"; when Julia asks what he means, he says, "It's nothing really. A landscape I've seen sometimes in a dream" (82).

Dreams in general form another layer of reality in the story; Winston dreams about his mother and sister (21–22), he dreams about the Golden Country, he dreams about someone he identifies with O'Brien. His dreams can be oddly clairvoyant: He dreams about the Golden Country before he sees it, and the phrase from a dream "We shall meet again in the place where there is no darkness" (18) is repeated in his conversation with O'Brien (118).

The past is thus a source of nostalgic sentiment, but it is also the realm of bitter memories; these memories are also linked to dreams: "There was the dream itself, and there was a memory connected with it had swum into his mind in the few seconds after waking" (106). The memories are about his mother and his sister, and his own cruel selfishness when he was a child. The central event was a fight over a piece of chocolate: His mother gives him more than his fair share, but he grabs the rest anyway (81). This memory, this dream, is linked back to Winston's first tryst with Julia; she has brought with her a piece of black-market chocolate, which stirs up a "memory moving around the edges of his consciousness. . . . He pushed it away from him, aware only that it was the memory of some action which he would have liked to undo but could not" (81).

As painful as this memory is, it is also an example of some of the deepest values expressed in the novel, related to his mother: "He did not suppose, from what he could remember of her, that she had been an unusual woman, still less an intelligent one; and yet she had possessed a kind of nobility, a kind of purity, simply because the standards that she obeyed were private ones" (109). These private standards have become impossible in the narrative present: "The terrible thing that the Party had done was to persuade you that mere impulses, mere feelings, were of no account." In the past, "what mattered were individual relationships, and a completely helpful gesture, an embrace, a tear, a word spoken to a dying man, could have value in itself" (110).

The past in Winston's world has no stability. As devoted to the past as he is, his job is to change it. The reader is given a very detailed explanation of the process, including Winston's discovery of the photo of Jones, Aaronson, and Rutherford, the proof that they were not guilty of the crimes for which they were condemned. Orwell describes both the techniques and the tools used to change the past. The tools include the speak-write, the pneumatic tubes that transport documents, and the memory holes (26–27). The techniques consist of constant revisions and replacements of the documentary record.

The mutability of the past is an essential feature of the ideology of the Party: According to the Party slogan, "Who controls the past controls the future, who controls the present controls the past" (165). In the third part of the novel, O'Brien goes to great lengths to convince Winston that the past has no objective existence.

The connection between the past, the present, and the future has been important in Winston's thinking from the very beginning of the novel: "How could you communicate with the future? Either the future would resemble the present, in which case it would not listen to him, or it would be different from it, and his predicament would be meaningless" (7). "He wondered again for whom he was writing the diary. For the future, for the past—for an age that might be imaginary" (20).[44] Can a similar question be applied to the narrative situation of the novel? For whom—past, present, or future—is Orwell writing?[45] Either the readers' world would resemble the world of the story, in which case they would not listen, or it would be different, and Winston's predicament would be meaningless. And yet Orwell's project is possible only if one world can communicate with another world about another possible world. Mimesis implies and perhaps requires difference.

Orwell also describes in detail the techniques of torture, both mental and physical: the beatings and the electrical shocks and the rat cage and the brainwashing. After Winston has been tortured, O'Brien makes Winston look in a mirror to see the results:

> A bowed, gray-colored, skeleton-like thing was coming toward him. Its actual appearance was frightening, and not merely the fact that he knew it to be himself. He moved closer to the glass. The creature's face seemed to be protruded, because of its bent carriage. A forlorn, jailbird's face with a nobby forehead running back into a bald scalp, a crooked nose and battered-looking cheekbones above which the eyes were fierce and watchful. The cheeks were

---

44. See also 24, 100, 103, 117, etc.

45. "What people of the future will think about Orwell's book we cannot know, nor can we say what it might mean to those who will remember so little about the time of totalitarianism they will need an editor's gloss if they chance upon a copy" (Howe 3).

seamed, the mouth had a drawn-in look. Certainly it was his own face, but it seemed to him that it had changed more than he had changed inside. The emotions it registered would be different from the ones he felt. He had gone partially bald. For the first moment he had thought that he had gone gray as well, but it was only the scalp that was gray. Except for his hands and a circle of his face, his body was gray all over with ancient, ingrained dirt. Here and there under the dirt there were the red scars of wounds, and near the ankle the varicose ulcer was an inflamed mass with flakes of skin peeling off it. But the truly frightening thing was the emaciation of his body. The barrel of the ribs was as narrow as that of a skeleton; the legs had shrunk so that the knees were thicker than the thighs. . . . The curvature of the spine was astonishing. The thin shoulders were hunched forward so as to make a cavity of the chest, the scraggy neck seemed to be bending double under the weight of the skull. At a guess he would say that it was the body of a man of sixty, suffering from some malignant disease. (180)

In *Out of the Silent Planet*, C. S. Lewis used a defamiliarizing description to jolt the reader into a new understanding of the human from an alien perspective; Orwell's description shows that Winston has become alien to himself.

At this point, however, despite the damage to his body, Winston still retains something of his own mind. The final pages of the book show even this taken from him. When he is faced with the rats, he begs that Julia be tortured instead (190), and the story ends with the famous sentence, "He loved Big Brother" (197).

1984 sits somewhat uneasily in Phelan's conception of the mimetic. The characters, including Winston, are thin, inconsistent, and implausible.[46] Their behavior is often determined by the needs of the plot, and events are often coincidental. It is a fantasy, even if it borrows some of the techniques of the realistic novel. It is the kind of fantasy that builds an unreal world and then demands that we compare that world to our own. Perhaps all fantasies ask for this comparison; perhaps realistic fictions do so as well. Each narrative builds its own relationship to reality, its own mimesis. An adequate theory of the mimetic aspect has to be able to account for the whole range of relationships between the fictive and the real.

---

46. Howe 6, for example, defends but does not deny the unreality of the characters and actions, but Phelan, *Reading* 33–34 argues that Orwell's initial treatment of Winston "is directed toward emphasizing his mimetic function." If he means that we care about Winston, I agree, but as I have argued, we can care about unrealistic characters. He further argues that Orwell attempts "to create a realistic individual psychology for Winston" (37), but the thematic needs of the story regularly trump realistic psychology.

CHAPTER 3

The Thematic Aspect

MATTHEW CLARK

I. DEFINITIONS OF THE THEMATIC

In the MST model, the thematic component is "that component of a narrative text concerned with making statements, taking ideological positions, teaching readers truths"; it is also "that component of character directed to its representative or ideational function" (Phelan, *Living* 219). The thematic dimensions of character can be "viewed as vehicles to express ideas or as representative of a larger class than the individual character" (Phelan, *Reading* 12).

In the MTS model, the thematic component is restricted to meanings that can be expressed or paraphrased as statements, positions, or truths; moreover, these meanings must be consciously intended by the author, since making statements, taking positions, and teaching truths are all intentional actions. Other kinds of meanings—meanings that are not paraphrasable propositions and meanings that are not intended—are not thematic, and narratives that do not primarily express intentional paraphrasable propositions are not thematic.

In the MTS model, each component is linked to a narrative type: "Some narratives (including most so-called realistic fiction) are dominated by mimetic interests; some (including allegories and political polemics such as *Animal Farm*) stress the thematic; others (including the *nouveau roman* and much postmodern metafiction) put priority on the synthetic" (Phelan and Rabinowitz in Herman et al. 7). Thus the thematic component carves out a group of narrative types in which the thematic component is dominant. There is no universally accepted name for this group, but it includes apologues, allegories, fables, and probably also satires. (I will have more to say about terminology below.) This group notably does not include the majority of realistic novels, which the MTS model would consider mimetic rather than thematic.

In the SMT model, however, the thematic aspect does not carve out a particular group of narratives. It is designed to cover meaning in all kinds of narratives, including meanings that are not paraphrasable as statements, positions, or truths, and including those that are not consciously intended by the author. Some of these meanings are created by the structure of narration or the manner of representation, and therefore the thematic is understood in relation to the synthetic and the mimetic. If the synthetic is something like syntax, while the mimetic is something like referential semantics, then the thematic is something like the kinds of meanings carried by complete utterances, including whole narratives.

The meaning of a narrative is built up gradually, sentence by sentence, in the course of reading. Some meanings will become foregrounded; others will fade into the background—though these, too, contribute to the gradual construction of meaning. Each reading of a text is different; new interpretations develop as different meanings are foregrounded. No meaning is excluded in principle from the thematic, and each interpretation has to make its own case for its choice of themes.

In the first book of the *Odyssey*, Athena, disguised as Mentes, comes to Ithaca to give advice to Telemachos. Telemachos welcomes her; she asks if he is the son of Odysseus, and he replies: "My mother says indeed I am his. I for my part do not know. Nobody really knows his own father" (Od.1.215–16). Telemachos is ostensibly talking about his father, but he is implicitly talking about his mother—if he is not the son of Odysseus, then Penelope has been unfaithful. Nothing much is made of this hint at the moment, but as the story develops, the question of Penelope's faithfulness is posed many times in many different ways, and the question of Penelope's faithfulness is crucial in the final recognition scene (Od.23.174–204). This hint does not make a statement, take an ideological position, or teach a truth, nor can we know what Homer intended by it, but it is surely meaningful, and the SMT model would include this meaning in the thematic aspect.

A little later in the same episode, Athena, still disguised as Mentes, tells Telemachos a lie about how she came to know Odysseus. He had gone to ask Ilos of Ephyre for poison to smear on his arrows, but Ilos had turned him down, fearing the judgment of the gods. "But my father"—that is, the fictitious father of Mentes—"did give it to him, so terribly did he love him" (Od.1.264–

65). Thus Mentes and Telemachos have an established family friendship. We don't know if anything like the incident is supposed to have happened, since Athena is telling a lie, but her lie suggests that Odysseus might have wanted to poison his arrows, and furthermore that the gods might well have disapproved. Does this story influence our evaluation of the moral character of Odysseus? The incident is not developed in the rest of the story; it seems to drop into relative insignificance, and it has received very little critical attention. Nonetheless, it introduces a flashing moment of doubt, and I would entertain an interpretation that could make something of it.

Narratives are full of hints and suggestions and meanings that do not translate into propositions. The resources of meaning are countless. All of the various narrative structures I have described in chapter 1 can contribute to the thematic aspect of a narrative. For instance, the kind of large-scale ring composition I have called ending with the beginning often invites a comparison between two situations; the great ring in the *Iliad* invites the audience to compare Agamemnon's rejection of Chryses's supplication to Achilles's hospitable and sympathetic treatment of Priam.

Style can be thematic. The following passage, from a story by Austin Clarke, implicitly makes a claim about the social status of dialect:

> I had never see a "coloured" girl in Toronto that look so good and so pretty, and with such a lovely "clear skin," in the three years that I did a student at Trinity College, playing I studying to be a political scientist and the saviour o'Barbados, and then afterwards, when I finish-up at Trinity, bound-'cross the English Channel, enter Middle Temple, tek torts, become a barrister-at-law and gone-back straight home, back to Barbados, to help run the country. (Clarke 95)

There is a long tradition of dialect writing in English, but the meaning of dialect differs from narrative to narrative. In George Eliot's *Adam Bede*, the dialect of many of the rustic characters is quite different from the dialect of the central characters, and different from the narrator's use of "standard" English. Eliot's use of dialect marks and perhaps reinforces social distinctions. In Twain's *Huckleberry Finn*, the primary voice is the narrator's dialect; Twain's use of dialect suggests that Huck can be a worthy narrator, despite his lack of education. Austin Clarke, in the passage quoted above, presents an educated narrator who chooses to use patois. This use of dialect claims that the culture of Barbados is not inferior to the culture of the imperial center.

Allusion can create meaning through the interaction of two texts. James M. Cain's *The Postman Always Rings Twice* alludes to the story of the murder of Agamemnon—the narrator, Frank Chambers, often calls Nick Papadakis "the Greek"; Frank and Cora try to kill Nick when he is taking a bath. Cain may be suggesting that his story has a mythic element, or he may be suggesting that the heroic figures of Greek myth were no better than common adulterers, or he may be suggesting some combination and interaction of these two meanings.

These few examples show that interpretation of the thematic aspect relies on analysis of the synthetic and the mimetic. The thematic aspect of a narrative is built up gradually, sentence by sentence, over the course of the narrative. Restriction of the thematic to some general meaning of the narrative as a whole impoverishes the reading experience.

II. NARRATIVE TYPES AND THE THEMATIC

Prose fictions, according to Sheldon Sacks, "are organized according to one of three mutually exclusive types: satire, apologue, or action" (Sacks, *Fiction* 25).[1] He defines these three types as follows:

> A satire is a work organized so that it ridicules objects external to the fictional world created in it.
>
> An apologue is a work organized as a fictional example of the truth of a formulable statement or a series of such statements.
>
> An action is a work organized so that it introduces characters, about whose fates we are made to care, in unstable relationships which are then further complicated until the complication is finally resolved by the removal of the represented instability. (26)

Gulliver's Travels is a satire, *Rasselas* is an apologue, *Tom Jones* is an action.[2]

David Richter distinguishes two kinds of apologues: An allegory presents "a one-to-one correspondence between objects and characters in the fiction and beings, persons, and ideas in the real world external to the fiction"; a fable is "a rhetorical fiction in which each detail of plot, characterization, and

---

1. For the third type, Sacks also uses the terms "represented action" and "novel"; he uses "example" as nearly synonymous with "apologue." David Richter uses "novel" generally to include all three types, which are then distinguished as satires, apologues, and actions.

2. Sacks's system is not the only way to cut the narrative pie. For example, R. S. Crane distinguishes novels of action, character, and thought (66), and Northrop Frye distinguishes novel (extroverted and personal), romance (introverted and personal), confession (introverted and intellectual), and satire (extroverted and intellectual) (303–9).

language is chosen in order to make us understand something in the external world . . . but in which the individual details generally do not have symbolic significance that can he detached from the fiction and equated on a one-for-one basis with ideas in the external world" (Richter 14–16). (I will have more to say about allegory below.)

The thematic component as defined in the MTS model certainly applies to apologues. When an apologue expresses a formulable statement, it is making a statement, taking an ideological position, or teaching a truth: "In an apologue all elements of the work are synthesized as a fictional example that causes us to feel, to experience as true, some formulable statement or statements about the universe" (Sacks, "Golden" 276–77). *Rasselas,* for example, expresses the following statement: "Earthly happiness does not exist, but its absence does not result in unbearable misery in this world for the reasonably virtuous who, in addition, may turn their eyes with hope toward heaven" (Sacks, *Fiction* 55).

Satire, by Sacks's definition, is organized around a "pattern of ridiculed objects," rather than "the exemplified thematic statement of apologue" (Sacks, *Fiction* 61). I am not sure if the thematic component of the MTS model applies to satire: On the one hand, the ridicule characteristic of satire probably can be expressed in a formulable statement; on the other hand, many satires, including *Gulliver's Travels,* direct their ridicule at a host of objects, so that a satire is likely to lack the unity of meaning found in an apologue.

The type of fiction Sacks calls an action does not express a formulable statement or any combination of formulable statements. An action is not concerned with statements or ridicule, but with "characters, about whose fates we are made to care" (Sacks, *Fiction* 26; see also Richter 10). Actions, as Sacks defines them, do not fit the thematic component of the MTS model. They are, however, full of meaning, perhaps more full of meaning than apologues and satires (Sacks, *Fiction* 249). The thematic aspect of the SMT model includes all kinds of meanings, paraphrasable or not, intended or not.

III. CRITIQUES OF THEMATIC CRITICISM

Thematic interpretation has had a special importance in literary criticism: "The interpretive maneuver most widely practiced by contemporary critics can be summarized in a two-word slogan: 'Always thematize!'" (Phelan, *Reading* 27). And Phelan quotes Robert Scholes's comment that "interpretation proper is the thematizing of a text" (Phelan, *Reading* 61, quoting Scholes, *Textual* 29), where thematizing presumably consists in finding the central unifying idea of a text, the text's theme.

If thematic interpretation has been the dominant form of criticism, it has not gone unchallenged. Some critics might deny that literary texts can have themes because language in general lacks any relation to external reality. I am not sure if anyone now seriously holds, or perhaps ever held, this position in its extreme form. A less extreme form, which certainly has been held, would claim that whatever meaning a text has is entirely internal and without reference; works of literature are only about works of literature or about the impossibility of meaning. Gerald Graff notes "the recent discovery that every text can be interpreted as a commentary on its own textual problems" (60), and Robert Scholes comments, "Criticism has taken the very idea of 'aboutness' away from us. It has taught us that language is tautological, if it is not nonsense, and to the extent that it is about anything it is about itself" ("Fictional Criticism" 233). Self-reference and internal reference are certainly interesting and important features of narrative, but they are not the whole story.

A second critique argues that while meaning and reference occur, they are not always at the heart of the literary experience. Helen Vendler, in her discussion of Shakespeare's sonnets, says that "the wish of interpreters of poems to arrive at something they call 'meaning' seems to me misguided. . . . Lyric poetry, especially highly conventionalized lyric of the sort represented by the *Sonnets,* has almost no significant freight of 'meaning' at all, in our ordinary sense of the word" (Vendler 13). Vendler does not mean that the poems are nonsense, or that their meaning is entirely internal or self-reflexive. She often notes the moral and emotional content of the sonnets, but these are not themes in the ordinary sense of the word. "The appeal of lyric lies elsewhere than in its paraphrasable argument" (14); that is, it does not lie in themes. "Where, then, does the charm of lyric lie? The answers . . . are as various as the sonnets. . . . However, they can be summed up in the phrase 'the arrangement of statement.' Form is content-as-arranged; content is form-as-arranged" (Vendler 14).

Vendler distinguishes the interpretation of lyrics from the interpretation of plays and novels: "Very few lyrics offer the sort of philosophical depth that stimulates meaning-seekers in long, complex, and self-contradicting texts like Shakespeare's plays or Dostoevsky's novels" (Vendler 13). But even long philosophical narratives create meaning through "the arrangement of statement."

A third critique of thematic interpretation is presented at some length by Richard Levin.[3] Thematic criticism, according to Levin, "is the approach

---

3. See also the discussion of Levin's critique in Phelan, *Reading* 45–50. Levin is mostly concerned with plays, but his argument is easily generalized to other kinds of literature.

that interprets a literary work as the representation or expression of some abstract concept, which will therefore give the work its unity and its meaning" (11). The theme can be simply an abstract concept, such as avarice or folly; or a problem, such as the discrepancy between appearance and reality; or a proposition, such as the proposition that avarice is evil (56–57). This mode of interpretation tends to turn a work of literature into "an analysis or exploration or examination of some idea or issue, an argument or debate, a commentary, a critique, a discussion, an essay, an inquiry, an investigation, a meditation, a sermon, a statement, a tract"—rather than a play or a story (12). Thematic interpretation tends to leave out the emotional effect of a work of literature (12–13). The themes discovered in thematic interpretation are usually vague and general: "We find the same central theme attributed to very different plays, and very different central themes attributed to the same play" (13). Moreover, the themes found in the plays turn out to be "banal platitudes and pieties. . . . If the meaning and purpose of the plays really can be found in this kind of general proposition, if *that* is what they add up to, then it is hard to see why any adult would be interested in them" (59).

Thematic interpretation requires a distinction between real and apparent meaning: "The play cannot really be about what it seems to be about, because it must be about an idea if it is about anything, or anything important" (18). Moreover, "very many different abstractions can be derived from any particular object," and there is no way in principle to decide which of these should be considered the theme (28).

The primary method of thematic interpretation, which Levin calls the thematic leap, "consists of seizing upon some particular components of the drama and making them the representatives or exemplars of a general class, which then becomes the subject of the play and of the critic's analysis" (23). The thematic leap transforms concrete particulars, the apparent meaning, into abstract ideas, the real meaning.

In practice, the determination of the class represented by a particular is arbitrary, but classes of greater generality are preferred: "Thus one thematic leap tends to beget another, and the result is a kind of thematic leapfrog. . . . Once the critic has taken the decisive step (or leap) by declaring that a character is not to be regarded as an individual but as a class representative, he finds himself in a competition to make that class as general as possible" (25).

The generalizations of thematic interpretations come at a price. Some characters can legitimately be seen as representative members of a class—many of the characters in Greek New Comedy, for instance, and their descendants in later literature. But characters in modern literature, especially major characters, are usually individualized: "What makes Lear's story so important to us—so interesting, so memorable, so moving—is surely not his representativeness but his uniqueness, his complex and extraordinary personality that differentiates him from every other character in the play" (27). Thus, in thematic interpretation, as Levin describes it, the richness of the experience of reading, including the richness of characterization and action, is abandoned in favor of a search for abstractions, and the abstractions that are found are usually trivial.

The MTS concept of the thematic may seem to be vulnerable to the charge of abstraction: The thematic component of character concerns "its representative or ideational function," and thematic dimensions of character can be "viewed as vehicles to express ideas or as representative of a larger class than the individual character" (Phelan, *Reading* 12). Moreover, "the importance of thematizing derives from the assumption that a narrative achieves its significance from the ideational generalizations it leads one to," and "the component of character contributing to these generalizations is the most important" (Phelan, *Reading* 27). In the MTS model, those aspects of character neglected by the thematic component are the province of the mimetic component, which is complementary to the thematic. "The distinction between the mimetic and thematic components of character is a distinction between characters as individuals and characters as representative entities" (Phelan, *Reading* 13). Phelan argues that "in order to account for the complex relations of the mimetic and the thematic components of character the alternatives presented by the thematists and the anti-thematists need to be transcended" (Phelan, *Reading* 28). "That Lear is a character who is more than the embodiment of general ideas does not necessarily mean that he is not also such an embodiment. In short, Levin's belief in the mimetic–didactic distinction leads him to present an either/or choice when a both/and solution is more likely to be adequate" (Phelan, *Reading* 50).

Taken as a whole, the MTS model is more flexible and comprehensive than thematizing as described by Levin. The MTS model does tend, however, to divide the mimetic from the didactic; the meanings of the didactic belong to the thematic component, and the thematic component tends to favor general propositional themes consciously intended by the author—statements, positions, truths—and thus it moves towards the allegorical. The thematic aspect of the SMT model, on the other hand, recognizes that not all meanings are intended and not all meanings are propositional; that the experience of reading is a part of meaning; that the thematic grows out of the synthetic and the mimetic; and that many narratives are open to a multiplicity of interpretations depending on which elements of the narrative are foregrounded by the author and the audience.

IV. THE THEMATIC ASPECT AND THE EXPERIENCE OF MEANING

Any long narrative expresses many meanings. These meanings gradually develop over the course of a story and interact with each other; some are reinforced and take on a particular prominence, some fall into the background. Themes are built up gradually by the accumulation of composition and representation. A critical interpretation can usefully point out one or several of these strands of meaning, but no interpretation can reproduce the richness of experience of the text itself. This experience is fundamentally temporal (at least on first reading), though readers can supplement the linearity of time through memory and anticipation; second and later readings are different experiences with different meanings.

Consider the first sentence of *Emma*:

> Emma Woodhouse, handsome, clever, and rich, with a comfortable home and happy disposition, seemed to unite some of the best blessings of existence, and had lived nearly twenty-one years in the world with very little to distress or vex her. (5)

The reader has been primed by the title to expect that Emma will be the central character of the story and thus also primed to pay special attention to this first characterization. The sentence means what it says, but it also has a tone: "Seemed" is a sort of warning, and "nearly twenty-one years" adds a note of amused irony. This tone is part of the meaning of the sentence.

When Emma's attributes are first mentioned, they function mimetically; as the story progresses, they are thematized by repetition and emphasis. In chapter 4 of volume 1, when Mrs. Weston and Mr. Knightley discuss Emma at some length, parts of the initial characterization are reinforced. "Emma is spoiled by being the cleverest of her family" (29), as Mr. Knightley says, and a little later, "I shall not attempt to deny Emma's being pretty," and "I confess that I have seldom seen a face or figure more pleasing to me than her's [*sic*]," and "I love to look at her; and I will add this praise, that I do not think her personally vain" (30). Emma's wealth, or her status in Highbury, which is due to her wealth, is implied throughout this conversation. The thematic importance of these characteristics is reinforced also through the contrast with other characters: Jane Fairfax is handsome and clever, but not rich; Harriet is handsome but neither clever nor rich; and Mrs. Elton is rich, though not as rich as Emma, and handsome, though not as handsome as the others, and certainly not clever.

The characterization is also reinforced and reinterpreted through the action of the story. Emma's cleverness is displayed, for instance, in her interpretation of riddles, but the limitation of her cleverness is shown by her incorrect interpretation of the behavior of the others in the story.

It would be possible to go through the whole text sentence by sentence to show the accumulation of meaning—in the style of commentaries on the great works of classical literature, such as the Homeric epics—but one further example will have to do for many. Austen clearly enjoyed writing monologues for Miss Bates, and no doubt she would welcome a reader who enjoys reading them. These monologues are part of the total experience of the novel, and thus part of the total meaning. Here is a short selection from Miss Bates's monologue at the ball:

> "Jane, Jane, my dear Jane, where are you?—Here is your tippet. Mrs. Weston begs you to put on your tippet. She says she is afraid there will be draughts in the passage, though every thing has been done—One door nailed up—Quantities of matting.—My dear Jane, indeed you must. Mr. Churchill, oh! You are too obliging! . . .
>
> . . . .
>
> "Well, where shall we sit? where shall we sit? Any where, so that Jane is not in a draught. Where *I* sit is of no consequence. Oh! do you recommend this side?—Well, I am sure, Mr. Churchill—only it seems too good—but just as you please." (226–27)

At times Austen, always an economical writer, uses these passages to drop little hints for the attentive reader—perhaps on a second reading. Here, for example, we see that Frank Churchill is paying special attention to Jane's comfort. And of course Emma's unsympathetic reaction to Mrs. Bates's tiresome chatter becomes one of the pivotal elements in the plot. These monologues contribute to larger themes, but they also provide pleasure in themselves. Their meaning is an experience of reading rather than a paraphrasable argument.[4]

V. MEANING AS ARGUMENT

Some narratives, of course, do express a paraphrasable argument. *1984* is among them. The argument of *1984*, in simplistic terms, is that totalitarianism

---

4. Compare Sacks, *Fiction* 12–13, who denies that these monologues have any satirical meaning.

is bad; moreover, totalitarianism is bad because (a) it is in the interests of the state to keep the population in poverty, (b) there will be constant surveillance, (c) children will be pitted against their parents, (d) the state will manipulate standards of truth and history, (e) the natural sexual drives will be frustrated, and so on. All of this was relevant to political questions at the time the book was written, and much of it remains relevant today. What is the value in stating these propositions in narrative rather than directly in argument? Part of the answer must be that narratives can act as examples, and examples, especially vivid examples, can make an argument more persuasive. Another part of the answer is our interest in individuals: We want to know more than an abstract lesson about totalitarianism; we want to see how this particular person, Winston Smith, lives his life in a totalitarian state. Narrative has never lost its roots in gossip.

The meaning of *1984* is not exhausted by a single theme. A long narrative, even an argumentative narrative, will almost inevitably introduce meanings other than those connected to the main theme of the argument. In the previous chapter, I noted Orwell's persistent attachment to a kind of romantic naturalization of the past, as seen, for example, in his references to clocks: Totalitarianism is bad because it takes away our natural twelve-hour way of keeping time. Another, but related, theme is expressed in the episode when Julia puts on makeup:

> She must have slipped into some shop in the proletarian quarters and bought herself a complete set of makeup materials. Her lips were deeply reddened, her cheeks rouged, her nose powdered; there was even a touch of something under the eyes to make them brighter. It was not very skillfully done, but Winston's standards in such matters were not high. He had never before seen or imagined a woman of the Party with cosmetics on her face. The improvement in her appearance was startling. With just a few dabs of color in the right places she had become not only very much prettier, but, above all, more feminine. Her short hair and boyish overalls merely added to the effect. As he took her in his arms a wave of synthetic violets flooded his nostrils. He remembered the half-darkness of a basement kitchen and a woman's cavernous mouth. It was the very same scent that she had used; but at the moment it did not seem to matter.
>
> "Scent, too!" he said.
>
> "Yes, dear, scent. And do you know what I'm going to do next? I'm going to get hold of a real woman's frock from somewhere and wear it instead of these bloody trousers. I'll wear silk stockings and high-heeled shoes! In this room I'm going to be a woman, not a Party comrade." (95)

Totalitarianism is bad because it prevents women from using makeup. This passage seems to suggest that there is something naturally feminine about wearing cosmetics and dresses and high heels and stockings, something naturally feminine about using perfume. This natural femininity, however, is produced artificially, and the scent is synthetic. But this episode of naturalization reminds Winston of one of the most unpleasant episodes in the story, his encounter with the aging prostitute, who used the same scent. However one finally decides to interpret the passage, it seems to go beyond the theme of totalitarianism. Thematic interpretation of *1984* generally ignores this passage, but surely it is part of the meaning of the novel.

If narrative meaning were exhausted by making statements, taking positions, or telling truths, there would be no need to tell stories. As Herman notes, following Bonnie Lynn Weber and others, "the objective of discourse is not to send ideas back and forth like so many packages, more or less carefully wrapped" (*Story* 19).

An assertion is good if it is true; an argument is good if it is valid; a joke is good if it is funny. It is the experience of a joke that matters, the experience of getting it, and thus a joke loses its force if it has to be explained. Narratives also are tested by experience, but each narrative experience is unique, and there is no single standard of judgment.

Logical arguments are tested by their truth or validity; an invalid argument is defeated and replaced by a valid argument. Narratives, however, are not in competition with each other, at least in this way. They present views of life—perhaps this is what Bruner means by lifelikeness—but one view of life does not necessarily invalidate another view of life. In William Golding's *Lord of the Flies* (1954), a group of boys is stranded on an island, and they quickly become uncooperative, violent, savage. In Robert Heinlein's *Tunnel in the Sky* (1955), a group of adolescents is stranded on an uninhabited planet with no expectation of rescue, but these young people manage to create a functioning and even happy constitutional government. Clearly, Heinlein presents a more optimistic view of human nature. I don't know that Golding is right and Heinlein wrong, or the reverse. Both authors present views of the human condition, and both say something of interest and value.

VI. NONPROPOSITIONAL MEANING

A narrative such as *1984* does present something like a paraphrasable argument, though this argument is only a small part of what makes the book worth reading. Arguments and assertions are only a small part of language and only a small part of narrative. Other kinds of utterances, such as commands, promises, and baptisms, have been explored, for example, by J. L. Austin; these are evaluated not by their truth but by other standards, such as felicity or efficacy.[5] Figurative language also escapes the test of argumentative truth. The cognitive force of metaphor has been studied extensively, but other figures also can express ideas.[6] And the various larger structures of narrative also carry meaning. A part of the project set by the SMT model is the identification of narrative figures and the investigation of their potential for meaning.

The meanings of these larger narrative figures can be difficult or impossible to paraphrase, and the experiential part of the meaning may be lost in the attempt. Moreover, narrative figures ordinarily do not have fixed meanings; the meaning has to be understood in the context of the work as a whole. As I mentioned above, ending with the beginning often can be understood as an invitation to reassess the initial situation, but how the reassessment works depends on the particularity of each story. Examples are countless; here I look briefly at ending with the beginning in *The Return of the Native* and *1984*.

At the beginning of Thomas Hardy's *The Return of the Native*, Diggory Venn is bringing Thomasin Yeobright home from her failed wedding with Damon Wildeve. Clearly, things are out of joint. The events of the story are too complex to be briefly summarized; as I noted in chapter 1, there is a complex set of relationships among five characters: Clym Yeobright > Eustacia Vye > Damon Wildeve > Thomasin Yeobright > Diggory Venn. Clym marries Eustacia, and Thomasin marries Damon, but Eustacia and Wildeve are also engaged in a romantic intrigue. By the end of the story, Eustacia Vye and Damon Wildeve have died, and Thomasin and Diggory marry.[7] Their marriage day recapitulates in part the initial journey, but this time with a successful marriage of the right couple. The very end of the story also recapitulates another part of the opening, as Clym stands on the barrow: "From a distance there simply appeared to be a motionless figure standing on top of the tumu-

---

5. See Austin on performatives.
6. The literature on metaphor is enormous; see, for instance, Kittay; Kövecses; Ricoeur; and Lakoff and Johnson.
7. Hardy, in a footnote, tells the reader that he had not originally intended that Diggory should marry Thomasin: "He was to have retained his isolated and weird character to the last, and to have disappeared mysteriously from the heath, nobody knowing whither—Thomasin remaining a widow. But certain circumstances of serial publication led to a change of intent. Readers can therefore choose between the endings, and those with an austere artistic code can assume the more consistent conclusion to be the correct one" (413). But which is more consistent?

lus, just as Eustacia had stood on that lonely summit some two years and a half before" (422). But while Eustacia was alone, waiting for a signal from Wildeve, Clym is preaching to a group of the residents of the heath. The various symmetries correct the tensions established at the beginning. An argumentative paraphrase would leave out the detail of the experience of reading about these particular characters as they work out their destinies.

The ending of *1984* recapitulates an event from part 1 of the novel, when Winston sees the three discredited leaders of the party, Jones, Aaronson, and Rutherford, sitting at the Chestnut Tree Café:

> They were men far older than himself, relics of the ancient world, almost the last great figures left over from the heroic early days of the Party. . . . But also they were outlaws, enemies, untouchables, doomed with absolute certainty to extinction within a year or two. . . . They were corpses waiting to be sent back to the grave. . . .
>
> It was the lonely hour of fifteen. . . . The place was almost empty. A tinny music was trickling from the telescreens. The three men sat in their corner almost motionless, never speaking. Uncommanded, the waiter brought fresh glasses of gin. There was a chessboard on the table beside them, with the pieces set out, but no game started. (52)

The last section of the novel begins:

> The Chestnut Tree was almost empty. A ray of sunlight slanting through a window fell yellow on the dusty tabletops. It was the lonely hour of fifteen. A tinny music trickled from the telescreens.
>
> Winston sat in his usual corner, gazing into an empty glass. . . . Unbidden, a waiter came and filled his glass up with Victory Gin. . . .
>
> . . . A waiter, again unbidden, brought the chessboard and the current issue of the *Times,* with the page turned down at the chess problem. (190–91)

These repetitions and more show that Orwell has contrived the ending to repeat a number of themes from the first part of the story. It is not easy to say exactly what the repetitions mean. They could suggest that just as Winston watched the earlier dissidents sit at the café, some budding dissident could be watching him. They could also suggest that Winston's fate was inevitable—what happened to the earlier dissidents has happened to him, and the same will happen to any later dissidents. They may also tend to elevate Winston: He was not just a mid-ranking functionary, but someone equal to the dissident founders of the Party—a failure, but on a heroic scale.

VII. ALLEGORICAL INTERPRETATIONS

Allegorical composition occurs when an author intends the ostensible meaning of a text to carry another meaning; allegorical interpretation, also known as allegoresis, occurs when an interpreter claims that a text has two (or more) meanings. Many theorists insist on the fundamental difference between allegory and allegoresis, but they are really two ends of the same stick. Allegorical composition calls for allegorical interpretation, and allegorical interpretation usually comes with the claim, explicit or implicit, that the allegory was intended by the author and is there to be seen in the text. If we agree with the interpretation, we will say that's what the text means; if we disagree, we will say that an allegory has been imposed. Most any text can somehow be read allegorically. As C. S. Lewis remarked, "Some published fantasies of my own have had foisted on them (often by the kindliest critics) so many admirable allegorical meanings that I never dreamed of as to throw me into doubt whether it is possible for the wit of man to devise anything in which the wit of some other man cannot find, and plausibly find, an allegory."[8]

I have noted above that Sacks (*Fiction*) divides narrative into three major categories—satire, apologue, and action—and he makes allegory a subcategory of apologue. Richter follows him, and further distinguishes allegory from fable: Both allegory and fable relate the world inside the story to the world outside, but an allegory makes a one-to-one match of internal and external elements, while a fable makes a general correspondence of story to world without a one-to-one match.

The term "apologue," however, is not widely used; it also lacks useful cognate forms (such as "apological," "apologesis," and "to apologuize").[9] Critics who do not use the term "apologue" tend to have a fairly broad understanding of allegory, not restricted to the kind of one-to-one internal-to-external correspondence required by Sacks and Richter. According to Scholes and Kellogg, for example, allegory is "the kind of didactic narrative which emphasizes the illustrative meaning of its characters, setting and action" (107); they note that "allegory demands a fairly consistent symbolism," but also that "allegorical narrative in practice has been anything but mechanical and simple-minded"

---

8. Quoted in Loomis 164. Lewis's Narnia tales (I would say) are Christian allegories, as are his three scientific romances.

9. Scholes and Kellogg, for example, use the general term "didactic fiction," which is then divided into "satire" and "allegory" (105). I do not find the term "apologue" in Tuve; Fletcher; Honig; or Quilligan. It is not indexed in Frye; Auerbach; Curtius; Wimsatt and Brooks; Alastair Fowler; or Altman, all of which do index allegory. There is little discussion of either allegory or apologue in recent narratological works.

(109). As I use the term, an allegorical composition involves some kind of significant correspondence to something external to the narrative, such as another narrative, a concept of the cosmos, the structure of society, a system of images, and the like; the correspondence does not have to be one-to-one, but it should be more than an incidental allusion. A formulable theme without some kind of correspondence does not make an allegory: *1984*, I would say, is allegorical; *Rasselas* is didactic but not an allegory.

Allegory is scalar rather than all-or-nothing. Ken Kesey's *One Flew over the Cuckoo's Nest*, I would argue, is a clear Christian allegory: The hero McMurphy enters the ward, just as Christ entered the world, and sacrifices himself to save others. This allegorical interpretation is supported by certain symbolic references. For instance, toward the end of the story, McMurphy and Chief Broom are given electric shock treatment: "They put the graphite salve on his temples. 'What is it?' he says. 'Conductant,' the technician says. 'Anointest my head with conductant. Do I get a crown of thorns?'" (237). The allegory, however, lies in the structure of the story rather than in explicit allusions, which are just indications to look for the structural parallels. James M. Cain's *The Postman Always Rings Twice*, as I have mentioned above, clearly alludes to Aeschylus's *Agamemnon*, but I suspect that many readers have read the story perfectly well without catching the hints. Robert Louis Stevenson's *Kidnapped* has something like the general plot structure of the story of Jason and the Golden Fleece: An uncle wants to deprive his nephew of his nephew's rightful inheritance and manages to send him on a trip in the hopes that the nephew will die on the way, but the nephew returns and takes vengeance on his uncle. So far as I can see, Stevenson makes no explicit reference to the myth, but the correspondence is there if the reader sees it. Of these stories, *One Flew over the Cuckoo's Nest* is the most allegorical, while *Kidnapped* is the least, but all of them have allegorical elements, and the recognition of the allegory enhances the reading.

A simple dichotomy between literal and allegorical meaning does not do justice to the variety and complexity of narrative. Dante (among others) interpreted four levels: literal, allegorical, moral, and anagogical. The literal level says what happened, the allegorical what you should believe, the moral what you should do, and the anagogical what you should hope for.[10] In his letter to Can Grande, Dante gives a fourfold interpretation of a passage from Psalm 114: "When Israel went out of Egypt, the house of Jacob from a people of strange language, Judea was his sanctuary, and Israel his dominion." At the lit-

---

10. For discussion of the fourfold method in Dante, see Anderson 329–45. The Jewish philosopher Philo used a threefold method of interpretation: literal, ethical, and metaphysical; see Lamberton, *Homer the Theologian* 47.

eral level, the passage recounts as historical fact the departure of the Children of Israel from Egypt; at the allegorical level, the passage signifies redemption through Christ; at the moral level, it means the struggle of the soul in conversion from sin to grace; at the anagogical level, it means the passage of the soul from the slavery of mortal existence to the freedom of eternal glory.

The four-level model of interpretation was developed for biblical exegesis, but it may be applicable to other texts, with a little adjustment.[11] For example, the literal sense of *1984* is just the story of Winston and Julia and O'Brien, told as if it were the true history of what was, at the time of writing, the future. The allegorical level could include the evident similarities between Big Brother and Stalin, between Emanuel Goldstein and Trotsky, and perhaps the general sense that the world of the novel is not really so different from Orwell's England. The moral level is the implied exhortation to make sure this world never does become reality. And the anagogical level could be Winston's repeated insistence that hope lies in the proles.

Allegorical composition goes back to our earliest texts from ancient Greece; there is clear allegory in the Homeric epics, in the poems of Archilochus and Alcaeus, and in Aesop's fables. Allegorical interpretation of the Homeric epics began as early as Theagenes of Rhegium, in the sixth century BCE. Allegorical rationalization of myth is found in Plato: Phaedrus (in the dialogue named after him) asks Socrates if he believes the story that Boreas, the god of the wind, abducted the Athenian princess Oreithyia; Socrates says that the sophistic explanation would be that the princess was simply blown off a cliff by the wind. And Palaephatus, an obscure writer perhaps of the late fourth century BCE, produced a collection of rationalizations, now known as *On Unbelievable Tales*. According to Palaephatus, Aktaion (for example) was not turned into a deer by Artemis and was not eaten by his own dogs, as in the myth; what really happened was that Aktaion spent all his money on hunting dogs, and so the story developed that he was eaten by his dogs.[12]

In book 4 of the *Odyssey*, Menelaus tells Telemachus what happened when he and his followers on their way home from Troy were stranded off the coast of Egypt. Eidothea, the daughter of Proteus, the Old Man of the Sea, took pity on Menelaus and told him to wait in ambush for her father as he slept surrounded by seals. She gave Menelaus and three of his companions sealskins to

---

11. See W. R. Johnson 16–22 for a fourfold interpretation of the *Aeneid*.
12. On allegorical interpretation in general, see Fletcher, whose broad interpretation of allegory includes westerns and detective stories, and Quilligan, who counts Nabokov's *Pale Fire* and Pynchon's *The Crying of Lot 49* as allegories. On allegorical interpretation of Homer, see Lamberton, *Homer*, and the articles collected in Lamberton and Keaney. Palaephatus, *On Unbelievable Tales*, is available in a translation by Jacob Stern.

use as disguises. Menelaus then caught hold of Proteus, who changed himself into many shapes; finally he resumed his original shape and answered Menelaus's questions.

The Neoplatonic philosopher Proclus (412–485 AD) interpreted this story in terms of his own very complex system of metaphysics: Being proceeds from The One ("to hen" in Greek), which is beyond Being and beyond Thought. Also at this level are the "henads," which are identified with the Greek gods. Other levels of Being proceed from these henads. The level of Being below The One and the henads is Mind or Intellect ("nous" in Greek), and below Mind is Soul ("psyche"). In the story of Proteus, according to Proclus, Proteus proceeds from the henad called Poseidon and represents an "angelic soul . . . holding and containing in himself the forms of all things that come to be and pass away" (Lamberton, *Proclus* 141). Eidothea, the daughter of Proteus, is a daemonic soul immediately inferior to the angelic soul. The seals represent other souls, rational and eternal. "And so, the partial souls that observe Proteus—who is an intellect with multiple powers and glutted with forms—apply the discursiveness of their own intellects now to one of his forms, now to another, and they imagine change in what their mind apprehends. . . . [I]n the partial apprehension of those who contemplate him, he seems in turn to become all the forms that he holds and contains, or rather, all those things that he continuously and eternally is" (Lamberton, *Proclus* 141). This allegory is very distant from the story as it appears in the epic; Proclus has taken what he needs from the story in order to make a correspondence with his system, but he has no interest in the story itself. Few modern readers would find this interpretation attractive, but as Lamberton remarks, Proclus's allegorical interpretations are "no more absurd than Claude Lévi-Strauss's perception that a vast number of myths and folktales are concerned with the dichotomy between nature and culture" (Lamberton, *Proclus* 201).

A modern allegorical interpretation of the *Odyssey* has been elaborated by Max Horkheimer and Theodor Adorno. This interpretation is presented primarily as support for their philosophic position rather than as literary criticism of the epic. The motive of their study was "the discovery of why mankind, instead of entering into a truly human condition, is sinking into a new kind of barbarism" (Horkheimer and Adorno xi). The problem, they say, is "the indefatigable self-destructiveness of enlightenment" (xi).[13] Enlightenment has two aims: to free humanity from fear and to establish human sovereignty

---

13. Horkheimer and Adorno discuss "*enlightenment*" as a general term and more specifically "the *Enlightenment*," often without clear distinction.

over nature—"yet the enlightened world radiates disaster triumphant" (3). Enlightenment is usually understood in opposition to myth, but according to Horkheimer and Adorno, "myth is already enlightenment, and enlightenment reverts to mythology" (xvi)—in a sort of return of the repressed. Enlightenment also seeks mastery and domination over external nature and over nature within the self. In their account, enlightenment is understood as the reduction of nature to position and arrangement (7). But "men pay for the increase of their power with alienation from that over which they exercise their power" (9). Horkheimer and Adorno find many of these themes in the story of Odysseus and the Sirens, from book 12 of the *Odyssey*:[14]

> [The Sirens'] allurement is that of losing oneself in the past. But the hero to whom the temptation is offered has reached maturity through suffering. Throughout the many mortal perils he has had to endure, the unity of his own life, the identity of the individual, has been confirmed for him. The regions of time part for him as do water, earth, and air. For him, the flood of that-which-was has retreated from the rock of the present, and the future lies cloudy on the horizon. (32)

Odysseus has his crew plug their ears with wax to keep them from hearing the Sirens. He has them bind him to the mast, so he will be able to hear without danger. Thus, the crew "reproduce the oppressor's life together with their own, and the oppressor is no longer able to escape his social role" (34).

> Odysseus is represented in labor. Just as he cannot yield to the temptation to self-abandonment, so, as proprietor, he finally renounces even participation in labor, and ultimately even its management, whereas his men—despite their closeness to things—cannot enjoy their labor because it is performed under pressure, in desperation, with senses stopped by force. The servant remains enslaved in body and soul; the master regresses. (35)

> The restriction of thought to organization and administration, practiced by rulers from the cunning Odysseus to the naïve directors of today, necessarily implies the restriction which comes upon the great as soon as it is no longer merely a question of manipulating the small. . . . The stopped ears which the pliable proletarians have retained ever since the time of myth have no advantage over the immobility of the master. (36)

---

14. Horkeimer and Adorno also discuss a number of other episodes in the *Odyssey*.

This episode surely deserves interpretation, and Horkheimer and Adorno are right to note the importance of the unequal power relationships here and throughout the epic. When they stay close to the text, they often make insightful observations. At times, however, the story is just a point from which they can jump off into their own speculations. I am particularly dubious about their repeated insistence that Odysseus represents the bourgeois and his crew the proletarians—"the hero of the adventures shows himself to be a prototype of the bourgeois individual" (43). Odysseus embodies "the principle of capitalist economy" (61). This interpretation is wildly unhistorical, and it casts doubt on their whole argument.[15]

Proclus and Horkheimer and Adorno show how not to do an allegorical interpretation, but they do not show that the *Odyssey* is not allegorical. Recent work by classical philologists has revealed a complex layering of communication in the epic, sometimes in shorter passages but also in the overall structure of the story. Is it likely, after all, that a story deeply connected to a rich mythological tradition, a story involving the interactions of gods and mortals, a story that reaches its conclusion during a festival to Apollo, a story that takes the reader from Olympus to the land of the dead, would not have layers of meaning?[16] The epic from start to finish is filled with deceptive appearances and ambiguous communications: Athena's various impersonations, the many omens and portents that need interpretation, Odysseus's lies, Penelope's dream, and so on. The *Odyssey* constantly means something other and something more than its surface.

VIII. IDEOLOGY AND THE THEMATIC ASPECT

According to Phelan, a narrative is "the act of somebody telling somebody else on a particular occasion for some purpose that something happened" (Phelan, *Living* 217). This definition is very like Terry Eagleton's characterization of ideology: "Ideology is less a matter of the inherent linguistic properties of a pronouncement than a question of who is saying what to whom for what purpose" (Eagleton, *Ideology* 9).[17] Usually, however, ideology is taken to

---

15. Peter Rose notes that "the fundamental Marxist assumption . . . is that Western society has always been characterized by class struggle" (35). I do not doubt the importance of class in the *Iliad* and the *Odyssey*, but class in archaic Greece is not structurally the same as class in modern society; Odysseus, for instance, does not think of wealth as capital. See also Rose 120.

16. See, for instance, Norman Austin; Murnaghan; Slatkin; Cook; and Levaniouk.

17. Phelan's most extensive discussion of ideology is found in Phelan, *Narrative,* particularly chapter 8, but his interest there is primarily political bias in a nonfiction text, rather than the ideological aspect of fictional narratives.

cover a restricted set of themes, particularly gender, class, and race; I would add religion and nationalism.[18] What these topics have in common is a concern with ideas particularly linked to social formations. Most novels touch on more than one of these ideological topics. Ideology usually involves networks of ideas, and ideological analysis is thus more complex than thematic analysis as described by Levin.

Ideological criticism often overlaps with allegorical interpretation, especially if characters are taken to represent positions within society. In Rudyard Kipling's *Captains Courageous,* for example, it is easy to see the boy protagonist, Harvey Cheyne Jr., as a representative of the capitalist class, while the fishermen who save him, and especially Harvey's counterpart Dan Troop, are representatives of the working class. The plot, then, is a story of the education of the prince, and also a demonstration that there is no fundamental antagonism between the boss and the workers. The novel certainly functions ideologically, but it is also a rousing adventure story. Harvey and Dan may represent social positions, but they are also just boys.

The ideological aspect of *Captains Courageous* is certainly there, but those who read it as a boy's adventure story may not pay much attention to ideology. Many novels, however, are explicitly ideological. Still within the nineteenth-century realistic tradition, Elizabeth Gaskell's novels *Mary Barton* and *North and South* are explicitly concerned with issues of class in the new industrial society. Mark Twain's *Pudd'nhead Wilson* deals with race. Anne Brontë's *Agnes Grey* and *The Tenant of Wildfell Hall* are feminist novels. George Eliot's *Adam Bede* is largely about religion. The reader may easily supplement this list. I don't mean to suggest that the interest of any of these is exhausted by its ideology, but a reading that ignores the ideology would be deficient.[19]

Some critics would argue that all novels are fundamentally ideological. According to Eagleton,

> The feminist critic is not studying representations of gender simply because she believes that this will further her political ends. She also believes that gender and sexuality are central themes in literature and other sorts of discourse, and that any critical account which suppresses them is seriously defective. Similarly, the socialist critic does not see literature in terms of

---

18. I would also add that ideology can be expressed through all sorts of structures and actions; in the Homeric epics, for instance, social status is expressed by the serving of meat at banquets (see Nagy).

19. Just as allegorical composition can be distinguished from allegorical interpretation, so it is possible to distinguish ideological composition from ideological interpretation, but again, composition and interpretation are two ends of the same stick.

ideology or class-struggle because these happen to be his or her political interests arbitrarily projected on to literary works. He or she would hold that such matters are the very stuff of history, and that in so far as literature is an historical phenomenon, they are the very stuff of literature too. (*Literary*, 209–10)

Emma is not explicitly ideological in the way that *Agnes Grey* is, or *Mary Barton*. *Emma* is about Emma and her gradual coming to some degree of self-awareness. And yet in a sense it is deeply ideological. The story deals with questions of gender (how could it not?), but it also provides a complex analysis of class in an English village in the early nineteenth century—up to a point. *Emma* is a story about character, but Austen understands character in a social setting, and so an analysis of class comes with the story. Certainly Austen's view of society has its blind spots; overall she communicates complacency rather than critique. But so far as it goes, her vision is very sharp. No doubt many readers, and some critics, read *Emma* without thinking much about class, but recent critical discussion has noted the importance of class in Austen's novels. I would argue that class is foregrounded in the text and therefore it should find a place in a comprehensive interpretation.[20]

When Emma is introduced to the reader, in the first sentence, she is characterized by her good looks, her cleverness, and her wealth—wealth is considered as a personal trait, in the way that good looks and intelligence are traits. Austen quickly places Emma at the highest point in her society:

> Highbury, the large and populous village almost amounting to a town, to which Hartfield, in spite of its separate lawn and shrubberies and name, really did belong, afforded her no equals. The Woodhouses were first in consequence there. All looked up to them. (6–7)

All of the other characters are placed within a clear hierarchy, though movement within the system is occasionally possible. Volume 1, chapter 2, for instance, offers an extensive account of Mr. Weston's place in the social structure of Highbury.[21] He was "born of a respectable family, which for the last

---

20. Some critics have noted the importance of social analysis in Austen's novels, but others take them simply or primarily as studies in character. Gard notes briefly that servants are largely invisible in *Emma*, but otherwise class has little place in his interpretation. Craig supplies useful social and political background, but her argument that Austen wrote state-of-the-nation novels seems extreme. McMaster provides a detailed analysis of the social hierarchy of Highbury. Parker argues that *Emma* expresses bourgeois ideology. Handler and Segal is generally useful for Austen's view of society.

21. Compare the account of Jane Fairfax's situation in volume 2, chapter 2.

two or three generations had been rising into gentility and property" (12). He joined the military and then married up, against the wishes of his wife's family. He and his wife lived beyond their means. When, after three years, his wife died, Weston was "rather a poorer man than at first, and with a child to maintain" (12). His wife's wealthy family took the child in as their own.

Mr. Weston then went into business with his brothers and did well—well enough to retire young and to buy a small estate, and well enough "to marry a woman as portionless even as Miss Taylor. . . . He had made his fortune, bought his house, and obtained his wife" (13). His son Frank, meanwhile, had adopted the last name of his mother's family and expected to be his uncle's heir. This chapter—almost a miniature novel in itself—tells a complex story of a family of the rising middle class, a double-edged marriage, a son taken over by rich relatives, success in business leading to retirement from business, and a marriage to a woman who brings no wealth with her.

Emma herself is of course acutely aware of social distinctions. She is, in fact, a snob. She is not, however, consistent. She wants Harriet to marry up; she persuades Harriet to refuse Robert Martin's proposal and to set her sights on Mr. Elton. Mr. Knightley warns Emma that Mr. Elton is "a very good sort of man, and a very respectable vicar of Highbury, but not at all likely to make an imprudent match" (48). But when Mr. Elton proposes to her instead of to Harriet, Emma is repelled by his social presumption—as much as Mr. Elton is shocked by the idea that he would marry Harriet: He understands "the gradations of rank below him," but he is "so blind to what rose above, as to fancy himself showing no presumption in addressing her!" (96).

Emma's social world includes the landed gentry, such as Mr. Knightley; professionals, such as the lawyer, Mr. Cox, or the apothecary, Mr. Perry; the vicar, Mr. Elton; Mrs. Goddard, the school mistress; and, at the bottom of the hierarchy, Mrs. Bates, the poor widow of the previous vicar, her daughter Miss Bates, and her niece, Jane Fairfax. It does not include a farmer, such as Robert Martin. Emma explains to Harriet that Robert Martin is both too low and too high to attract her attention: "A farmer can need none of my help, and is therefore in one sense as much above my notice as in every other he is below it" (22; see also 130). Nor is Emma alone in her sensitivity to social distinctions; Mr. Knightley worries that Harriet will not gain by her friendship with Emma: "Hartfield will only put her out of conceit with all the other places she belongs to. She will grow just refined enough to be uncomfortable with those among whom birth and circumstances have placed her home" (29).

Emma's sense of social gradation is tested by the Coles' dinner party. The social background of the Coles is explained in some detail in volume 2, chapter 2: "They were of low origin, in trade, and only moderately genteel" (143).

But success in business allowed them to add to their house and to hire more servants. Emma at first wants to teach them their place: "The Coles were very respectable in their way, but they ought to be taught that it was not for them to arrange the terms on which the superior families would visit them. This lesson, she very much feared, they would receive only from herself; she had little hope of Mr. Knightley and none of Mr. Weston" (144). They are not such snobs as she is. But when she does not receive an invitation to the dinner party, she is put out: "She felt that she should like to have had the power of refusal." (144). She does eventually receive an invitation, and she is glad to take the Westons' advice to accept it.

More often, Emma's social exclusions are strict. She scorns Mrs. Elton's mercantile background (127). When she takes Harriet to visit the Martins (129), she does not herself enter their house. She does visit the poor, but only as an act of charity, and the narrator does not take the reader along on the visit (63–64). The Gypsies represent a frightening world beyond knowledge.

Servants are almost invisible. The Woodhouses have at least four servants—James, the footman; Searle, the cook; a butler; and Emma's maid (146)—and probably more. But tea appears as if by magic, the supper table sets itself, and doors are opened evidently by no one. The servants are not, however, outside all awareness. Both Emma and her father try to be considerate to James, who keeps and drives their carriage (8), and Mr. Woodhouse maintains that Searle, their cook, is the only person who understands how to boil an egg (19).

Miss Bates lives at the intersection of classes in Highbury; she associates with those at the highest level—Emma and Mr. Knightley—and she also counts William Larkins as an old acquaintance:

> "The very same evening William Larkins came over with a large basket of apples, the same sort of apples, a bushel at least, and I was very much obliged and went down and spoke to William Larkins and said every thing, as you may suppose. William Larkins is such an old acquaintance! I am always glad to see him. But however, I found afterwards from Patty, that William said it was all the apples of *that* sort his master had; he had brought them all—and now his master had not one left to bake or boil. William did not seem to mind it himself, he was so pleased to think his master had sold so many; for William, you know, thinks more of his master's profit than anything; but Mrs. Hodges, he said, was quite displeased at their being all sent away." (165)

Emma's view of Highbury is for the most part quite selective; just once the narrator presents a wider view of the village through Emma's eyes, as she stands in the door of Mrs. Ford's shop:

Emma went to the door for amusement.—Much could not be hoped from the traffic of even the busiest part of Highbury;—Mr. Perry walking hastily by, Mr. William Cox letting himself in at the office door, Mr. Cole's carriage horses returning from exercise, or a stray letter-boy on an obstinate mule, were the liveliest objects she could presume to expect; and when her eyes fell only on the butcher with his tray, a tidy old woman travelling homewards from shop with her full basket, two curs quarrelling over a dirty bone, and a string of dawdling children round the baker's little bow-window eyeing the gingerbread, she knew she had no reason to complain, and was amused enough; quite enough still to stand at the door. (161)

The very end of the story, however, sees some change in Emma's attitudes. She is pleased and relieved when she learns that Harriet has accepted Robert Martin's proposal: She invites him to Hartfield, and she acknowledges his virtues—or at least "the appearance of sense and worth" (322). Married to Robert Martin, Harriet would be "retired enough for safety, and occupied enough for cheerfulness. She would be never led into temptation, nor left for it to find her out" (322). But the contours of society are ultimately secure:

> Harriet, necessarily drawn away by her engagements with the Martins, was less and less at Hartfield; which was not to be regretted.—The intimacy between her and Emma must sink; their friendship must change into a calmer sort of goodwill; and, fortunately, what ought to be, and must be, seemed already beginning, and in the most gradual, natural manner. (332)[22]

Class is an almost constant concern of the novel, and Austen's analysis of class is detailed and precise. It is not, however, easy to determine Austen's (or the implied author's) ideological stance. As Mark Parker notes, there is a progressive reading of class in *Emma* and a reactionary reading—a reading that sees "the insidious workings of class," and a reading that "accepts this working as part of the price of social stability" (358–59). The lack of critical agreement suggests that *Emma* does not present a paraphrasable argument.

IX. THE THEMATIC ASPECT OF THE *ILIAD* AND THE *ODYSSEY*

No Western texts other than the Bible and perhaps the plays of Shakespeare have been studied more thoroughly than the Homeric epics. The following

---

22. According to Duckworth, "Emma and Knightley will remain friends of the Martins," and "the social gaps which individual actions threatened to widen will be closed around the marriage of the central figures" (176). This interpretation simplifies a complex situation.

discussion is not intended as a comprehensive account of the thematic aspect of the epics, but as a brief application of some of the modes of analysis presented earlier in the chapter, with a concentration on the *Iliad* and a shorter examination of the *Odyssey*, particularly in its relation to the *Iliad*.

Here is a literal translation of the first line and a word of the *Iliad*, with the word order of the original retained: "**Anger** sing goddess of Peleus's son Achilles / destructive"—or, in better English, "Goddess, sing about the destructive **anger** of Peleus's son Achilles" (Il.1.1–2) In Greek, the first word is *mênin*, the accusative case of a noun that means something like "anger"; I will return to the meaning in a moment. The poet asks the goddess, presumably the Muse, to sing about this anger; evidently this anger is a theme of the poem.[23]

Other epics also begin by naming a theme. The *Odyssey*, for instance, begins, "**Man** to me tell about Muse of many turns," or "Muse, tell me about the **man** of many turns" (Od.1.1). The first word announces that this story will be about a man—Odysseus, of course, though he is not named until line 21. The *Aeneid* begins, "**Arms** and a **man** I sing," or "I sing about **arms** and a **man**" (Aen.1.1). Vergil begins with two themes, more or less the themes of the *Iliad* and the *Odyssey*, and the two Homeric epics are the lumber from which he constructs his own epic. Petrarch's *Africa* begins, "Tell me, Muse, about the **man** noted for his valor and feared in war, to whom noble Africa, broken under Italian **arms,** first gave her eternal name" (1.1–2)—that is, Scipio Africanus. And Milton's *Paradise Lost* also begins by stating a theme: "Of man's first disobedience, and the fruit / Of that forbidden tree, whose moral taste / Brought death into the world, and all our woe, / With loss of Eden, till one greater man / Restore us, and regain the blissful seat, / Sing, heavenly muse" (1.6). Tasso's *Gerusalemme Liberata* and Camoens's *Os Lusiádas* also begin by stating themes, and both clearly allude to the beginnings of the *Iliad*, the *Odyssey*, and the *Aeneid*, but the passages are too long to quote here.

The first enunciated theme of the *Iliad*, then, is *mênis*. There is no adequate English translation of this complex Greek word. Some translators use "anger," others use "rage"; Cunliffe's *Lexicon of the Homeric Dialect* gives "wrath" or "ire." Leonard Muellner, after examination of relevant passages in the *Iliad*, the *Odyssey*, and the *Homeric Hymns*, concludes that *mênis* "is not just a term for an emotional state. *It is a sanction meant to guarantee and maintain the integrity of the world order*; every time it is invoked, the hierarchy of the cosmos is at stake" (26). It is "the irrevocable cosmic sanction that prohibits some characters from taking their superiors for equals and others from taking their

---

23. We should note here also the role of the Muse in the creation of epic poetry; this is an interesting recurring theme both in the *Iliad* and in the *Odyssey*, but I will not be able to explore it here.

equals for inferiors" (31).²⁴ In the *Iliad*, this sanction operates against groups rather than against individuals. Thus the whole of Troy suffers because of the crime against hospitality committed by Paris, but in the *Odyssey*, the word has somewhat different implications, where it is more directed against the blameworthy rather than against the community as a whole (44).²⁵

The poem announces the *mênis* of Achilles at the very beginning, but it takes a while for the action to catch up. In the first event of the story, Chryses, a priest of Apollo, comes to the Achaean camp to offer ransom for the return of his daughter, who has been taken as a war prize (the technical term is *geras*) and apportioned to Agamemnon. Agamemnon refuses Chryses's supplication and orders the old man to leave under the threat of violence. Agamemnon's refusal, which goes against the decision of the army as a whole, violates fundamental principles of cosmic order. Chryses prays to Apollo, who sends a plague to the Achaean army; the whole army suffers for the actions of Agamemnon. Apollo's punishment of the Greek army is the first instance of *mênis* in the story (Il.1.75). After angry deliberation among the chiefs, Agamemnon relents, the girl is returned to her father, and the plague comes to an end.²⁶

Achilles's *mênis* is a by-product of this little episode. When Agamemnon agrees to give up Chryses's daughter, he demands compensation, and after a long and increasingly angry argument with Achilles, he demands Achilles's war prize, a woman named Briseis. Achilles's rage is caused by this demand. He threatens to kill Agamemnon, but Athena (seen only by Achilles) stops him. He then declares that he will no longer fight against the Trojans, and for most of the rest of the story he keeps to his promise.

Book 1 ends on the divine level; the transitional figure is the goddess Thetis, the mother of the mortal Achilles. After he leaves the Achaean camp, he calls to her to ask Zeus for help: "Since, my mother, you bore me to be a man with a short life, / therefore Zeus of the loud thunder on Olympus should

---

24. Homeric language typically emphasizes the external manifestations of what later came to be internalized as emotions. Thus *phobos* in Homer means "flight," and only later means "fear."

25. Passages examined by Muellner include Il.V.34; Il.5.444; Il.16.711; Il.1.247; Hymn to Demeter 350 and 410; Od.5.146; Hymn to Aphrodite 290; Il.22.358; Od.11.73; Il.5.178; Il.13.624; Od.14.283; Od.2.66; Od.17.14; and Il.1.75.

26. It is notable that Achilles calls the council where the chiefs discuss the plague. Homer never makes the point directly, but surely the meaning of this detail is that Achilles is performing the functions that should be performed by Agamemnon. I have previously discussed book 1 of the *Iliad* in Clark, "The Concept" and "Chryses' Supplication."

grant me / honor [*timé*] at least" (Il.1.352–54)."²⁷ Once, when all the other gods attempted to dethrone Zeus, Thetis saved him, and now Achilles asks her to call in this debt. Thetis appeals to Zeus aside, and he agrees to help Achilles by favoring the Trojans. As Muellner notes, Zeus takes on Achilles's *mênis* (124). But he also displays what amounts to *mênis* on his own account; though the word itself is not used, much of the associated vocabulary appears. Hera has seen him conferring with Thetis and she confronts him angrily, but he warns her not to interfere: "Now sit down and be silent, and obey my command, / lest all the gods on Olympus be of no help to you / coming nearer, when I lay my untouchable hands upon you." (Il.1.565–67).

Hephaistos intervenes to settle the impending dispute, which he says would be devastating, since Zeus is stronger than all the other gods together. He reminds Hera of the time when Zeus threw him down from Olympus and mortal men had to care for him. He then limps around to serve wine to all the gods; they laugh, the order among the gods is restored, and the threat of Zeus's *mênis* is avoided.

The theme of *mênis* must be understood within a set of ideas and attitudes that have come to be called the heroic code.²⁸ The basic elements of the code can be summarized as follows: Human life is short, especially as compared to the immortality of the gods. The compensation for a short life is honor, which is achieved by facing death in battle. But the hero also has to resist the appeals of those who would try to persuade him not to fight.²⁹ During life, honor is made manifest by material rewards and by status in rituals, such as sacrificial feasting; the technical term for this honor is *timé*. In the world of the *Iliad*, honor and status are measured by its external manifestations, such as the prizes awarded to heroes for their bravery in battle. The apportioning of prizes is a fundamental sign of social structure and the esteem in which a warrior is held. Honor that does not have a material manifestation is hardly conceivable. After death, honor is made manifest by fame, particularly in the form of epic poetry; the technical term for this fame is *kleos*.

The principal theme of the *Iliad* is thus deeply ideological. This ideology is expressed through a set of key terms, it is expressed through the actions of the story, and it is also directly expressed by the characters: Why (Sarpedon asks his countryman Glaukos) are we honored above others and given the best

---

27. Here we learn for the first time that Achilles is fated to have a short life. Thetis repeats this point a few lines later (Il.1.415–16). In book 9, we learn that Achilles has a choice: either a short life with fame, or a long life without fame.

28. The heroic code is discussed by many scholars; see, for example, Whitman; Griffin; and Clarke, "Manhood."

29. As Andromache to Hektor (Il.6.406–65) or Priam to Hektor (Il.22.38–76).

meat and wine, why are we given orchards and vineyards and ploughland? It is our duty to stand in the front lines so the Lykians will praise us. If we could live forever, then I would not fight in the front lines nor would I urge you to do so. But since death stands close beside us and no man can escape it, let us win glory for ourselves, or give it to others (Il.12.310–28).

Like most ideological systems, the heroic code is subject to certain stresses, and the *Iliad* in many ways is an exploration of these stresses. Agamemnon feels that his own status is threatened if he has to give up his war prize, but his attempt to get compensation violates the rules of communal distribution and also threatens Achilles's status. Achilles feels that he is no longer part of the community, now that the prize the community awarded him has been taken back, and so he withdraws from the fighting. Achilles comes to doubt his place in the heroic code, and perhaps ultimately he comes to doubt the code itself. His place in the heroic system has been challenged; his response to this challenge is *mênis*; his *mênis* is expressed by his absence from fighting; and his absence from the fighting will bring disaster on the Achaean army.

Thus the three incidents of wrath in book 1 set the primary theme of the epic through a combination of key words—*mênis*, *geras*, and *timê*—and actions manifesting those words. As always, the thematic is created by the synthetic and the mimetic. The poem will be about the wrath of Achilles, caused when Agamemnon takes his war prize from him and threatens his status. Each of these heroes claims to be the best of the Achaeans—Agamemnon because he commands more men, Achilles because he is the best warrior. Their contest and wrath are seen, in the context of the divine wrath of Apollo and Zeus, as fundamental disturbances to the order of the cosmos. According to Rose, in this conflict Achilles represents meritocracy while Agamemnon represents plutocracy: "In the *Iliad* the transition from a meritocracy to a plutocracy, from inherited demonstrable excellence to inherited wealth and status, emerges as the central contradiction within ruling-class ideology" (94).

When Achilles leaves the fighting, he also more or less leaves the story, at least until book 9. Thematic discussion of *mênis* therefore could jump to book 9 and pick up the story and themes there. Such a jump, however, would fail to account for another thematic aspect of the epic, the experience of reading (or hearing) the story in the order it is presented. This experience in fact matches an important element of the wrath of Achilles: The reader (or audience) has to experience Achilles's absence from the narrative between book 1 and book 9 just as the Achaeans experience his absence from the battlefield.

A narrowly thematic approach, an approach that insists on a single organizing theme, is left with not much to say about a number of important episodes. In book 2, for example, Agamemnon tests the troops by suggesting that they abandon the war. The troops all rush for the ships, and only the swift actions of Odysseus save the day.[30] Also in book 2 Thersites criticizes Agamemnon, and Odysseus beats him. These events implicitly comment on the dispute between Agamemnon and Achilles.

In book 3 there is the inconclusive duel between Menelaus and Alexandros (Homer's usual name for Paris); when Alexandros is about to lose, Aphrodite snatches him away and takes him back to Troy. Also in book 3 we see Helen for the first time. As the duel is about to begin, Iris, the messenger of the gods, comes to Troy in disguise. She finds Helen weaving a robe and working into the weaving representations of the Achaeans and the Trojans fighting over her; in effect, she is making this garment into a textile version of the epic itself. Iris takes Helen up to the walls, where King Priam and the other Trojan elders are watching the fighting. They question her about some of the Achaean leaders—Agamemnon, Odysseus, Aias—as if the war were just beginning. Here also Helen reproaches herself: She wishes she had died rather than being the cause of the war; her judgment of herself is harsh.

After Aphrodite snatches Alexandros away from the duel, she then goes to Helen and tells her to come back to her apartment, where Alexandros is waiting for her, but Helen replies angrily. If you love Alexandros so much, she says to Aphrodite, then why don't you marry him yourself? But Aphrodite warns Helen not to get her angry, or else she will grow to hate her as much as she loves her now (Il.3.399–417). Evidently the favor of a god has a double edge.[31]

The theme of the relationship of gods to mortals is constant throughout the epic. In book 1, Athena comes to the Achaean camp, invisible to all except Achilles, and she pulls his hair and stops him from killing Agamemnon. Later in book 1 Achilles appeals to his mother, who is a goddess. In book 2 Zeus sends a deceitful dream to Agamemnon. In book 3, Aphrodite saves Alexandros from the duel. In book 4 Athena, disguised as a Trojan warrior, persuades the Trojan archer Pandaros to shoot an arrow at Menelaos. In book 5 the Achaean warrior Diomedes actually wounds Aphrodite, who rushes off to Olympus to be comforted by her mother, Dione. Such interactions continue throughout the epic. The gods are close to mortals—indeed, several mortals are the children of gods—but the gods live on a different plane. They take

---

30. Note the repetition of Il.2.110–18 and Il.9.18–25; surely this is a significant repetition. In book 2 Agamemnon does not mean what he says, but in book 9 he does.

31. Helen reappears several times: In book 6, for instance, when Hektor goes to the city, he meets and talks first with his mother, Hekebe; second with Helen; and third with his wife, Andromache. Then in book 24, at the very end of the story, these three women mourn over the body of Hektor: first Andromache, then Hekebe, and finally Helen, who speaks almost the last words of the epic.

sides in the war, but they also can watch it unfold with a kind of pleasure. And no matter what happens, no god will die, while death looms over the head of every mortal in the poem.

The theme of death is particularly poignant in book 6, when Hektor, on his way from the city to the battlefield, meets his wife and their infant son, Astyanax. She is afraid that he is going to his death (and in fact she never sees him alive again), and she says that when he dies it would be best if she could die, too. Achilles has killed her father and all seven of her brothers; he captured her mother and released her for ransom, but she died shortly after. "Hektor," she says, "thus you are father to me, and my honored mother, you are my brother, and you it is who are my young husband" (Il.6.429–30), and she asks him to stay on the rampart and draw the army back to the city. But Hektor refuses: "I would feel deep shame before the Trojans, and the Trojan women with trailing garments, if like a coward I were to shrink aside from the fighting" (Il.6.441–43). He knows that the city is doomed, and he is most troubled, not for his father and mother and brothers, but "the thought of you, when some bronze-armored Achaean leads you off, taking away your day of liberty, in tears; and in Argos you must work at the loom of another" (VI.454–56). Here working at the loom has a sexual connotation. Hektor then holds out his arms for his son, who shrinks back in fear from Hektor's helmet with its crest of horse hair (Hektor's usual epithet is "Hektor of the shining helmet"). Hektor takes Astyanax into his arms and prays to Zeus that his son may surpass him in valor. Though the story isn't told in the *Iliad,* the original audience probably knew the tradition that Astyanax was killed when the Achaeans captured Troy.[32]

In this passage, Homer (or the text, or the tradition) seems to want us to feel and think about death, and the destruction of a city, and the experience of women and children in war. The MTS model would count feeling as part of the mimetic component and thinking as part of the thematic component. I see no benefit in dividing thinking from feeling; compartmentalizing defeats the particular virtue of narrative, which brings thinking and feeling together in a seamless experience. In the SMT model, the thematic aspect, signification, is created through the mimetic aspect, representation.

In book 9, the story returns to Achilles, who is still sulking in his hut. Without him, the Achaeans are being pushed back toward their ships. At a meeting of the chiefs, Nestor proposes that Agamemnon offer Achilles recompense. Agamemnon agrees and makes a lavish offer, but he adds a stipulation:

---

32. This passage can be compared to Andromache's speech in book 24, which develops these points under even more poignant circumstances, after Hektor's death.

"Let him yield place to me, inasmuch as I am the kinglier and inasmuch as I can call myself born the elder" (Il.9.160–61).[33]

Three ambassadors are selected to convey the offer: Odysseus, Ajax, and Phoinix, Achilles's friend and surrogate father. When they reach Achilles's camp, they find him playing the lyre and singing about the famous deeds of men. The Greek word translated "famous deeds" is *kleos* (here in the accusative plural). Etymologically it means something like "things that are heard about," and so it can mean "report," "rumor," "reputation," "fame," or "glory." In the *Iliad*, it can mean the undying fame that a hero achieves, as in the phrase *kleos aphthiton*, "undying glory." Whereas *timé* is the material sign of honor received by the living hero, *kleos aphthiton* is the reward that lasts after the death of the hero. Epic itself becomes the record of the hero's undying glory. When Achilles sings the famous deeds of men, he is singing an epic within the epic. His singing is similar in some ways to Helen's weaving, as both show a kind of epic awareness.[34] This epic awareness of the characters within the story can be seen as part of the thematic aspect of the poem—though of course it also can be understood synthetically and mimetically.

Achilles entertains the ambassadors according to the epic ritual pattern; the importance of hospitality is a recurring theme in both the *Iliad* and the *Odyssey*. The ambassadors then make their appeals, first Odysseus, second Phoinix, and last the blunt soldier Aias. Odysseus's long speech repeats Agamemnon's offer of compensation, but without Agamemnon's final demand; it fails utterly. Achilles replies that he hates as he hates the gates of Hades the man who hides one thing in his heart but says something different (Il.9.312–13). Ostensibly he means Agamemnon, but of course his description fits Odysseus, who has hidden the demand at the end of Agamemnon's offer.

Achilles then seems to call the whole enterprise of the war into doubt. Those who fight and those who hold back both die; the brave and the coward have the same honor (Il.9.318–20). Why are Argives fighting the Trojans? The army was assembled because of Helen, but are the sons of Atreus the only men who love their wives? Achilles loved Briseis, even if she was a captive (Il.9.337–43). After a long denunciation of Agamemnon, Achilles explains his own situation. His mother has told him he has two possible destinies: If he

---

33. Even without Agamemnon's direct demand for subservience, the recompense is ambiguous at best. Agamemnon offers one of his daughters to Achilles, who would then be Agamemnon's son-in-law. Achilles scornfully tells Odysseus, "Let him pick some other of the Achaeans, someone who is kinglier" (Il.9.391–92). Muellner 141 argues that the very excess of the offer signifies Agamemnon's superior wealth and power.

34. Helen shows her epic awareness also in her conversation with Hektor (Il.6.354–58), where she notes that they will be matters of song for people in the future.

stays to fight at Troy, he will have no homecoming (*nostos*), but he will have everlasting glory (*kleos aphthiton*); if he goes home, he will have no glory but a long life (Il.9.410–16). The choice, then, is between *nostos*, return home, and *kleos*, fame; in the *Iliad* (but not in the *Odyssey*), these form an exclusive opposition.³⁵

The resolution of the argument between Achilles and Agamemnon could have come in book 9, with Agamemnon's offer of restitution. But Agamemnon's offer does not satisfy Achilles. Many of the crucial issues of the epic depend on how one interprets Achilles's intransigence. The other Achaean warriors feel that he is being unreasonable—but they are not disinterested judges. It seems clear, at any rate, that Achilles no longer feels bound by the heroic code, and arguments based on the code do not move him.

What moves him, ultimately, is the death of his companion, Patroklos, who has entered the battle, in Achilles's armor. At first he manages to rout the Trojans, but eventually he is killed by Hektor, assisted by the god Apollo. Since Patroklos is wearing Achilles's armor, his death in a sense prefigures the death of Achilles.

The death of Patroklos brings Achilles back into the battle, but not as a participant in the heroic code; he wants only to avenge the death of his companion, even though he knows that his own death will follow soon after Hektor's.³⁶ As soon as he gets new armor from Hephaistos, he calls a meeting of the army, where Agamemnon repeats his offer of gifts of compensation; Achilles has no concern for these gifts and urges the army to go straight into battle. Odysseus, however, argues that the army should eat before they fight, and he insists that the gifts of compensation be brought into the middle where all can see them, and that Agamemnon shall swear that he never entered the bed of Briseis, the woman he took from Achilles. And so, against Achilles's desires, it is done. Achilles may have no interest in the heroic code and its symbols, but Odysseus understands that he must be brought back into the community and into the heroic code.

Achilles in battle now is quite berserk. His violence and cruelty are contrasted directly with the restraint he showed in his previous fighting. In book 19, we are given the example of Priam's son Lycaon, whom Achilles had captured and sold into slavery once before. After Lycaon was ransomed he returned to battle, and once again he faces Achilles. He falls at Achilles's feet

---

35. The episode continues with the attempted persuasions of Phoinix and Aias. Phoinix introduces the idea of an ascending scale of affections, which will become important especially when Patroklos dies (see Nagy 103). Aias, the least rhetorical speaker, is the most persuasive.

36. I omit here several important episodes, in particular the forging of the new armor for Achilles and the funeral games for Patroklos.

as a suppliant and begs for mercy, but Achilles refuses the supplication. Before Patroklos was killed, he says, I took many Trojans alive, but now no Trojan will escape death, and especially the children of Priam. Why make such a clamor about your death? Patroklos was greater than you are, and he is dead. Look at me, how splendid I am, born of a great father and a goddess, but I too will die (Il.19.99–113). Achilles cuts his head off and throws him in the river to be food for the fish.

It is instructive to compare this passage with the passage summarized above in which Sarpedon explains the essential features of the heroic code. Death looms over both passages, but the deductions are somewhat different. Sarpedon finds the compensation for death in the honor bestowed by the community; Achilles finds the compensation for death only in the death of his enemy, and the only community he recognizes at this point is the community of the slayer and the slain.

Achilles's rage comes to a climax when he meets Hektor. Before they fight, Hektor asks for mutual assurances of decent treatment: If he defeats Achilles, he promises not to defile the body and to return the body to the Achaeans, and he asks Achilles for the same promise. But Achilles refuses: There are no agreements, he says, between men and lions, or between wolves and lambs (Il.22.256–67). When Achilles has delivered the mortal blow, Hektor again appeals to him; Achilles answers, "I wish my fury would drive me to eat your raw flesh; I would not give up your body, not even if Priam himself were to come with your weight in gold; instead the dogs and birds will feed on you" (Il.22.345–54).

This final battle is only the extreme manifestation of the fundamental impulse of the epic, which is violence, or, as Simone Weil calls it, force. Force, she says, is manifested in three ways: First there is the force that kills, the force that turns someone into a corpse. Second, there is the force that turns a person into a thing even while that person is still alive. As Weil says, "A man stands disarmed and naked with a weapon pointing at him; this person becomes a corpse before anybody or anything touches him" (5). "He is alive; he has a soul; and yet—he is a thing. An extraordinary entity this—a thing which has a soul" (4). And third is the force that intoxicates, that keeps the possessor of force from reflection, justice, and prudence. Weil says, "Force is as pitiless to the man who possesses it, or thinks he does, as it is to its victims" (11). "The man who is possessor of force seems to walk through a non-resistant element; in the human substance that surrounds him nothing has the power to interpose, between the impulse and the act, the tiny interval that is reflection. Where there is no room for reflection, there is none either for justice or prudence. Hence we see men in arms behaving harshly and madly" (12–13). This is the image of Achilles at the moment of Hektor's death.

Achilles exceeds the socially sanctioned forms of violence. After he kills Hektor, he mistreats the body in a shameful way; he pierces the ankles of the corpse behind the tendons, pulls thongs through the holes, fastens the thongs to his chariot, and drags the body around the city.[37] Apollo feels that Achilles has gone too far: "Achilles has destroyed pity," he says (Il.24.44). Hera, however, argues that Achilles, born of a goddess, has a higher regard among the gods than Hektor. Zeus settles the disagreement. He summons Thetis and tells her to tell her son that he must give up the body of Hektor for ransom. He then sends Iris, the messenger of the gods, to tell Priam to go to Achilles to ask for the body.

Hekabe tries to dissuade Priam: Where has your wisdom gone? How can you face this man who has slaughtered so many of your sons? Your heart is iron. And she wishes she could eat Achilles's liver (Il.24.201–16). Achilles's savage wish has been transferred to Hekabe.

Priam, guided by Hermes in disguise, goes to Achilles's camp. He finds Achilles, who has just finished dinner. He grasps Achilles's knees and makes a long appeal in supplication.[38] Achilles is astonished to see him: How could you have dared to come to the ships of the Achaeans and to my camp, when I have killed so many of your sons? Your heart is iron (Il.24.517–21). Achilles repeats exactly the words Hekabe had used, "Your heart is iron," but with a very different meaning. The difference in meaning between these two passages shows that the formulaic style is capable of considerable sophistication.

Achilles tells Priam that grief is given to mortals by Zeus, and even the person who is given blessings at one time will receive suffering at another. My father Peleus, he says, was honored by the gods with wealth and an immortal wife, but the gods gave him evils as well: He had only a single son, who will die in Troy. And you, Priam, were known for your wealth and for your children, but now there is fighting around your city and your sons have been killed. But there is no advantage in endless mourning (Il.24.522–51).

Priam is not much interested in Achilles's thematic essay; he just wants the body of Hektor. Achilles warns him not to go too far. Yes, he will give the body back, in obedience to the orders of Zeus, but clearly he is still angry about the death of Patroklos and he finds it difficult to control his sorrow and anger. He

---

37. Achilles also sacrifices twelve young Trojan men during the funeral of Patroklos; however a modern audience may react, there is no indication that the other Achaeans or any of the gods believe that this action has violated any moral standard.

38. On supplication in general and this supplication in particular, see Crotty.

and his attendants, Automedon and Alkimos, go out and tend to the body and place it onto the wagon. Achilles returns to Priam and urges him to eat. He tells the story of Niobe, whose twelve children were all killed by Apollo and Artemis, but even Niobe remembered to eat (Il.24.599–620).[39] Here Achilles seems to have learned something from Odysseus.

At the end of the story, Achilles and Priam remain enemies. After Hektor's funeral, the war will continue, and eventually Achilles will die. There is no happy ending. But many readers, I among them, feel that there is some community of feeling established between Achilles and Priam:

> But when they had put aside their desire for drinking and eating,
> Truly Dardanian Priam wondered at Achilles,
> How great and of what sort he was; for it was like facing the gods.
> But Achilles wondered at Dardanian Priam,
> Looking at his beautiful face and hearing his words. (Il.24.628–32)

In this story, the community of enemies is perhaps the most that can be expected, but it is not nothing.

I have noted already in chapter 1 that there is a remarkable formal similarity between book 1 and book 24 of the *Iliad*—a formal similarity but a thematic difference: Achilles's treatment of Priam is very different from Agamemnon's treatment of Chryses. This similarity and difference has to count in the thematic interpretation of the epic: Agamemnon's callous treatment of Chryses has only led to disaster; Achilles's respect for his enemy will not bring peace, but it does bring a kind of understanding. And the amazing artistry of the poem as a whole as it represents the grief of war perhaps shows one human response to the mortal condition.

The events of the *Odyssey* follow after the *Iliad*, though the relationship between the two epics remains a matter of scholarly controversy. According to Denys Page, "nowhere [in the *Odyssey*] is there any allusion to the wrath of Achilles or to the death of Hector, or indeed to any other incident, large or small, described in the *Iliad*" (158).[40] Page concludes, therefore, that the traditions of the two poems are unconnected. Gregory Nagy argues, on the other hand, that such a strict exclusion could hardly be accidental: "If the avoidance was indeed deliberate, it would mean that the *Odyssey* displays an awareness of the *Iliad* by steering clear of it. . . . [T]he traditions of the *Iliad* and the

---

39. This is the only known version of the story in which Niobe eats. Some scholars argue that Homer has altered the traditional story to fit the situation; see Willcock.

40. This observation is known as Monro's Law, named after the late nineteenth-century Homeric scholar David Monro.

Odyssey constitute a totality with the complementary distribution of their narratives" (21).

This complementary distribution can be noted even at the level of diction. The word *gaster*, which means "belly" or "stomach" or (just once) "womb," is used in both epics, but in rather different ways. The word is used thirteen times in the *Iliad*.[41] Ten times, the word refers to a part of the body that is wounded in battle; for instance, at Il.4.531 Thoas strikes Peiros in the middle of the belly and kills him. At Il.5.539 Agamemnon strikes Deïkoön, and the sword drives through his belt into the deep part of the belly. (This line is repeated at Il.17.519, when Automedon kills Aretos.) At Il.5.616 Telemonian Aias strikes Amphios in the lower part of the belly. And so on. It seems that in the *Iliad*, the *gaster* is a point of vulnerability. There are three partial exceptions. At Il.6.58, the word is used to mean womb: Agamemnon says to Menelaos that they should kill all the Trojans, even the child carried in its mother's *gaster*. At Il.16.163 the word is used in a simile: Achilles's soldiers, the Myrmidons, are like wolves who eat raw flesh; their hearts are fearless and their bellies are glutted. Both of these uses continue the theme of violence associated with *gaster* in the *Iliad*. The thirteenth instance I will take up in a moment.

The word is used seventeen times in the *Odyssey*.[42] In thirteen of these, the belly is the location of hunger. In book 4, for example, Menelaos is telling the story of his homecoming; for a time he and his men were becalmed on the island of Pharos, off the coast of Egypt, and during that time hunger oppressed their bellies (Od.4.369; the same line is used at Od.12.332, when Odysseus and his men are trapped on the island of Helios). In book 6, Odysseus has been cast ashore on the island of the Phaiakians and has crawled under a bush to sleep. In the morning, he is awakened by the sound of Nausikaa and her attendants playing ball, and he crawls out from the thicket; the narrator compares him to a lion, beaten by the rain and the wind, going after cattle or sheep or deer, because his belly urges him (Od.6.133). In book 7, Odysseus has come to the palace of Alkinoös; he asks for dinner, since there is nothing more shameless than the belly (Od.7.217). In book 15, Odysseus, disguised as a beggar, tells his host, the swineherd Eumaios, that people endure sorrows because of the cursed belly (Od.15.344).

---

41. The complete list is Il.4.531; Il.5.539; Il.5.616; Il.6.58; Il.13.372; Il.13.398; Il.13.506; Il.16.163; Il.16.465; Il.17.313; Il.17.519; Il.19.225; and Il.21.180.

42. The complete list is Od.4.369; Od.6.133; Od.7.216; Od.9.433; Od.12.332; Od.15.344; Od.17.228; Od.17.286; Od.17.473; Od.17.559; Od.18.2; Od.18.44; Od.18.118; Od.18.53; Od.18.364; Od.18.380; and Od.20.25. The single example I do not examine in detail comes in book 9: When Odysseus escapes from the cave of the Cyclops, he holds himself under the belly of Polyphemus's ram (Od.9.433).

In books 17 and 18, there are eight passages in which the word is used in the sense "belly," and two more where it means "sausage," that is, something like haggis. Odysseus has arrived at his palace, still in disguise, and his beggar's belly receives much discussion. Then at the beginning of book 18, a new character is introduced, another beggar, Iros, known for his ravenous belly (Od.18.2). The suitors stage a fight between the two beggars, and Odysseus agrees to the match because of his belly (Od.18.53). The prize for the winner is a sausage, so the two beggars are fighting over a stuffed belly (Od.18.44 and 118). In one additional passage the word means "sausage": At the beginning of book 20, Odysseus is lying awake trying to plan the next steps in his revenge on the suitors; he twists and turns like a sausage on a fire (Od.20.25). So Odysseus himself has become the *gaster*, which is both the ravenous belly and the food that fills it.

With these examples in mind, we can return to the one passage left unexamined from the *Iliad*. This comes in book 29, after the death of Patroklos. Achilles wants to rejoin the Achaean army and engage the Trojans without delay, but Odysseus says that the army must eat first: In no way do the Achaeans mourn a dead man with the belly—that is, by fasting. We bury the corpse, and when we have wept, then we eat and drink, so that we can fight all the more strongly (Il.19.225-32). The word thus seems to be in complementary distribution—in the *Odyssey*, the belly is the source of hunger, but in the *Iliad*, it is a point of vulnerability, except when Odysseus speaks. It is as if Odysseus drags the contexts of his own poem with him into Achilles's poem. This distribution is directly related to the different thematic interests of the two epics.

The *Odyssey* is in part a reassessment of many of the themes of the *Iliad*; as Erwin Cook notes, "the *Odyssey* consistently asserts its views and its claim to greatness at the expense of the *Iliad*" (10). This contest between the poems can be understood partly through a number of related semantic oppositions. Sometimes an opposition is expressed by different meanings of a single word or phrase, as *gaster* is used one way in the *Iliad* and a different way in the *Odyssey*. But often there is a contrast of two terms (or two terms and their synonyms), such as the contrast between *biê*, "force," and *metis*, "cunning"; or the contrast between *kleos*, "fame," and *nostos*, "homecoming"; or the contrast between *muthoi*, "words," and *erga*, "deeds." Sometimes a contrast occurs within one of the epics, sometimes the two epics are contrasted. All of these oppositions are interrelated, and to discuss one is to discuss them all.

An important phrase with different applications is *aristos Achaiôn*, "best of the Achaeans." The initial conflict in the *Iliad* sets Agamemnon against Achilles, each with a claim to be the best of the Achaeans—Agamemnon because he has more followers, Achilles because he is the best fighter.[43] But the conflict is also seen between the two epics: The *Iliad* proposes that Achilles is the best of the Achaeans because of his excellence in fighting, while the *Odyssey* proposes that Odysseus is the best because of his excellence in thinking. This contest between two versions of excellence is implicit throughout the *Odyssey*, but at times it rises to the surface. In book 8, the Phaiakian bard Demodokos sings about a time when Achilles and Odysseus quarreled: Agamemnon was pleased, because Apollo had issued an oracle that when the two best of the Achaeans quarreled, then the end of Troy would be near (Od.8.73–82). (Agamemnon evidently misconstrued the oracle, which was referring to the quarrel at the beginning of the *Iliad*.) According to Nagy, the quarrel between Achilles and Odysseus can perhaps be reconstructed: Will Troy fall through force (*biê*) or through cunning (*metis*) (23)?[44]

The *Iliad* is the poem of force, and Achilles is the hero of force, manifest in deeds (*erga*). The *Odyssey* is a story of cunning, and Odysseus is the hero of cunning, manifest in words (*muthoi*)—though each hero has some claim to excellence in the special realm of the other. In the *Iliad*, Achilles gains fame, *kleos*, because of his force, *biê*, but he loses his return, his *nostos*. In the *Iliad*, at least for Achilles, these two goals are mutually exclusive. But they are not mutually exclusive in the *Odyssey*; if epic poetry itself constitutes heroic *kleos*, then Odysseus's *kleos* is his *nostos*, his return.[45] At the beginning of book 9, when Odysseus reveals his identity to the Phaiakians, he says, "I am Odysseus, the son of Laertes, known to all people for my tricks, and my *kleos* reaches heaven" (Od.9.19–20).[46] As Cook notes, "the *Iliad* . . . offers a paradigm of the heroic warrior in which kleos aphtiton is purchased with an early death. In the *Odyssey*, by contrast, Odysseus must choose between a long life with fame and eternal obscurity as the husband of Calypso" (30).

The contest between the two poems is expressed very forcefully in book 11, when Odysseus meets Achilles in the Land of the Dead. No man, he tells Achilles, has been so blessed; when you were alive, you were honored as no man has been, and now you have authority among the dead. Achilles is not

---

43. Agamemnon is called "best of the Achaeans" at Il.1.91, Il.2.82; Achilles at Il.2.769. See Nagy 22–41 for an extensive discussion of various claims to the title. In the *Iliad*, Odysseus is never called the best of the Achaeans, but he contends for the title in the *Odyssey*.

44. See Cook: "In the *Odyssey*, the alignment of *mêtis* with Greek cultural norms results in a theodicy, while the *Iliad*, the poem of *biê*, is populated by gods who cause undeserved suffering" (10).

45. For *kleos* in the *Odyssey*, see Segal 85–109.

46. The qualifier "all" could modify either "people" or "tricks": "I am known to all people for my tricks" or "I am known to people for all tricks."

consoled; he would rather be the slave of a poor man than king over the dead. The hero of the *Iliad* rejects the values that made him a hero.

There is, of course, much more to be said about the thematic aspect of the *Odyssey*.[47] Many of the important themes can be understood simply within the *Odyssey* itself, but an intertextual reading certainly adds an important thematic element. The Homeric epics may seem like a special case of intertextuality, but I think in fact they are not so unusual. Other narratives in the epic tradition draw from the *Iliad* and the *Odyssey*—the *Aeneid* clearly expects its readers to know the Homeric poems. But other narratives outside the epic tradition also benefit from intertextual readings. *Huckleberry Finn* reassesses themes from *Tom Sawyer*, in somewhat the way the *Odyssey* reassesses themes from the *Iliad*.[48] Many narratives are more or less modeled on earlier texts—examples are too numerous to count—but even when there is no specific intertext, it is often possible to detect a kind of generic intertextuality.

Homeric intertextuality, and intertextuality in general, involves all three narrative aspects. To return to the word *gaster*, the deployment of the word within each poem is clearly synthetic, and comparing the usages in both poems is also synthetic, as the diction of one poem is compared to the diction of the other. Each usage can also be seen mimetically: The belly in the *Iliad* is represented as a point of vulnerability, while in the *Odyssey* it is represented as the source of hunger; the realities of the two poems are different. And of course these usages have thematic implications: The *Iliad* is a story of force, the *Odyssey* is a story of desire. Intertextuality thus involves all three aspects, and the three aspects are simultaneous, because they are simply different ways of looking at a unified experience of meaning.

---

47. For discussion of other thematic issues in the *Odyssey*, see, for example, Rose on the ideology of inherited excellence. See Thalmann on class. On gender, see Katz; Heitman; Felson; and Cohen. Dougherty considers the *Odyssey* in the context of Mediterranean cultures. On the gods in Homer, see Kearns. Ahl and Roisman offer a reading of the *Odyssey* against the grain.

48. Huck is in some ways like Odysseus: He is a traveler, he tells lying stories, and he succeeds by his wits, but the episode when he is disguised as a girl is reminiscent of the story of Achilles on Scyros. Another important intertext is *Don Quixote*.

CHAPTER 4

Narrative as Rhetoric and the MTS Model

JAMES PHELAN

I AM DEEPLY GRATEFUL to Matthew Clark for his rich engagement with rhetorical narratology's concepts of the mimetic, the thematic, and the synthetic (hereafter MTS). His detailed unpacking of the various aspects of these three concepts—their multiple dimensions and subtypes—is an excellent contribution to narrative theory. At the same time, I am more persuaded by some parts of his analysis than others, and, indeed, I find that we ultimately have very different theoretical commitments, so I am also grateful for this opportunity to respond. At the outset, I want to spell out my goals, and in so doing, I shall also sketch some big-picture differences between Clark's approach and mine, differences whose consequences I will subsequently explore in more detail.

1. Both Clark and I want to reexamine the three concepts, individually and collectively, and to modify them in ways that increase their explanatory power. In his introduction, Clark notes that the concepts form a model that "usefully distinguishes three kinds of responses and interests a reader may have, . . . relates these responses and interests to elements of the text or the reading experience," and thus "encourages a sharper and more discriminating critical attention" (1). At the same time, Clark notes that his efforts to work with this model, especially in teaching, have led him to identify some difficulties and problems that he proposes to correct. Clark, I believe, exemplifies a very valuable method of scholarly progress: Work with ideas that have proven to be at least somewhat productive and then seek to refine, extend, or other-

wise revise them in order to enhance their explanatory power. In following his example, my goal is not to dig in defensively and say that my previous discussions of MTS got everything right and so there's no need for any revisions. Instead, I want to do my own reexamination and revision through a triangulation of Clark's analyses, my own further thinking, and the practice of some narrative artists. In this connection, I believe it will be helpful to sketch the history of my own work on the concepts.

As Clark notes, when I initially defined and developed them in *Reading People, Reading Plots* (1989), I saw them primarily as a way to identify three simultaneously existing components of fictional character.[1] Over time, I gradually realized that they could be used to enhance a broader rhetorical account of authorial and readerly interests and the relation of those interests to textual phenomena. Consequently, I have continued to rely on the concepts as I investigated other issues over the last thirty years (e.g., character narration, character–character dialogue, narrative progression, narrative ethics, and probability, to name just a few), but I have not gone back and engaged in the reexamination that Clark's work now prompts me to do.

2. I want to explore not just the surface overlaps and divergences between Clark's views and mine but also the underlying reasons for them—and what's at stake when we diverge. To his credit, Clark notes that my work on the concepts is part of my larger effort to develop a rhetorical narratology—what I now refer to as a rhetorical poetics of narrative. In his introduction, Clark declares that

> My revisions are intended as a contribution to rhetorical narratology, but I am sympathetic to other schools of narratological theory, particularly unnatural narratology, cognitive narratology, and ideological narratology (which, as I take it, includes feminist narratology, but also the analysis of class, race, religion, and so on). My revision of the MTS model is partly designed to accommodate these other narratologies within the framework of rhetorical narratology. (13)

---

1. Clark mildly objects to my using the term "component" rather than "aspect" on the ground that "component" suggests something too modular—like a home entertainment system—rather than something integrated into a larger whole. But he goes on to use both terms. I'm going to stay with "component" because I don't think that the link between "component" and "modular" is a necessary one (anatomists talk about three components of the brain, for example, without impeding their ability to talk about the brain as single, larger organ). I also think "component" gives each concept greater weight than "aspect." At the same time, I emphatically underline Clark's point about the interdependence of the three.

Clark's practice bears out his claim to be sympathetic to rhetorical narratology (and to other approaches), but I also want to put pressure on his phrase "partly designed" because doing so generates the question, What is the whole design? Clark does not explicitly answer that question, but I believe his analyses implicitly do. Consider his discussion of the mimetic. He contends that the term should be understood in a way that covers not just realism but also various forms of nonrealistic representation. This assertion and the analyses more broadly indicate that Clark's main goal is not to revise rhetorical narratology but rather to offer a viable descriptive poetics of narrative rooted in his ideas about "the triad." A good scholar, he wants that model to be informed by and to contribute to multiple schools of contemporary narratology, and given my previous work on MTS, he gives special attention to it. But ultimately he advances a case for narrative as a synthesis of construction (the synthetic), representation (the mimetic), and signification/meaning (the thematic)—or to put it another way, for *narrative as a three-pronged textual composition*.

This conception of narrative is ultimately significantly different from a conception of it as rhetoric, which regards narrative not primarily as a textual structure but as an action: somebody telling somebody else on some occasion and for some purposes that something happened. Thus, within the rhetorical view, the MTS model functions neither as a summary nor as a foundation. Instead it is one (important) means for explaining how authors use the resources at their disposal—elements of narrative such as character and space, audiences and their interests, and more—to achieve their purposes in relation to specific audiences. In *Somebody Telling Somebody Else*, I develop a model of narrative communication rooted in the relationships among Authors, Resources, and Audiences (ARA). I see authors and audiences as the constants of the communication, and the elements of narrative (events, characters, temporality, paratexts, genre, etc.) as resources whose significance will vary from one narrative to another. The resources in the ARA model, then, constitute the basic units of narrative communication, and the MTS model describes various ways in which authors shape those building blocks to activate particular kinds of readerly interest in the service of achieving particular purposes in relation to particular audiences.

To put this point another way, rhetorical narratology, while greatly interested in textual composition (and its components), subordinates that interest to the author–audience–purpose nexus in narrative. It's telling that Clark describes my model as identifying "responses and interests a reader may have," but then makes textual composition the center of his. I want to keep "responses and interests" at the center of my model, though I'll tweak the phrase to "authorial shaping of readerly interests and responses" in order to better tap into rhetorical theory's interest in the author–text–audience relationship.

In sum, I find that Clark's MTS model leads him to a text-centric descriptive poetics, while mine leads to a rhetorical poetics that regards the text as itself determined by the author–audience–purpose nexus. Delving more deeply into this difference between Clark's model and mine will help sharpen my own views about both the MTS model and its relation to the larger project of rhetorical poetics.

3. Given Clark's sympathetic attitude toward rhetorical narratology, I state my final goal as our reaching a consensus—one that readers of this book will also come to share—about the superior explanatory power of the MTS model within rhetorical narratology. In short, I want Clark and all my readers to respond affirmatively to my call, "Come home to rhetoric!" Come home to rhetoric, I urge, not because the text-centric descriptive poetics is fundamentally erroneous but rather because it gets subsumed (and appropriately modified) by the more capacious and supple rhetorical poetics. Where Clark's model offers new and substantial insight into the what and even some of the how of MTS, the rhetorical model adds the why—and a more nuanced account of the what and the how—via its attention to authors, audiences, and purposes. In so doing, it offers a more adequate account of the interrelations of the three components.

I hasten to add that I regard this goal as more aspirational than realistic—and that I think failure to reach it can still be part of a positive outcome of our dialogue. Not reaching consensus can be positive if our exchange productively clarifies the nature and the significance of our differences—and invites others to join and advance the conversation.

I. NARRATIVE AS RHETORIC, THE PROJECT OF RHETORICAL POETICS, AND THE MTS MODEL

I begin by placing the MTS model within the conception of narrative as rhetoric and the project of rhetorical poetics. I conceive of narrative as rhetoric not only because I believe it is one viable way of understanding the remarkable phenomenon of storytelling, but also because I believe it captures something significant about why we humans have invented narrative, and why so many have invested in the highly crafted narratives we deem to be literary.[2] We tell stories to come to terms with one or more aspects of what Heidegger called our "thrownness," our finding ourselves in the world and needing to cope with our condition. That coming to terms can itself take multiple forms in relation to multiple purposes. And that coming to terms can vary across the modes of fiction and nonfiction. Perhaps the teller simply wants to understand something more deeply and to communicate that understanding to her audience. Perhaps the teller perceives some particularly pressing issue that she wants to communicate her stance on. Perhaps the teller wants to imagine an alternative to the world as she knows it and to invite the audience to share that alternative. Perhaps the teller finds the very act of creating and sharing stories an intrinsically pleasurable activity. Perhaps the teller combines aspects of all these purposes. Perhaps the teller wants to stick closely to things that actually happened to actual people, perhaps the teller wants to invent characters and events that can exist only in the imagination, or perhaps the teller wants to blur the line between the actual and the invented. In all cases, however, the teller wants to use the storytelling in order to come to terms with one or more aspects of the actual world and to convey that coming to terms to an audience in such a way that it influences the audience. That influence may be an increase in knowledge, understanding, sympathy, empathy, or other cognitive or affective responses; it may be a change in belief, or even a decision to act in new ways; it may be to provide entertainment or even an escape—or of course some combinations of two or more of these things. At the most general level, rhetorical poetics seeks to understand narrative as a way of doing things in the world.[3]

Moving from the motivations and goals of rhetorical poetics toward its workings, I note first that it highlights the multilayered nature of narrative communication. In literary narrative, these layers typically include at least the intellectual, the affective, the ethical, and the aesthetic, and these layers typically interact—though the exact prominence of each layer can vary from one

---

2. When I say "one viable way," I deliberately leave room for other viable ways. These different ways can give us different kinds of valuable knowledge. Furthermore, sometimes one way can generate results that can be integrated into another way. And sometimes different ways lead to productive disagreements. I see the dialogue between Clark and me as evidence for all these points.

3. In response to this paragraph, Peter J. Rabinowitz asked, "What about storytelling with lower stakes—jokes, simple exchanges of information, and so on?" I agree that this description is a better immediate fit with higher-stakes storytelling and that it's important to recognize different stakes. But I would suggest that there's something similar in the underlying rhetorical dynamics of both high-stakes and low-stakes storytelling: a teller responding to some phenomenon in a way that she wants to share with an audience.

narrative to another.[4] Since nonliterary narrative does not aspire to aesthetic effects, the aesthetic will be a less significant layer. The (utopian) project of rhetorical poetics is to offer a comprehensive, precise, and coherent account of the what, the how, and the why of narrative communication in general, including its layers and their interactions. Rhetorical poetics also seeks to make that account simultaneously substantive and supple; that is, it wants to develop explanatory concepts with real content and with the flexibility to apply across a wide range of individual narratives.

For example, I identify unreliable narration as involving the communication by an author to an audience that a narrator's telling is in some way off-kilter. I also note that narrators perform three main functions with their telling—reporting, interpreting, and evaluating—and thus that a narrator can be unreliable in three main ways that may or may not influence each other. That is, tellers can be unreliable as they perform one function but reliable as they perform the others. Or they can be unreliable as they perform two—or even all three—functions. And their unreliability can vary over the course of a narrative. Furthermore, I contend that authors can shape the unreliability for a broad spectrum of effects. These effects can vary from radically estranging the narrator from the audience to strongly bonding narrator and audience. I realize that not all narrative theorists find this model satisfactory, but I propose it as one that is both sufficiently substantive and sufficiently nuanced that those who disagree with it should have no trouble locating their specific points of contention.[5]

I would like the MTS model to perform a similar function within rhetorical poetics, even as I recognize that it encompasses far more phenomena: characters, events, space, time, techniques, progression, audience, and more. Understanding this set of authorial and readerly interests and how they interact in any particular narrative can be a powerful way of accessing and accounting for the multilayered nature of narrative communication. Furthermore, while some components of the MTS model will be more closely linked to some layers of the narrative communication than others (for example, the thematic with the ethical, and the synthetic with the aesthetic), I resist the idea that there is any one-to-one correspondence between components and

---

4. This list of layers is illustrative rather than comprehensive—some religious narratives, for example, focus on a spiritual layer—and some of the categories could themselves be subdivided. The intellectual, for example, includes many kinds of cognition.

5. The most common objection is that I give too much credit to authorial agency and not enough to readerly activity. For more on this view of unreliable narration, see *Living to Tell about It* and *Somebody Telling Somebody Else*. *STSE* also includes theoretical proposals about reliable narration and "deficient" narration (in which actual audiences find fault with reliable narration).

layers of response. On the contrary, the layers of response will typically result from the interactions of the MTS components.

II. COMPARING THEORIES: SOME METHODOLOGICAL PRINCIPLES

Clark's "revised model" and his comments on it form the basis of my claim that he offers a conception of narrative as a three-pronged textual composition:

> Every narrative can be considered from three aspects, the synthetic, the mimetic, and the thematic; these aspects are simultaneous and interdependent. Every text can be seen as synthetic, mimetic, and thematic. Synthetic analysis concerns all kinds of verbal construction, from sentences to whole plots, and also the construction of characters and narrative worlds. Mimetic analysis concerns the representation of characters and worlds constructed in a narrative, realistic or not. Thematic analysis concerns all kinds of meaning imparted by or derived from a text, direct and indirect, intended by the author or not. (11)

Clark goes on to make things even more succinct: "The synthetic aspect of narrative looks at narrative as construction in general, the mimetic aspect looks at narrative as representation in general, and the thematic aspect looks at narrative as signification in general" (12).

Given that Clark and I are working with fundamentally different conceptions of narrative, is it possible for one of us to legitimately argue that his MTS model is actually better than the other? Maybe it's just a case of my saying "potato" and Clark saying "potahto," and we should call this whole thing off. Obviously, I don't think so, but these questions and concerns do highlight the need to be clear about the grounds upon which I claim that rhetorical poetics can appropriately subsume (and modify) Clark's model as part of an ultimately more powerful account of MTS.

When we compare hypotheses designed to answer the same question, to explain the same phenomena, as, for example, when we juxtapose divergent interpretations of the same text, or, in this case, test different models of narrative, we can productively appeal to three main criteria.[6]

---

6. There are other possible relevant criteria, such as "legitimacy," that is, the extent to which the explanation of the details constitutes an accurate construal of them. For example, if I notice that in the "London, 1999" segment of *Atonement*, Briony refers to her vascular dementia, and I build a reading based on her being cured rather than diagnosed with the

1. Comprehensiveness: How adequately does the explanation account for all the generally-agreed-upon significant parts of the phenomenon? An account of a narrative divided by its author into multiple parts (e.g., *The Sound and the Fury, Invisible Man, Atonement*) that does not explain one of its parts does not meet this criterion. A theory of narrative that explains character but is silent about plot also would not meet this criterion. To be sure, there can be disputes about whether some feature of a text or a theory should count as significant, but such disputes themselves point to the utility of this criterion.
2. Correspondence or precision: Does the explanation offer a description of the parts that accounts for their specific rather than their general features? Does the explanation fit loosely or tightly? Does the explanation account for the relative salience of different elements of the phenomenon? For example, an account of *Atonement* may better meet the comprehensiveness criterion by discussing the narrative's movement from Parts One, Two, and Three (which tell the story of Briony Tallis's misidentification of Robbie Turner as a rapist and its consequences for Robbie, Cecilia Tallis, and Briony), to the final section, "London, 1999," with its surprising revelation that those three parts are actually written by Briony. But if that account gives the same weight to Robbie Turner and Cecilia Tallis's brief discussion of Fielding and Richardson in Part One as it does to "London, 1999," it would not meet this criterion of correspondence.[7] Similarly, an account of "London, 1999" that stops with the observation that it is a way for McEwan to have Briony comment on her writing of Parts One, Two, and Three but does not address why McEwan uses a diary entry on the occasion of Briony's seventy-seventh birthday does not do as well on this criterion as one that does. As for theory, I initially made the case for the MTS model of character on the grounds that it would yield greater correspondence to readerly interests than other

---

condition, that explanation would fail the test of legitimacy. But I don't see any issues with legitimacy in Clark. More generally, bringing in criteria for adjudicating between explanations opens up some deeper questions in hermeneutics and epistemology; for example, does the object itself stay stable as we move from one model of explanation to another? But to get into those questions here would sidetrack me from my purpose of responding to Clark. My claim is just that these criteria of coherence, comprehensiveness, and correspondence work well for that purpose.

7. Of course, if we switch the question from one about McEwan's larger purposes to one about his drawing on the tradition of the English novel, then the answer might very well find Robbie and Cecilia's discussion more in need of explanation than significant events that aren't directly concerned with that tradition.

models, especially the then-prominent structuralist view that character was just a group of predicates organized under a proper name.
3. Coherence: Does the explanation account for how the particular details of the phenomena are integrated (or fail to be integrated) into a larger whole? An account of *Atonement* that notes it has four equally compelling parts and discusses what makes each one compelling without discussing how the parts contribute to (or fall short of contributing to) McEwan's overarching novelistic project does not meet this criterion. As the parenthetical phrases in the previous sentences indicate, not all phenomena are themselves coherent. Meeting this criterion in those cases involves offering an account that identifies possible principles of coherence and explains how the construction of the parts is not consistent with those principles. As for theory, an account of narrative that lists its elements but does not explain how they relate to one another would not meet this criterion.

Although Clark does not explicitly appeal to these criteria, he does so implicitly. For example, when he says that my conception of the mimetic fails to do justice to antimimetic or unnatural narratives and that my conception of the synthetic neglects style, he implies that both conceptions fail the test of comprehensiveness. When he says that my conception of the thematic tends toward the allegorical, he suggests that it fails the test of correspondence. (If "fails" is too strong, then substitute "he claims that his model does better on those tests.") Thus, in order to convince Clark and others to adopt the rhetorical model, I will need at minimum[8] to demonstrate that it actually does better on those tests than his model. The challenge is significant because Clark's model does very well on the tests of coherence and comprehensiveness (though I do find one small inconsistency in his discussions of the thematic and the synthetic). My case ultimately, then, will be that the (revised) rhetorical model is equally coherent and comprehensive and more correspondent to the details of both reading and texts than Clark's model.

Let's look more closely at the underlying differences in the two models. Again, from the rhetorical perspective, construction, representation, and signification—like plot, character, and narration—are less important than how authors use them to influence audiences in some ways rather than others. Clark, on the other hand, with his ultimate focus on textual composition, unmoors construction, representation, and signification from how they're

---

8. It's possible, of course, that I could make a convincing case for the rhetorical model as more adequate than Clark's and that some readers will respond by saying, "Okay, fine, but I prefer this other model."

used by authors in order to accomplish purposes in relation to audiences. This difference is perhaps most evident in his claim about the thematic: "Thematic analysis concerns all kinds of meaning . . . direct and indirect, *intended by the author or not*" (11; my emphasis).

The difference is also evident in the way he approaches the task of accommodating other narratologies within rhetorical theory, especially unnatural narratology. Implicitly guided by the criterion of comprehensiveness, Clark accommodates by adding. In dealing with the mimetic, for example, he reasons that putting together what rhetoric has said with what unnatural narratology has said yields a more satisfactory account. That move works for Clark because unnatural narratology is another text-centric approach. But it won't work for me, because adding a rhetorical and a text-centric approach will yield an incoherent model built on divergent first principles. So my challenge will be to integrate both Clark's insights and those of unnatural narratology into a coherent account of the mimetic that meets the criteria of both comprehensiveness (and thus is equal to Clark's) and correspondence (and thus stakes its claim for superiority).

Before I offer my own fresh definitions of the three components, I want to offer some additional grounds for my giving greater weight to the authorial shaping of readerly interests and responses than to textual composition. I do so to suggest that the power of readerly interests and responses exists independently of rhetorical theory's calling attention to them, and, thus, that any model of MTS would do well to account for them. In that respect, I want to suggest that accounting for readerly interests is one part of meeting the test of correspondence. I make this case by temporarily moving away from Clark's commentary and considering the observations of two other distinguished and accomplished theorists.

Here's Catherine Gallagher:

> We already know . . . that all of our fictional emotions are by their nature excessive because they are emotions about nobody, and yet the knowledge does not reform us. Our imagination of characters is, in this sense, absurd and (perhaps) legitimately embarrassing, but it is also constitutive of the [novel as a] genre. (352)

Gallagher emphasizes the persistence of readers' affective responses to fictional characters in the face of the presumed ultimate truth that they are nobodies, a truth based in both the undeniable textuality and fictionality of those characters.[9] This presumed truth renders those emotions "excessive,"

---

9. As this passage indicates, Gallagher is both influenced by and not totally accepting of the structuralist view of character as all and only textual.

"absurd," and "(perhaps) legitimately embarrassing," even though they help define the novel as a genre. But notice what happens if we question that ultimate truth by starting from those readerly emotions. Rather than being excessive and a potential source of embarrassment, they become a legitimate and fascinating phenomenon that narrative theory needs to explain.[10] Granting legitimacy to readerly interest and emotions does not deny that characters are also textual constructs, but it does reject the assumption that their essence is to be found in their textuality. Furthermore, it opens the door for an account that seeks to explain rather than apologize for readers' regarding fictional characters as possible people and having emotional responses to them.

Here's Robyn Warhol, whose commentary dramatizes her shift from a view of character as pure textuality to a view of character as possible person—although she does not comment explicitly on the significance of her shift. Early on in her feminist-narratological discussion of Anne Elliot in Jane Austen's *Persuasion*, Warhol declares,

> For both narrative theory and feminist criticism . . . remembering that characters are not people is crucially important. Characters are marks on the page, made up of the alphabetical characters that spell out who they are. (in Herman et al. 119)

After discussing Anne's character in some detail, however, Warhol concludes that "every page of *Persuasion* contains passages of free indirect discourse reflecting Anne's thoughts, feelings, and bodily sensations, adding up to the powerful illusion of an independent psychology comparable to that of a 'real person.' . . . For me as a feminist narratologist, the fullness with which the novel represents this strongly gendered interiority is what gives the character its interest" (124). For me as a rhetorical theorist, the trajectory of Warhol's commentary provides telling evidence of the power of readerly interests in and responses to characters as possible people. For me as a rhetorical theorist, both Gallagher's and Warhol's observations point to the need for an MTS model that accounts as accurately as possible for those powerful interests.[11]

---

10. Proceeding in this fashion would not rule out the possibility that in some cases readerly emotions can be excessive, but that possibility actually reinforces the idea that in general, readerly emotions are legitimate. The other option would be to go all in on the idea that readerly emotions are bogus and therefore embarrassing. But I doubt that any readers of this book would want to take this option.

11. Both commentaries also suggest to me that Gallagher and Warhol are recognizing at some level the significance of the narrative audience in reading fiction. I wouldn't insist on that point, and it's too complicated to get into now. But I invite my readers to return to these remarks by these distinguished critics after my discussions of the narrative audience.

One final methodological point—about the organization of what follows. Because the MTS model is just one part of rhetorical poetics and because I have tried to construct rhetorical poetics as a coherent theory, my version of the MTS model intersects with several other aspects of that theory. The most relevant ones are the rhetorical model of audience, the concept of narrative progression, the distinction between the ethics of the telling and the ethics of the told, and a conception of fictionality and nonfictionality. In order to keep the discussion focused on Clark's proposals and challenges, however, I will not deal with all these aspects of rhetorical poetics in relation to every narrative I analyze and how the MTS model illuminates it. Instead, I will bring them in selectively as they are most relevant to the specific issues raised by my effort to respond to Clark. More specifically, I will bring in the model of audience in relation to the mimetic and synthetic, and the concept of narrative progression and the ethics of the telling and the told in relation to the thematic. At the end of my discussion, I will do a brief but more broadly oriented reading of all three components in a single narrative that also brings in a conception of fictionality and nonfictionality. As a way to show how the MTS model extends to nonfiction and particularly to a nonfiction narrative that gives prominence to all three components, I will analyze the chapter called "Old China" from Tobias Wolff's remarkable memoir, *In Pharaoh's Army: Memories of the Lost War*.[12]

III. THE RHETORICAL MTS MODEL: DEFINITIONS

I now follow Clark's good example by explicitly defining the mimetic, the thematic, and the synthetic. I deliberately craft the definitions so that they apply to both fictional and nonfictional narrative.

The mimetic component refers to the results (evident in both textual phenomena and readerly response) of authorial shaping of readerly interests in the narrative's imitations of—or references to—the actual world, including such matters as events following the cause-effect logic of the extratextual world, characters functioning as possible people or being representations of actual people, time and space following the known laws of physics, and so on. I agree with Clark that (a) the mimetic does not involve direct copying of the extratextual world but rather the author's take on features of that world and that

---

12. I hasten to add that I believe Clark's model could also apply to nonfiction. But since he focuses mostly on fiction and since I developed the original model while working on fiction, I want to show how it applies to nonfiction—even as I acknowledge that one example can't do justice to the range and variety of nonfiction.

(b) over time authors and audiences establish general conventions that apply to mimetic representation (e.g., dialogue in fiction is clearer, cleaner, and more coherent than most dialogue in our everyday interactions). Indeed, this agreement provides one basis for my stipulating "imitations of—or references to—the actual world" in my definition. Although, as I shall discuss in some detail when I take up my rhetorical approach to fictionality, I find important differences between fictional and nonfictional narrative, I also find the concept of the mimetic relevant to both.

This conception of the mimetic also helps address the objection from David Herman, quoted by Clark, saying that the concept of the mimetic is caught on the horns of a dilemma:

> On the one hand, if mimesis is defined narrowly as imitation or reproduction, the very concept becomes untenable—since there can be no direct representation of the world, no bare encounter with reality, without mediating world-models. On the other hand, if mimesis is defined as part of a family of strategies for deploying world-models, then the concept cannot do the work my co-authors [Phelan and Rabinowitz] try to get it to do—for example, when they set mimesis up as a standard or touchstone against which "antimimetic" stories, or the "synthetic" and "thematic" dimensions of narrative, can be measured. (Herman in Herman et al. 16)

As the emphasis on "authorial shaping" indicates, I don't define mimesis as unmediated representation, and, thus, the concept is not caught on the first horn. And since I view mimetic–thematic–synthetic relations as variable and interdependent (and tied to the nexus of author–audience–purpose relationships), the concept is not caught on the second horn. In other words, the mimetic isn't the standard against which to measure the synthetic and the thematic, but rather one kind of authorial shaping and readerly interest that can have a wide range of relationships with those other two kinds of shaping and interest. Read on for further demonstration of this point. (See also my comments on infrastructure and superstructure following my definition of the synthetic as well as my comments on Roman Jakobson's concept of the dominant shortly after that.)

Of course, by linking the mimetic to the actual world, I may seem to be confirming Clark's objection that my conception is too narrow, too tied to realism. But I want to retain that link because my experiences as a reader and teacher of narrative fiction and nonfiction has convinced me that questions about the relation of the textual world to the extratextual world are fundamental to author–audience relationships and thus to the experience of reading narrative. The issue, then, is whether this conception, in combination with those of the thematic and synthetic components, is supple enough to account for the diversity of narrative projects. Read on and draw your own conclusions.

The thematic component refers to the results (evident in both textual phenomena and readerly response) of authorial shaping of readerly interests in the ideational, ethical, and ideological dimensions of the narrative. Authors reveal these dimensions through a wide range of strategies that often work together; these strategies include, but are not limited to, the arrangement of sequences of action, explicit generalizations about the nature of the world by narrators or characters, and characters functioning as representatives of larger groups or embodiments of ideas.

The synthetic component refers, first, to narrative as itself a constructed object—something artificial rather than natural, something fashioned rather than found—including the various elements that go into that construction, and, second, to the results (evident in both textual phenomena and readerly response) of authorial shaping of readerly interests in a narrative as a constructed object. Clark and I agree that the synthetic is the "infrastructure" of narrative, its necessary condition. But my rhetorical orientation leads me to add the issue of authorial shaping of readerly responses to and interests in that infrastructure to the definition. Consequently, my rhetorical orientation leads me to reject any strict binary between infrastructure and superstructure, because it calls attention to the way authors sometimes make the infrastructure part of the superstructure.

Authors have various means of drawing readers' interests to or away from the synthetic component. The chief means for drawing attention away is what I call the mimetic illusion, about which I'll have a lot more to say below. The chief means for drawing attention to the synthetic is employing the devices that have drawn the attention of unnatural narratology (e.g., flouting established conventions of narratives that rely on the mimetic illusion; deploying logically or physically impossible tellers, characters, and events or event sequences) and overtly calling attention to such material features of the text as typography, page layouts, and so on. As the necessary infrastructure of narrative, the synthetic component will be present in both fiction and nonfiction, and authors can draw attention to it in both modes and in those that blur the boundaries.

My definitions also give more weight to the content of the acts involved in textual composition than Clark's do. This difference is perhaps most immediately apparent in our respective locations of unnatural or antimimetic narratives. For Clark, the unnatural belongs in the domain of the mimetic because it is one kind of representation. For me, the unnatural belongs in the domain of the synthetic because it flaunts its rejection of imitation, and because, as I noted above, I find that that move leads to a qualitatively different reading experience than the one we have with texts that embrace imitation. The key to my case will be the rhetorical model of audiences, since it will allow me to go beyond asserting that there is a qualitative difference between these kinds of narratives to showing that the model offers a more precise account of how each kind of narrative works. In order to make this case, I find it necessary to consider the mimetic and the synthetic together rather than in sequence (as Clark does). Considering them together will inevitably lead to my bringing the thematic into the discussion to some degree, but I will save a full comparison between Clark's conception of the thematic and mine for its own section.

More generally, in thinking about interactions among the components, I find it helpful to adapt Roman Jakobson's concept of the dominant, which he developed as part of his account of verbal communication. Jakobson identifies six general functions of messages between senders and receivers: referential, aesthetic/poetic, conative, emotive, phatic, and metalingual. Any message will have multiple functions, but typically each message will have a single dominant function, which the others will support, and around which the whole message is organized. I adapt Jakobson's concept for the rhetorical MTS model by emphasizing that with narrative, the entire range of dominant/subordinate/equal relationships is possible. Although all three components will be present to some degree (at least, I have not yet encountered a narrative in which one is absent), sometimes a single component will be dominant. For example, authors of allegories such as George Orwell's *Animal Farm* typically subordinate their readers' mimetic and synthetic interests to their thematic ones; authors of portrait narratives such as Alice Munro's "Prue" typically subordinate their readers' thematic and synthetic interests to their mimetic ones; and authors of some metafictions such as John Barth's "Menelaiad" subordinate their readers' mimetic and thematic interests to their synthetic ones. Sometimes authors will make two components dominant. For example, most authors working in the realist tradition of the novel—including, as I will explain below, Austen in *Emma*—emphasize the mimetic and the thematic and subordinate readerly interest in the synthetic. Some authors of metafictions will shape readerly interest to emphasize the synthetic and thematic and subordinate the mimetic, as Italo Calvino does in *If on a winter's night a traveler*. Although I cannot currently think of examples in which authors emphasize the mimetic and the synthetic and subordinate the thematic, I believe it would be foolish to conclude that this arrangement is impossible. Finally, sometimes authors will make readerly interests and responses to all three components prominent—as McEwan does in *Atonement,* as Toni Morrison does in *Beloved*, and as Tobias Wolff does in "Old China," to name just three examples.

These three points—about avoiding a strict binary between infrastructure and superstructure, about the salience of content, and about the variability of the dominant—underlie my response to one of Clark's striking formulations about the relationship among the three components: "If the synthetic is something like syntax, while the mimetic is something like referential semantics, then the thematic is something like the kinds of meanings carried by complete utterances" (96). Although this formulation does reflect our shared view that the three components are interrelated, I do not want to endorse it for two main reasons. The formulation fixes the components in specific roles (when an author such as Barth makes the synthetic infrastructure part of the superstructure, then the synthetic becomes "something like semantics"), and it implicitly assigns the fixed dominant role to the thematic.

CHAPTER 5

The Mimetic, the Synthetic, and the Criterion of Correspondence

Or Audiences, the Mimetic Illusion, and Ghosts

JAMES PHELAN

CLARK SUCCINCTLY EXPRESSES both his general view of the mimetic and his sense of the inadequacy of the rhetorical view in a single paragraph. This paragraph also displays his appeal to the criterion of comprehensiveness.

> The range of representation in narrative is enormous; the MTS model tends to reduce that range to a dichotomy of the "mimetic" or realistic and the "antimimetic." Even within realism there is a range of representation, and the dividing line between the realistic and the nonrealistic is not easily drawn. My proposed revision to the model takes mimesis as all sorts of representation; it is then the task of further analysis to distinguish among the various ways representation can occur. (69)

Clark devotes much of the chapter to that further analysis as he takes up representation under a very wide range of topics: visual mimesis, descriptive mimesis, narrative mimesis, mimesis as world-building, the mimetic illusion, plausibility and realism, time and space, objects, action, and characters. He ends this way: "An adequate theory of the mimetic aspect has to be able to account for the whole range of relationships between the fictive and the real" (93). In its context, that sentence implies that rhetorical poetics cannot offer—or at least has not yet offered—such an account.

As for the synthetic, in addition to defining it as construction of all kinds, Clark argues, as I noted above, that it is the "infrastructure" of narrative, the necessary substrate on which the mimetic and the thematic are built. As he does with the mimetic, he then identifies a range of subtypes: style and patterns of textual composition, including various kinds of repetition, then links, ring composition, ending with the beginning, anticipations, juxtapositions, character sets, and the broad category of architecture. Clark also finds that my model fails to do justice to the synthetic either because it overlooks or minimizes its role or claims that it is covert when readers can easily recognize it. In this sense, Clark implies that my model does not do well on the tests of comprehensiveness and correspondence. Clark's overall assessment comes through in his summary remarks after his impressive discussion of the various synthetic features in *Emma*: "*Emma* is a realistic novel—in Phelan's terms, a mimetic narrative. It is also synthetic, and many of the synthetic devices are quite overt—and those that are covert, or that are not foregrounded, can be noticed with a little attention" (52).

I find considerable insight in Clark's efforts to develop a descriptive poetics of "the various ways representation can occur," and I'm similarly impressed by his efforts to highlight the importance of style[1] and to identify various patterns of textual composition. I can incorporate much of what he says into rhetorical poetics. Furthermore, in keeping with my stance of welcoming Clark's engagement with the MTS model, I concede that my previous work on both components has not gone far enough. As a first step toward building a better model, I turn to the rhetorical account of audiences and some necessary corrections to Clark's view of that account.

I. AUDIENCES AND THE MIMETIC ILLUSION

In discussing the mimetic illusion, Clark claims that

> Phelan's concept of the mimetic illusion divides the flesh-and-blood reader into two parts, one of which (the authorial audience) knows that the fiction

---

1. One reason I'm pleased about Clark's attention to style is that style was the subject of my first book, *Worlds from Words* (1981). I wrote it before I had proposed an MTS model, but today I can express its argument in terms of that model. For the most part, style is a subordinate synthetic element of fiction, but its degree of subordination—or alternatively, its degree of importance—varies from one fictional narrative to another in relation to the larger mimetic and thematic purposes of each narrative. Furthermore, style can become an object of readerly interest in its own right in parallel with readerly interests in character and event, and it can even become foregrounded to such an extent that it becomes the dominant interest of the narrative.

is a fiction, and one of which (the narrative audience) believes that the fiction is history; thus the flesh-and-blood reader is only half deluded.

The narrative audience is a purely theoretical entity. Its justification presumably is to account for the emotional engagement the reader feels for realistic fiction: "The mimetic component of narrative is responsible for our emotional responses to it, and these responses are a crucial part of the distinctive quality and power of narrative" (Phelan, *Living* 28). There is no reason to believe, however, that in order to have an emotional response to a narrative the reader needs to be deceived into false belief, and there is no reason to suppose that readers have no emotional response to nonrealistic narratives. (66)

Although Clark is typically a good reader of rhetorical theory, he's off-target here. Or perhaps the problem is with the way I've talked about the mimetic or with the way Peter J. Rabinowitz, who did the groundbreaking work, and I have described the rhetorical model of audiences over the years (see Rabinowitz, "Truth in Fiction" and *Before Reading*; Phelan, chapter 6 of *Narrative as Rhetoric*; and both of us in Herman et al.). In any case, let me redescribe the account. First, it is rooted in widely acknowledged experiences of reading fiction. (One way of distinguishing fiction from nonfiction is to note that nonfiction does not construct a narrative audience position.) Flesh-and-blood readers of fiction operate with a *double-consciousness,* simultaneously responding to a character such as Emma Woodhouse as a real person who acts autonomously in her world and knowing that she, like any fictional character, is an artificial construct whose specific traits and behavior are ultimately determined by her author. Furthermore, that tacit knowledge of authorial construction means that the flesh-and-blood reader also assumes that such construction is not random but purposeful. Rhetorical theory accounts for the first part of this response by saying that the flesh-and-blood reader enters the narrative audience, and it accounts for the second part by saying that the flesh-and-blood reader simultaneously enters the authorial audience. As I'll explain, the model has more to say about each audience and its activity, but everything starts from this initial distinction. (Note that this conception of the narrative audience as a role the actual reader takes on distinguishes it from the narratee, the audience, either explicit or implicit, addressed by the narrator.)

Let me emphasize, first, that rather than conceiving of actual readers as divided between the two audiences, this model insists that they simultaneously enter both—and often they do not feel any contradiction between the roles (though authors can shape a wide variety of relations between the two audiences). Furthermore, the experience of reading as a member of the narrative audience is nested within the experience of reading as a member of the authorial audience. Austen wants her audience to respond to Emma as a possible person while retaining an awareness that she is a construct. There's no delusion or deception involved, just the remarkable phenomenon of nested double-consciousness.

Shifting the situation from prose fiction to that of drama can efficiently illustrate the point. When, in the fifth act of a strong performance of *Othello*, the Moor is on the verge of strangling Desdemona, audience members are likely to be feeling pity and fear, and thinking something along the lines of "No, no, Othello, don't, both for Desdemona's sake and your own." Yet they feel no urgency to run onto the stage to stop Othello, and they make no negative ethical judgments of themselves for staying in their seats. The audience's pity and fear are a product of their participation in the narrative audience, and their staying in their seats is a product of their participation in the authorial audience subsuming their experience in the narrative audience. Furthermore, as members of the authorial audience, the spectators implicitly recognize that the emotions they are feeling—and the ones that will be generated once Othello does the deed—are being generated for some authorial purpose(s).

I can best address Clark's last point in the above passage—"there is no reason to suppose that readers have no emotional response to nonrealistic narratives"—within the context provided by his next set of remarks on the narrative audience.

> Even if one grants the existence of a narrative audience, it does not distinguish "mimetic" narratives from "nonmimetic" or "antimimetic" narratives. If the narrative audience stands within the story, it can also stand within a nonrealistic story. If the narrative audience of *Emma* can believe in Emma, then the narrative audience of *Dracula* can believe in Dracula. The same principle applies even to more difficult cases; the narrative audience of Samuel Beckett's *How It Is* would presumably believe in the reality of the characters, including the narrator and Pim. (66)

The correction here is that rhetorical theory does not view the concept of the narrative audience as exclusive to realistic narratives or as the sole means to distinguish between mimetic and nonmimetic or antimimetic narratives. When Clark says, "If the narrative audience of *Emma* can believe in Emma, then the narrative audience of *Dracula* can believe in Dracula," he is singing a stanza of the Rhetorical Theory Theme Song. And his point that actual readers can have emotional responses to nonrealistic narratives is one of the key lines ("Dracula, you make me shudder") in that stanza.

More importantly, I can now draw on these corrections and the rhetorical model of audiences to further develop my conceptions of the mimetic and the synthetic and how they relate to each other. For ease of reference, I restate my definitions:

The mimetic component refers to the results (evident in both textual phenomena and readerly response) of authorial shaping of readerly interests in the narrative's imitations of—or references to—the actual world, including such matters as events following the cause-effect logic of the extratextual world, characters functioning as possible people or being representations of actual people, time and space following the known laws of physics, and so on.

The synthetic component refers, first, to narrative as itself a constructed object—something artificial rather than natural, something fashioned rather than found—including the various elements that go into that construction, and, second, to the results (evident in both textual phenomena and readerly response) of authorial shaping of readerly interests in a narrative as a constructed object.

I start with a fresh look at the mimetic illusion. Recall Clark's summary comment about *Emma*. "*Emma* is a realistic novel—in Phelan's terms, a mimetic narrative. It is also synthetic, and many of the synthetic devices are quite overt—and those that are covert, or that are not foregrounded, can be noticed with a little attention" (52). First, for me, *Emma* is a realistic novel that, like all narratives, involves all three components. As Ralph Rader puts it, *Emma* and other realistic novels work by creating "a focal illusion of characters acting autonomously as if in the world of real experience within a subsidiary awareness *of an underlying constructive authorial purpose which gives their story an implicit significance and affective force which real world experience does not have*" (Rader, *Fact* 206). What Rader calls a "focal illusion" I call the "mimetic illusion," and, again, it arises from the actual audience's double-consciousness.

Furthermore, the mimetic illusion depends on the significant overlap in the beliefs and knowledge of the narrative and authorial audiences. In fact, the only significant difference is that the narrative audience believes that the characters and events are real and the authorial audience knows that they are constructed. Actual readers may not know everything that the authorial audience knows, but Austen constructs a storyworld that conforms closely to the actual world of England in 1815. The pleasures and payoffs of reading *Emma* depend to a great degree on the actual audience buying in to the idea that Austen's inventions are plausible representations of people and events in the actual world, and, thus, that Austen's fiction has a lot to say, both directly and indirectly, about that world.

Constructing and preserving the mimetic illusion does not require Austen to write in a "transparent" style, nor does it require her to hide any of the patterns of textual composition that Clark identifies. She need not hide these synthetic elements precisely because actual, narrative, and authorial audiences always already know that all narrative is constructed. Furthermore, to the extent that Austen's "well-turned sentences" in general and her particular deployments of such devices as "parallel structure, antithesis, and tricolon" contribute to her audience's fine-grained perceptions of her characters and their situations, Austen's style will enhance the mimetic illusion. The same goes for the patterns of textual composition Clark identifies. Furthermore, the authorial audience's awareness of these synthetic aspects of the novel will be one factor in their aesthetic appreciation of it.

Constructing and preserving the mimetic illusion does require Austen to handle the unfolding of the narrative in some ways rather than others. She needs to arrange it so that the answers to questions such as "Why does Emma insult Miss Bates at Box Hill?," "Why does Mr. Knightley rebuke Emma for that insult?," and "Why does Emma respond to Mr. Knightley's rebuke the way she does?" have different but equally plausible answers for the narrative audience and the authorial audience. That is, the answers to those questions need to be some version of "These actions are fully motivated by character and situation" (and thus satisfy the narrative audience) and "These actions serve the underlying mimetic and thematic purposes of the narrative" (and thus satisfy the authorial audience).

Austen would break the mimetic illusion, and, thus, violate the mimetic–synthetic relationship governing the narrative, if her construction undermined the apparent autonomy of the characters and their actions and the close matching of their world with the actual England of 1815. In other words, she would break the illusion by introducing elements to the narrative that would shift the authorial audience's subsidiary awareness of the synthetic to a dominant awareness. Austen could effect such a shift in three main ways: (1) She could introduce significant distance between the beliefs and knowledge of her narrative audience and her authorial audience. For example, if Austen suddenly had Emma's mother visiting from beyond the grave to advise her about, say, not giving her heart to Frank Churchill, and if Austen asked her narrative audience to accept that in this storyworld such events are par for the course, she would opt out of preserving the mimetic illusion. (2) She could flag the break in her narration. For example, when she arrived at volume 3, chapter 7, the chapter now given over to the events at Box Hill, she could have her narrator declare the following: "We have now come to the forty-fifth chapter of this novel, and since I pride myself on never taxing my reader's patience beyond that number, I shall now tell you the fates I have in store for Emma, Mr. Knightley, Harriet, and the various other puppets I have been playing with." (3) She could radically depart from the previously established logic of character and action. For example, she could bring about the engagement between Mr. Knightley and Emma by having him first propose to Harriet and then having Emma respond to the news with an outpouring of her own feelings for him. Both Mr. Knightley's proposal and Emma's response to it would be so far from their apparently autonomous previous actions that they would destroy the illusion of autonomy. In addition, Mr. Knightley's and Emma's—and Austen's—treatments of Harriet in this scenario would run counter to just about everything we've learned about them. To put this point another way, the narrative audience would not be able to answer the question "Why do Mr. Knightley and Emma come to be engaged this way?" with any satisfaction, and the authorial audience's best answer would be something like "Because Austen wanted to exercise her authorial powers."

Of course, not all authors seek to construct and preserve the mimetic illusion. But the relationship between the knowledge and beliefs of the authorial and narrative audiences is an important factor in the relative roles of the mimetic and the synthetic in any fiction, and, thus, I want to say more about how I conceive of both audiences. In a recent essay ("Fictionality, Audiences, and Character," written after Clark wrote his part of this book), I identify two moves that flesh-and-blood reader makes in entering the narrative audience.

1. With a nod to J. K. Rowling, I suggest that the actual reader adopts an Invisibility Cloak and takes up a position within the storyworld from which he or she can perceive (see, hear, etc.) without being perceived. This metaphorical description has the advantage of emphasizing the difference between the narrative audience as a role that the actual reader takes on and the narratee as the audience, characterized or not, addressed by the narrator. At the same time, of course, the reader under the Invisibility Cloak does not have the freedom of movement of Harry Potter under his Cloak, but instead is restricted to the author's presentation of some scenes and events rather than others.

2. Once in that observer position, the narrative audience adopts the normative beliefs and attitudes of that storyworld. For example, the narrative audience of *Dracula* believes in the reality of vampires, and the narrative audience of Rowling's Harry Potter novels believes that the world population can be divided into those with powers to do magic (wizards and witches) and those without such powers (muggles). Entering the narrative audience provides one basis for readers' affective responses to fiction, but, as I'll explain when I discuss the thematic in *Emma* below, it is not the only basis.

The authorial audience in fiction retains the awareness that the characters and events are synthetic constructs. The authorial audience in fiction also has a particular relation to the author's beliefs, knowledge, and ethical values. Sometimes an author will posit an authorial audience who shares her beliefs, knowledge, and values and then rely on that shared position in her representations of the characters and events. The dictum "Show, don't tell" is based in part on such an author–authorial audience relationship. But at other times, an author will posit an authorial audience that initially does not share one or more of her significant beliefs or values and will then use the narrative to move the audience to share her positions. See my discussion of *Wuthering Heights* below for an exemplary case. In addition, the authorial audience, though ultimately a hypothetical entity, is the author's projection of who her readers are and what they need to know to understand the narrative. This projection is typically based in the author's knowledge of actual readers.[2]

To introduce an example I'll soon do more with, if an author creates ghosts as characters in her narrative, that author may posit an audience that believes in ghosts or one that doesn't, especially since some actual readers believe and some don't. If as actual reader I believe in ghosts and the authorial audience does not (or if I don't believe in ghosts and the authorial audience does), then I will have trouble entering the authorial audience until I align my beliefs with theirs, if only for the duration of my reading experience. Once I finish, I may then find it profitable to talk back to the author about our different beliefs. The larger point here is that rhetorical reading involves a two-step process for actual readers: (1) trying to enter the authorial and narrative audiences and (2) evaluating the consequences of those efforts. For my immediate purposes of explicating mimetic–synthetic relationships and interactions, I will focus on step 1. Once I move to discuss the thematic, I will say more about step 2.

---

2. Some commentators on rhetorical theory focus on the idea that the authorial audience is an ideal reader who has the knowledge and interpretive skill to read the narrative "correctly," and then object when fallible rhetorical critics claim to know what the authorial audience does. Let me be clear that any such statements about the activity of the authorial audience I make here should be taken as hypotheses similar to the interpretive claims Clark—or any other critic—makes in his commentary on a narrative. In other words, I know I could be wrong and I'm open to learning from other critics. But that fallibility in the interpretation of the actual audience does not undercut the utility of the concept. In any case, in this dialogue with Clark, I am at least as concerned with the authorial audience's knowledge of and beliefs about storyworlds as with my hypotheses about the audience's interpretations. For a related discussion, see the special issue of *Style* (52 [2018], 1–2), which includes my essay "Authors, Resources, Audiences: Toward a Rhetorical Poetics of Narrative," twenty-four responses to that essay (including one by Clark), and my comments on those responses. Especially relevant are the exchanges I have with Jan Alber, Gerald Prince, and Emma Kafalenos.

II. A RHETORICAL VIEW OF THE UNNATURAL: GHOSTS AND MORE

These conceptions of the two audiences point to the possibility of a wide range of relationships between their respective knowledge and beliefs. Furthermore, the greater the distance between those two sets of knowledge and beliefs, the more likely the synthetic will become prominent.[3] Just as important, attending to these varied relations between the audiences makes the concepts of both the mimetic and the synthetic dynamic rather than static. That is, different relationships among the audiences can make the same phenomenon mimetic in one narrative and antimimetic/unnatural or synthetic in another.

Consider, for example, the difference between the two dominant readings of the ghosts in Henry James's *The Turn of the Screw*. In the first reading, which sees it as a traditional ghost story, the ghosts of Peter Quint and Miss Jessel are real, and the governess tells the tale of her heroic combat against them. In the second reading, the ghosts are her hallucinations, and she unwittingly tells the tale of the multiple negative consequences of her psychological breakdown. In this sense, James writes a realist novella. Clark would say that as representations, the ghosts in both readings fall under his category of the mimetic. The difference is that in the first reading, the mimetic extends to the nonrealistic ghosts, and in the second, it does not, because they are psychologically realistic hallucinations. Clark could of course flesh out these broad observations with more fine-grained analyses of the different kinds of mimesis he identifies. And he could complement this work by looking at James's style and the various other patterns underlying his composition of the novella. The results, I believe, would offer us genuine insight into both readings. But I believe the rhetorical approach through audiences provides an account of the two readings and of the differences between them that better meets the criterion of correspondence.

In the reading that the governess saw the ghosts, the narrative audience believes in ghosts and the authorial audience does not. Actual readers who take this option experience pleasure and satisfaction by simultaneously adopting the narrative audience's belief and tacitly sharing the belief of James and his audience that there are no actual ghosts. The pleasure and satisfaction, in other words, arise from exercising the license to believe within the safety of knowing that the actual world does not grant such license. In this experience, James's authorial audience has a dual awareness of the mimetic—the govern-

---

3. The relationships of these different audiences to the ethical and political values of the narrator and of the implied author are also worthy of attention, but these relationships are more relevant to the thematic than the mimetic component, so I'll discuss them in that section.

ess, her charges, and her challenges—and the synthetic, those ghosts (and James's style and his framing of the tale and so on). Both interests feed into James's thematizing of the governess's commitment and courage as she gamely tries to defend the children from the ghosts.

If we opt for the hallucination reading, as so many readers have since Edmund Wilson first proposed it in 1934, then we of course posit an authorial audience that does not believe in ghosts, but we have two possible narrative audiences, each of which provides the basis for a distinctive experience. In one variant, the narrative audience believes in ghosts but does not believe that the governess provides sufficient evidence that the ghosts of Quint and Jessel have actually appeared at Bly. This reading, in effect, contends that the narrative audience shares the view of Wilson and his followers that there's a psychological cause for the governess's belief that she sees the ghosts. The reading also contends that James, whose writings indicate that he took the idea of ghosts seriously, does enough to give the narrative audience a belief in their possibility.[4] Within this reading, much of the power of the tale stems from the possibility that for the narrative audience, the governess *could* have been right. The governess's story—what happens to her and especially to Miles—is so poignant precisely because she is wrong but she didn't have to be. The authorial audience's relative degrees of interest in the mimetic and synthetic components are similar to those in the ghosts-are-real version, but, of course, the specifics of the governess's mimetic component of character are radically different: She is not psychologically healthy and courageous but unstable and deluded. Consequently, the specifics of the thematic component also change, as James guides the audience to reflect on the issues—of gender, desire, repression, and others—that underlie the governess's hallucinations.

---

4. In the preface to the 1908 New York edition, James indicates that he believes in ghosts, while also indicating that his ghost story does not aspire to be mimetically accurate about them:

> Recorded and attested "ghosts" are in other words as little expressive, as little dramatic, above all as little continuous and conscious and responsive, as is consistent with their taking the trouble—and an immense trouble they find it, we gather—to appear at all. Wonderful and interesting therefore at a given moment, they are inconceivable figures in an <u>action</u>—and *The Turn of the Screw* was an action, desperately, or it was nothing. I had to decide in fine between having my apparitions correct and having my story "good"—that is producing my impression of the dreadful, my designated horror. Good ghosts, speaking by book, make poor subjects, and it was clear that from the first my hovering prowling blighting presences, my pair of abnormal agents, would have to depart altogether from the rules. They would be agents <u>in fact</u>; there would be laid on them the dire duty of causing the situation to reek with an air of Evil. Their desire and their ability to do so, visibly measuring meanwhile their effect, together with their observed and described success—this was exactly my central idea; so that, briefly, I cast my lot with pure romance, the appearances conforming to the true type being so little romantic. (230–31)

In the second variant, neither the authorial nor the narrative audience believes in ghosts. In this reading, the power of the narrative resides in the judgments and emotions attendant upon the governess's slow evolution into the frightening condition in which her repressed desires for her distant employer lead to her hallucinations—and to the disastrous consequences for Miles and Flora. In this view, James is working with his special version of the mimetic illusion, as the novella shifts from being a traditional ghost story to a study in psychological realism, with the mimetic dominant and the synthetic subordinate. The thematic component remains prominent even as the story puts a darker spin on the general issues explored in the version in which ghosts exist but the governess hallucinates Quint and Jessel.

Now, I would not claim that Clark's model would prevent him from seeing these two possible hallucination readings, because he is too good a practical critic. I will say, however, that his text-centric approach to the mimetic, with its focus on "representation of all kinds," makes it less likely for its practitioner to see both. Because the rhetorical approach, by contrast, explicitly raises questions about the beliefs and knowledge of the different audiences, its practitioner is more likely to see both. These issues aside, again my larger case is that the rhetorical approach to the relation between the mimetic and synthetic via the rhetorical model of audiences offers a more precise account of James's novella and the various mimetic–synthetic relationships its ambiguity gives rise to.

Lest Clark or others object that James's ambiguity makes *The Turn of the Screw* an anomalous rather than a representative case, let me step back and consider the broader issue of ghosts in fictional narrative. Are they mimetic or antimimetic? If we just measure the textual representation against most Western readers' beliefs about the actual world, then the answer is obvious: Ghosts are antimimetic. But, of course, as I noted above, some Western readers do believe in ghosts. And some writers of fiction believe in ghosts and some do not. So how do we adjudicate their status? I submit that rhetorical theory's approach through audience leads to an appropriately layered answer: Ghosts can be either mimetic or antimimetic depending on how the author constructs the relationship among the authorial and narrative audiences, and especially depending on whether she constructs an authorial audience that believes in ghosts. In step 2 of rhetorical reading, actual readers can then either adopt or resist the beliefs of the authorial audience and explore the consequences of doing either. More generally, I see four main options:

1. An author can construct narrative and authorial audiences that believe in ghosts; in such a construction, the ghosts would be mimetic characters

with spectral rather than bodily form. I suggest below that Emily Brontë works with a version of this option in *Wuthering Heights*.
2. An author can construct narrative and authorial audiences that don't believe in ghosts; in such a construction, the ghosts would be figments of a mimetic character's imagination, and thus signs of that character's delusions. This option is realized in the second variant of the reading that "the governess hallucinates the ghosts" in *The Turn of the Screw*.
3. An author can also construct narrative audiences that believe and authorial audiences that do not; in such a construction, the ghosts would be antimimetic. This option is realized in the "governess actually sees the ghosts" reading of *The Turn* as well as in standard ghost stories. I will suggest below that Toni Morrison works with a very different version of this option in *Beloved*.
4. An author can construct a narrative audience that does not believe in ghosts and an authorial audience that does; in such a construction, the ghosts would ultimately be mimetic.[5] I am not aware of an author who constructs this relationship between the two audiences, but that doesn't mean someone hasn't done it—or will do it in the future.

Let me give some additional texture to these theoretical points by saying more about the ghosts in *Wuthering Heights* and *Beloved*.

Brontë's narrative project is to engage her audience in her exploration of the origin, evolution, trials and tribulations, and eventual resolution of the remarkable relationship between Catherine and Heathcliff. Using Lockwood's and Nelly Dean's often unreliable interpreting and evaluating of what they report, Brontë depicts the depth and strangeness of that relationship, and how it violently disrupted both the Earnshaw and the Linton families until its resolution—Heathcliff's realization that he could meaningfully reunite with Catherine in the afterlife—also facilitated a new, positive integration of those families. Brontë's innovation is to arrange the narrative progression so that it *alters* the beliefs of both audiences about ghosts. She starts by constructing both audiences as nonbelievers by having Lockwood narrate what appears to be his very vivid *nightmare* about Catherine trying to enter his room at Thrushcross Grange. By the end of the novel, however, Brontë has used numerous strategies to convince the narrative audience that the deceased

---

5. I can readily imagine a narrative in which the authorial audience believes in ghosts and the narratee—the person(s) addressed by the narrator—does not. Furthermore, I can imagine that the progression of the narrative would include the narratee's either coming to believe in ghosts or being thoroughly discredited. But in such a case, the narrative audience would be standing with the believing authorial audience.

Catherine and Heathcliff walk the moors, despite Nelly's and Lockwood's beliefs that such a thing is impossible. In a sense, then, Brontë directs her narrative audience to accept a Catherine-and-Heathcliff exceptionality thesis—unlike other mortals, they have an existence in this world after death. Once convinced, Brontë's narrative audience reinterprets Lockwood's nightmare as an actual encounter with Catherine's ghost, and, thus, as additional evidence of her life beyond death—and something that fuels Heathcliff's own belief that she is not confined to her grave. Even more radically, Brontë uses the narrative audience's conversion—and her representation of the Catherine–Heathcliff relationship—as the basis for the authorial audience to take seriously the possibility that a love like theirs could continue beyond the grave. In other words, through the nesting of the audiences and the progression of the narrative audience's movement from nonbelief to belief, Brontë invites her authorial audience to buy into the possibility that the exceptionality thesis could apply in the actual world. (Of course, the authorial audience never believes that Catherine and Heathcliff actually walk the moors because the authorial audience retains its subsidiary awareness that they are fictional characters.)

In this way, Brontë challenges her audience to accept a more expansive conception of the mimetic, a move that has ripple effects on the synthetic and thematic components of their interest. While the authorial audience remains aware of some foregrounding of the synthetic in the novel's fascination with ghosts, that awareness has different consequences than it does in the readings of *The Turn of the Screw* in which the narrative audience believes in ghosts. In those variants, the authorial audience never wavers in its nonbelief, whereas the appeal of *Wuthering Heights* depends to a large degree on Brontë's ability to persuade the authorial audience to move from nonbelief to belief—or at least to much looser attachment to the nonbelief. At the same time, Brontë's handling of the mimetic–synthetic relationship moves the multiple thematic issues about love, hate, desire, and reconciliation touched on in the progression into a prominent place in the authorial audience's interest. As always, actual audiences may or may not buy into the authorial audience position, but I point to the long history of readers testifying about the peculiar power of the novel as evidence that many do buy in.

Morrison works with still another narrative audience–authorial audience relationship, which in turn sets up yet another kind of interrelationship between the novel's mimetic and synthetic components. Morrison's project is to write a historical novel that draws on the tradition of slave narratives even as it insists on the ongoing effects of slavery in the US. In the service of these ends, she incorporates or relies on the relevance of considerable nonfictionality. She situates the action of the novel in plausible fictional settings within nonfictional places (Sweet Home plantation in Kentucky, 124 Bluestone Rd., Cincinnati, Ohio). She also relies on both her narrative and authorial audiences to be knowledgeable about such historical events as the Civil War, the Emancipation Proclamation, and the Fugitive Slave Act, which gave slave owners the right to hunt down and re-enslave any slaves who escaped from bondage. Morrison then asks the narrative and authorial audiences to draw on this knowledge to understand the significant differences in cultural context surrounding the events of the two main time frames of the novel, 1855 and 1873. In pre–Civil War 1855, Sethe escapes from Sweet Home to Cincinnati but is pursued by her owner's slave catchers. In post–Civil War 1873, the time of the novel's primary narrative, Sethe lives with the consequences of her 1855 decision to kill her infant rather than have her grow up as a slave. In these ways, Morrison directs her audience to develop a deep interest in her novel's mimetic component.

Yet, at the center of this thoroughly historical novel, Morrison positions a character whose synthetic component she foregrounds for the authorial audience: Beloved, who has multiple incompatible identities, one of which is Sethe's "murdered daughter brought back to life." Furthermore, Morrison makes Beloved's ghostly presence part of the novel's donné. Morrison's first paragraph, set shortly after the Civil War, refers to years of ghostly activities at 124 Bluestone Rd. The middle of the narrative includes multiple events signifying the supernatural powers of a now-embodied Beloved, and the last chapter includes cryptic references to her continued presence in the present time of the narration (1987). In addition, Morrison gives Beloved a plausible identity as an escapee from the house of a recently deceased white man who had kept her in captivity, and as a representative of the slaves who lost their lives in the Middle Passage.

In previous work (*Narrative as Rhetoric*, chapter 10), I have identified Morrison's construction of Beloved as an instance of the stubborn, by which I mean a recalcitrant textual phenomenon designed not to yield to readers' efforts at overcoming its recalcitrance. Furthermore, I have argued that readerly engagement with Beloved's stubbornness—the ongoing but ultimately unsuccessful effort to achieve interpretive mastery of her character—is a central source of the novel's power. I now add that Morrison designs Beloved's stubbornness so that it is experienced by both her narrative and authorial audiences—and that each audience does something different with that experience. The narrative audience both buys into the reality of Beloved and comes to accept her ultimate unknowability. Recognizing the multiple facets of her identity, the narrative audience is unable to make them cohere into a larger intelligible whole and so comes away with a sense of Beloved as a fascinating enigma. The authorial audience responds to Beloved's stubbornness as a consequence of her synthetic construction, and, indeed, a signal that Morrison wants to foreground her synthetic and thematic components. For the authorial audience, the thoroughly synthetic Beloved becomes a rich thematic metaphor of the African American slave experience. Morrison directs her audience to recognize the metaphor's applications to multiple aspects of that experience, from the Middle Passage to the way it continues to haunt the whole nation. The novel's power lies in Morrison's ability to make Beloved simultaneously such a vivid and difficult presence for her narrative audience and such a powerful metaphor for the authorial audience. The novel's power also lies in Morrison's ability to engage both narrative and authorial audiences in the historical realities that provide the context for the experiences of all the characters, including Beloved.

This approach to ghosts indicates how rhetorical poetics would integrate the unnatural more generally. Faced with the questions, Is it unnatural? and What difference does the unnaturalness make?, the rhetorical theorist would follow these guidelines in answering.

1. An element of a narrative will be unnatural if the author invites her authorial audience to take it as such, and that invitation will entail a gap between the narrative audience's belief in the naturalness of the element and the authorial audience's belief in its unnaturalness. (This step does not of course guarantee that actual audiences will accept the invitation.)
2. The degree of unnaturalness will depend on the degree of distance between the beliefs and knowledge of the authorial audience and those of the narrative audience. In Western culture, a belief in ghosts is less radical than, say, a belief that a character can be in multiple places at the same time.
3. The overall effect of the unnatural element(s) on the mimetic–synthetic relationship in the narrative will depend on how it/they relate(s) to all the other elements of the narrative.

These guidelines indicate that the mimetic–synthetic–thematic relationships can vary widely in unnatural narrative. To add further support both to this point and to my claim that rhetorical poetics is well equipped to deal with that variation, I'll briefly consider two additional examples, Martin Amis's *Time's Arrow* and Julio Cortázar's "Continuity of Parks." In *Time's Arrow,* Amis foregrounds the unnatural right from the start, but he ultimately uses it in the service of his more dominant mimetic and thematic ends. In "Continuity of

Parks," Cortázar does not introduce the unnatural until the very end of his story, but its arrival radically transforms the whole into a narrative that makes the synthetic and thematic dominant.

Richardson and Alber both cite Amis's novel as an exemplary case of unnatural temporality because of its technique of backwards narration, one type of what Richardson calls antinomic narration ("Beyond Story" 49): Amis's unnamed character narrator (though for convenience's sake, critics typically refer to him as "Soul") experiences time's arrow as moving backward rather than forward. Thus, he narrates from the moment of his death back toward the moment of his birth. The unnatural technique has multiple consequences, including its reversal of the standard relation between causes and effects. Doctors don't heal wounds but inflict them, for example. But attention to audience highlights the way Amis's use of the technique allies it very closely with a mimetic representation of time. As the narrative audience accepts the reversal of time's arrow, the authorial and actual audiences reconstruct the normal, forward movement of time. Furthermore, as the narrative unfolds, the actual audience gets more accustomed to doing the conversion. The technique is clearly unnatural, but its simple reversal of temporal order connects it closely to natural temporality.

In addition, the key events of *Time's Arrow* are historical ones. Soul is the dissociated self of a fictional Nazi doctor, Odilo Unverdorben, who worked at Auschwitz, and the scenes there refer to such historical figures as Josef Mengele and Eduard Wirths. By using the backwards narration to represent the mass killings as mass resurrections, Amis defamiliarizes the genocide of the Holocaust in a way that makes it even more horrific. At the same time, Amis's handling of the unnatural temporality dramatically demonstrates his thematic point that doctors could participate in the genocide only by radically compartmentalizing that activity. In short, Amis's foregrounding of the synthetic in the backwards narration does not in itself make the synthetic component of *Time's Arrow* dominant. Instead, Amis ultimately marshals it in service to his more dominant mimetic and thematic ends.[6]

In "Continuity of Parks," Cortázar's unnamed protagonist, seated in a green velvet armchair with his back to the door of his study, resumes reading a favorite novel. Cortázar's narrator recounts the final stages of that novel's plot. Two lovers, a man and a woman, meet to review and then carry out their own plot against "another body it was necessary to destroy." The lovers part, with the woman heading north and the man, armed with a knife, entering a

---

6. See *Somebody Telling Somebody Else* for a more thorough discussion of Amis's technique and its relation to questions of reliable and unreliable narration.

house to carry out the deed. The narration tracks the man's movements until the story's end:

> Through the blood galloping in his ears came the woman's words: first a blue parlor, then a gallery, then a carpeted stairway. At the top, two doors. No one in the first bedroom, no one in the second. The door of the salon, and then the knife in his hand, the light from the great windows, the high back of an armchair covered in green velvet, the head of the man in the chair reading a novel. (65)

The standard way to analyze the story is by reference to the concept of ontological metalepsis, a sure sign of the unnatural. Cortázar's ending is effectively shocking because it breaks the seemingly secure ontological boundary between two distinct storyworlds, that of Cortázar's protagonist and that of the novel he is reading (see Cohn). That analysis is very good as far as it goes, but I think rhetorical poetics can take us even further. Cortázar's ending is effectively shocking because of how it transforms the relationships between the narrative and authorial audiences and ultimately between Cortázar and his authorial audience. Cortázar uses those transformations to radically reconfigure the relation between the mimetic and the synthetic components of the story and to add a significant new dimension to the thematic component.

Cortázar initially constructs nested mimetic illusions. The narrative audience believes in the autonomy of the protagonist in the armchair returning to his favorite book, while the authorial audience retains the subsidiary awareness that he is a character in Cortázar's fiction. That protagonist then enters into his own mimetic illusion. Indeed, Cortázar's description could serve as an epigraph in a treatise on double-consciousness:

> Without effort his memory retained the names and images of the protagonists; the illusion took hold of him almost at once. He tasted the almost perverse pleasure of disengaging himself line by line from all that surrounded him, and feeling at the same time that his head was relaxing comfortably against the green velvet of the armchair with its high back. (63–64)

Then, by gradually shifting from narration that summarizes what the protagonist reads ("a lustful yearning dialogue raced down the pages like a rivulet of snakes") to narration that could plausibly be in the book he is reading (e.g., those last sentences—"No one in the first room," etc.), Cortázar blurs the line between the two mimetic illusions. That blurring sets up the ontological metalepsis, even as that metalepsis destroys both mimetic illusions—albeit in radically different ways. For Cortázar's protagonist, the illusion gets replaced with the grim reality that the man with the knife is about to strike. For Cortázar's narrative audience, the belief that normal ontological boundaries apply in this storyworld suddenly gets replaced by the belief that such ontological border crossings are possible. Thus, safe under its Invisibility Cloak, the narrative audience watches in horror as the murderer approaches the protagonist. For Cortázar's authorial audience, the illusion that the storyworld imitates the actual world gets shattered, which in turn suddenly opens up a huge gap between its knowledge and beliefs and those of the narrative audience. By introducing this gap, Cortázar shifts the dominant mode of the story from mimetic to synthetic. In making this shift, he also thematizes both the power and the flimsiness of the mimetic illusion. In other words, he takes the infrastructure of the story and makes it part of the superstructure. In addition, Cortázar foregrounds his own relationship with his audience and makes it a central focus of the reading experience. It's as if he says, "Look, reader, what we can do together, if you follow my lead, because we both love the mimetic illusion—and are aware of its fragility."

III. THE MIMETIC COMPONENT OF *1984*

Lest Clark and others feel that my efforts to meet the challenge of demonstrating how rhetorical theory can integrate the unnatural have led me to neglect his more detailed discussions of his examples, I turn to his analysis of the mimetic component of Orwell's *1984*. I focus on two passages from his commentary, the first about time, the second his concluding paragraph. As part of his longer discussion of time, Clark moves toward a meta-commentary (I have not included his footnotes because I do not comment on them).

> The connection between the past, the present, and the future has been important in Winston's thinking from the very beginning of the novel: "How could you communicate with the future? Either the future would resemble the present, in which case it would not listen to him, or it would be different from it, and his predicament would be meaningless" (7). "He wondered again for whom he was writing the diary. For the future, for the past—for an age that might be imaginary" (20). Can a similar question be applied to the narrative situation of the novel? For whom—past, present, or future—is Orwell writing? Either the readers' world would resemble the world of the story, in which case they would not listen, or it would be different, and Winston's predicament would be meaningless. And yet Orwell's project is pos-

sible only if one world can communicate with another world about another possible world. Mimesis implies and perhaps requires difference. (92)

Here's Clark's conclusion (again minus a footnote):

1984 sits somewhat uneasily in Phelan's conception of the mimetic. The characters, including Winston, are thin, inconsistent, and implausible. Their behavior is often determined by the needs of the plot, and events are often coincidental. It is a fantasy, even if it borrows some of the techniques of the realistic novel. It is the kind of fantasy that builds an unreal world and then demands that we compare that world to our own. Perhaps all fantasies ask for this comparison; perhaps realistic fictions do so as well. Each narrative builds its own relationship to reality, its own mimesis. An adequate theory of the mimetic aspect has to be able to account for the whole range of relationships between the fictive and the real. (93)

I start with a clarification. I view *1984* as a novel whose thematic component, not its mimetic component, is dominant. Within this conception of the novel, I find Clark's comments on time good as far as they go but want to subsume them into a broader conception of Orwell's construction of and relation to his audiences. Orwell writes for an authorial audience that recognizes how he has deployed both mimetic and synthetic elements of the novel in the service of his thematic-dominant purpose of issuing an indictment of and a warning about totalitarianism. Orwell invites that audience to recognize how his inventions of a new world order with new nation-states and new technologies are fictional extrapolations from the actual world order of 1949, the year of the novel's publication. More than that, Orwell invites his narrative audience to don an Invisibility Cloak in that storyworld and closely observe the experience of Winston Smith, who follows a trajectory from suspicion of the state and its totalitarianism to rebellion against it to loving it. Because the trajectory is determined by Orwell's thematic purposes, Winston Smith and the other characters are not as richly realized possible people as, say, Emma Woodhouse and countless others in the realistic tradition. Nevertheless, Orwell shapes his authorial audience's interest in the trajectory of Winston's experience along mimetic as well as thematic lines. Winston's thoughts and behavior are well grounded in a plausible psychology attached to standard human desires, including those activated in his relationship with Julia, that are thwarted by the state. As I argue in *Reading People, Reading Plots*, Orwell's ending is so effective precisely because it relies on internal focalization, the dominant technique in 1949 for mimetic representation of consciousness, even as that representation reveals how the state has effectively colonized Winston's mind:

> He gazed up at the enormous face. Forty years it had taken him to learn what kind of smile was hidden beneath the dark moustache. O cruel, needless misunderstanding! O stubborn, self-willed exile from the loving breast! Two gin-scented tears trickled down the sides of his nose. But it was all right, everything was all right, the struggle was finished. He had won the victory over himself. He loved Big Brother. (197)

Thus, Orwell is writing for his present audience in 1949 and for future readers, using his combination of the mimetic, thematic, and synthetic components to send his warning about totalitarianism. He relies on his audiences to recognize both the difference between their world and Winston's and the trends in their world that point to the possibility of their world turning into something like Winston's. Orwell's capacity to think rhetorically about his current and future readers is one reason why the novel has increased in popularity in the age of Donald J. Trump.

CHAPTER 6

The Thematic and the Relation between Comprehensiveness and Correspondence

JAMES PHELAN

I BEGIN with a brief reminder of our respective definitions. For Clark, "*Thematic analysis concerns all kinds of meaning imparted by or derived from a text, direct and indirect, intended by the author or not*" (11). For me, *the thematic component refers to the results (evident in both textual phenomena and readerly response) of authorial shaping of readerly interests in the ideational, ethical, and ideological dimensions of the narrative.* Authors reveal these dimensions through a wide range of strategies that often work together; these strategies include the arrangement of sequences of action, explicit generalizations about the nature of the world by narrators or characters, and characters functioning as representatives of larger groups or embodiments of ideas.

Clark's conception of the thematic follows from his text-centric approach invested in as much coverage of narrative territory as possible. From that perspective, he finds the rhetorical approach too limited, because it does not take a sufficiently expansive view of the thematic (it is not sufficiently comprehensive) and because it has a tendency toward allegorizing (it doesn't do well with the criterion of correspondence). I will address the first concern by offering my reflections on the internal logic of Clark's expansive view and will address the second one when I discuss the rhetorical alternative. In my view, Clark's focus on comprehensiveness with the thematic leads him to sacrifice correspondence.

Clark's expansive view leads him to three basic categories of the thematic, each connected to a different feature of textual composition. (1) The thematic as the local, atomistic meaning of words and sentences. Clark's definition implies that every word and every sentence in a narrative is an aspect of its thematic component. (2) The thematic as a particular topic or subject matter. In discussing the *Iliad*, for example, he touches on the themes of *menis*, of the relationship of the gods to the mortals, of death, and of violence. (3) The thematic as one of five general (and disparate) kinds of meaning: meaning as the experience of reading, meaning as paraphrasable argument, structural meaning, allegorical meaning, and ideological meaning.

I. LIMITATIONS OF CLARK'S ACCOUNT

As with his discussions of the mimetic and the synthetic, Clark's commentary is insightful. Each subsection of the chapter offers perceptive analysis of its topics and of the texts he discusses, and his comparison/contrast between the thematic components of the *Iliad* and the *Odyssey* is one of the highlights of his analysis.[1] In addition, some of his general observations are astute, such as the point that readers don't have to choose between narrative fictions that offer opposed positions on particular issues. Nevertheless, I find that Clark's commitment to coverage and to the equivalence between meaning and the thematic leads him to flatten out or otherwise misrepresent the diverse phenomena that he includes under the thematic and to engage in some strained or relatively unpersuasive interpretive analyses.

Consider Clark's first category: words and sentences. While everyone would agree that they have meaning, focusing on this truism obscures the significant differences in the functions of those words and sentences. Sometimes words and sentences have deictic functions, sometimes they orient audiences in time and/or space, sometimes they describe people, places, or things, sometimes they report actions, sometimes they interpret those actions, sometimes they express ethical judgments, sometimes they ask questions, sometimes they give commands, sometimes they make explicit philosophical pronouncements, and on and on. In short, words and sentences in narrative can perform all the functions that they do outside of narrative, and I doubt whether Clark would label all those functions ("Hey, Matthew, it's Jim") thematic. Labeling all those functions

---

1. While I know the *Iliad* and the *Odyssey* well enough to be impressed by Clark's discussions of them, I lack both the necessary expertise and hubris to offer any competing commentary on them.

thematic gives them an equivalence that depends on a radical reduction of their differences, or, to put it another way, it stretches the term "thematic" beyond its breaking point.

Fortunately, Clark does not go too far astray in his practical criticism because he does not consistently follow through on this claim and because he pays more attention to the ways that narratives gradually develop their thematic components. Even so, there's often an unfortunate wobbling in his commentary that stems from his theoretical commitment. Consider, for example, this passage:

> The first sentence of *Emma*, for example, *certainly has meaning*:
>
>> Emma Woodhouse, handsome, clever, and rich, with a comfortable home and happy disposition, seemed to unite some of the best blessings of existence, and had lived nearly twenty-one years in the world with very little to distress or vex her.
>
> The reader has been primed by the title to expect that Emma will be the central character of the story and thus also primed to pay special attention to this first characterization. The sentence means what it says, but it also has a tone: "Seemed" is a sort of warning, and "nearly twenty-one years" adds a note of amused irony. This tone is part of the meaning of the sentence.
>
> *When Emma's attributes are first mentioned, they function mimetically; as the story progresses,* they are thematized by repetition and emphasis. (103; my emphasis)

The wobble here comes from the "meaning of meaning" in a context in which the thematic is equivalent to "meaning of all kinds." In this context, when Clark says the first sentence certainly has meaning, the claim entails that it has thematic meaning. But Clark's initial commentary does not follow through on that claim. Instead, it focuses on expectations and the effect of the tone. Furthermore, Clark acknowledges that (1) the words "handsome, clever, and rich" initially function mimetically and (2) they eventually become thematized by the narrative progression. Both acknowledgments create space between the "meanings" of the words and their thematic functions. Clark could eliminate some of the wobble in the analysis by simply quoting *Emma*'s first sentence and going right to the last sentence I quote here. But he wouldn't eliminate it entirely since the gap between initial (mimetic) meaning and eventual (thematic) meaning would remain.

Clark's last sentence here moves him into considering the second category of meaning, the topic and subject matters addressed by a narrative. And with this second category, I find that we have much in common: the specifics of a narrative's thematic component emerge as the narrative itself develops. Indeed, in my rhetorical view, I explicitly tie both the emergence and development of the thematic to the narrative progression. For me, Clark's "repetition and emphasis" are aids in thematizing, but I would add that beyond these verbal matters, authors use patterns of action as mechanisms for thematizing. See, for example, my discussion of Henry James's "The Beast in the Jungle" in *Reading People, Reading Plots*.

Clark's equivalence of meaning and the thematic also leads to some theoretical problems in his treatment of his third category, the broad types of thematic meaning. The problems arise in his discussions of "meaning as the experience of reading" and "structural meaning." The first remains at best a fuzzy category, defined more by what it is not than what it is, and the second involves mistaking a means of conveying the thematic for the thematic itself. Here's Clark's substantive discussion of meaning as an experience of reading:

> [Miss Bates's monologues] *are part of the total experience of the novel, and thus part of the total meaning.* Here is a short selection from Miss Bates's monologue at the ball:
>
>> "Jane, Jane, my dear Jane, where are you?—Here is your tippet. Mrs. Weston begs you to put on your tippet. She says she is afraid there will be draughts in the passage, though every thing has been done—One door nailed up—Quantities of matting.—My dear Jane, indeed you must. Mr. Churchill, oh! You are too obliging! . . .
>>
>> . . . .
>>
>> "Well, where shall we sit? where shall we sit? Any where, so that Jane is not in a draught. Where *I* sit is of no consequence. Oh! do you recommend this side?—Well, I am sure, Mr. Churchill—only it seems too good—but just as you please." (226–27)
>
> At times Austen, always an economical writer, uses these passages to drop little hints for the attentive reader—perhaps on a second reading. Here, for example, we see that Frank Churchill is paying special attention to Jane's comfort. And of course Emma's unsympathetic reaction to Miss Bates's tiresome chatter becomes one of the pivotal elements in the plot. These monologues contribute to larger themes, but they also provide plea-

sure in themselves. Their meaning is an experience of reading rather than a paraphrasable argument. (104; my emphasis)

Again we run into the problem of the "meaning of meaning" when meaning equals the thematic. Here the problem takes the form of circular argument. Experience is meaningful, so it must be thematic. But just how are Miss Bates's monologues thematic? They provide pleasure, they drop hints about characters, and one shows up in the crucial scene at Box Hill. (In the MTS model, the first function would follow from Austen's handling of Miss Bates's mimetic component and the other two would be part of the character's synthetic component.) Why are such functions thematic? Because they have meaning and anything that has meaning is thematic. They're obviously different from such paraphrasable arguments or, indeed, straightforward claims as we get in such statements from the narrator as "Seldom, very seldom, does complete truth belong to any human disclosure; seldom can it happen that something is not a little disguised or a little mistaken," so Clark needs a new label for them. Hence the category "meaning as the experience of reading." But Clark's circular reasoning means that the category doesn't really illuminate the thematic function of the monologues.

The problem with Clark's category of structural meaning is that according to his own logic, he should have located it in the domain of the synthetic. In this respect, it's a small problem in the overall coherence of his model, one that he could easily correct by eliminating the category from the domain of the thematic. In fact, he discusses the same parallel scenes from *1984*—scenes depicting Winston Smith in the Chestnut Tree Café—as an example of both structural meaning and of the synthetic category of "repeated events." The structural parallel is part of the synthetic component because Orwell is not making any thematic point about parallel structure but instead using it to make thematic points about the power of the totalitarian state. Clark works with such an expansive view of the thematic that it seems almost natural for it to encroach upon the synthetic.

II. THE RHETORICAL VIEW OF THE THEMATIC

In explicating the rhetorical view, I start by reiterating what I initially said about the project of rhetorical poetics.

I conceive of narrative as rhetoric not only because I believe it is one viable way of understanding the remarkable phenomenon of storytelling, but also because I believe it captures something significant about why we humans have invented narrative: to come to terms with one or more aspects of what Heidegger called our "thrownness," our finding ourselves in the world and needing to cope with our condition. That coming to terms can itself take multiple forms in relation to multiple purposes. And that coming to terms can occur across the modes of fiction and nonfiction, even as those modes can influence the effort to come to terms.

Authors of both fictional and nonfictional narratives engage with and seek to intervene in the actual world in some way. One consistent layer of their engagements and interventions involves engaging with ideational, ideological, and/or ethical matters that relate to the world beyond the narrative. Authors and readers approach narratives, fictional and nonfictional, with the presupposition that they have a thematic component, and authors seek to shape readerly interests in that component in some ways rather than others. Furthermore, authors typically use their construction of a narrative's progression as the primary mechanism for shaping readerly interests.

I break the thematic into the three dimensions of the ideational, ethical, and ideological in the interests of both comprehensiveness and correspondence. All three dimensions combine what Aristotle called "thought" with "value," and they overlap with one another. But I find it serves comprehensiveness and correspondence better to allow for the overlap than to draw rigid boundaries between and among these dimensions. By ideational matters, I mean the kinds of things Clark refers to in his second broad category of the thematic—subject matters or topics such as anger, death, violence, and "the best blessings of existence." In my rhetorical view, however, such topics don't become properly part of the thematic until authors communicate their stances on them via explicit statements or the narrative progression. By ethical matters, I mean the moral values at issue in the narrative. Furthermore, I distinguish between the ethics of the telling, the moral values informing the author–narrator–audience relationships, and the ethics of the told, the moral values relevant to the character–character situations depicted in the narrative.

By ideological matters, I mean the social and political values informing the narrative. My conception, then, is close to Clark's, since he defines ideology as "*ideas* particularly linked to social formations" (115; my emphasis), and he identifies the following as ideological issues: gender, class, race, religion, nationalism, and age. I would extend the list both by adding identity issues such as sexuality and disability and by moving beyond identity issues to such other matters as human–other species relationships, human–environment relationships, and human–planet relationships. And again, for me, an ideological issue doesn't become properly part of the thematic until an author expresses one or more stances on it. Consequently, I find that Clark's very perceptive discussion of class in *Emma* stops too soon. Clark admirably traces *Emma*'s variable attitudes toward class but refrains from making any determinate statements about *Austen's* stances on those attitudes. Instead, Clark is content with the two conclusions that "Austen's analysis of class is detailed and precise" and "It is not easy to determine her ideological stance." I will return to this point in my own discussion of the thematic in *Emma*.

This conception of the thematic has room for allegory, but it neither privileges nor disparages it. Allegory is one way of constructing a fictional narrative whose thematic component is dominant. Writers of allegory, such as Spenser in *The Faerie Queene* or Bunyan in *Pilgrim's Progress* or Orwell in *Animal Farm*, typically establish one-to-one correspondences between their characters and particular concepts, human types, or extratextual entities. Bunyan's Christian is every Christian seeker of salvation; Spenser's Error is, indeed, just that; and his Duessa is the Roman Catholic Church. Sometimes writers of allegory will extend this construction of one-to-one correspondences between narrative elements and abstract concepts beyond character, as Bunyan does when he has Christian fall into the Slough of Despond. Furthermore, writers of allegory construct plots that demonstrate how conflicts between and among, to borrow a phrase from Sheldon Sacks, such "walking concepts" (either people-as-concepts or concepts-as-people) arise, get complicated, and are eventually resolved. The readerly dynamics situate the narrative and authorial audiences on the side of the ethically superior walking concepts, and the audiences' affective responses are tied to the degree of success those ethically superior characters have as they work through the conflicts. As the term "walking concept" indicates, writers of allegory typically foreground the synthetic component of their narratives, but that foregrounding, like the subordination of the mimetic component, is in the service of the author's dominant thematic purpose.[2]

But of course, not all narratives that make their thematic components dominant are allegories. *1984* is a case in point. Orwell does not set up one-to-one correspondences between his characters and particular concepts or extratextual entities. Instead, as I discussed in chapter 5, he develops the mimetic components of his characters and guides his audience to align ethically and affectively with Winston. That strategy, as Clark nicely points out, also means

---

2. See Gary Johnson for a fascinating rhetorically based study of allegory that adds considerably more nuance to its narrative dynamics.

that Orwell can and does direct his audience's attention to multiple ideational and ethical dimensions of the narrative. That strategy also means that when Orwell shows how effectively and thoroughly the state defeats Winston, Orwell more powerfully indicts totalitarianism and more effectively warns his audience to beware of its encroachment.

I have written rather extensively about progression (*Reading People, Experiencing Fiction, Somebody Telling*), so here I will focus on the key points. It refers to the underlying principles that govern a narrative's movement from beginning through middle to ending. It is more comprehensive than the concept of plot because plot refers just to the logic governing the sequence of events, while progression refers to the synthesis of textual dynamics and readerly dynamics. Textual dynamics involve the internal logic of a plot or other principle of textual movement in interaction with the narration, and readerly dynamics involve the unfolding responses of the audience—cognitive, affective, ethical, as well as those related to mimetic, thematic, and synthetic interests—to those textual dynamics. Progression is a synthesis because readerly dynamics not only follow from but can also exert an influence on textual dynamics. Narratives that work toward appropriately surprising their audiences help illustrate this point. An author's influence in creating the effect of surprise greatly influences how she constructs the textual dynamics. More generally, an author's construction of the textual dynamics will be influenced by unfolding readerly dynamics. For example, at the end of *Emma*, when Austen needs to find a way to move Emma and Mr. Knightley from engaged to married, she faces a constructive/synthetic problem given two aspects of her mimetic characterizations and thematic commitments. Mr. Woodhouse dreads such a big change in his own life, and Emma and Mr. Knightley appropriately respect and defer to his interests. So Austen invents the incident of a burglary in the hen house at Hartfield to motivate Mr. Woodhouse's change of mind: With Mr. Knightley at Hartfield, he will feel safer. In arranging the incident, Austen flirts with breaking the mimetic illusion—she seems to rely on a "robber ex machina"—but by this point in the progression, her narrative and authorial audiences so strongly desire the marriage that the invention does not break the illusion.[3]

---

3. For a fuller theoretical discussion and more examples of this phenomenon, see *Somebody Telling Somebody Else*, chapters 2, 3, and 11.

III. THE THEMATIC COMPONENT OF *EMMA*: AN ILLUSTRATIVE ANALYSIS

Austen constructs the central track of the textual dynamics on the instabilities and complications that result from the intersection of Emma's mimetic character and her particular, privileged position in Highbury. Clark gives an excellent account of those textual dynamics in his analysis of the novel's three main movements, each involving a mistake of Emma's, and of Austen's skillful resolution of those instabilities and their complications. With his text-centric orientation, however, Clark pays less attention to the readerly dynamics. Given that Austen aptly described Emma as a character "whom no one but myself will much like," and given that Austen constructs the progression so that it will culminate in the happy union of Mr. Knightley and Emma, Austen faces some considerable challenges in constructing the readerly dynamics. Specifically, how can she simultaneously expose Emma's unwarranted pride and its negative consequences for others such as Harriet without turning her audiences against her protagonist? How can she get the audience to invest in Emma's happiness? To a large degree, Austen's strategy is to engage her audience in nuanced ethical judgments of Emma that then influence the audience's affective responses. She balances all the reasons not to like Emma against reasons that point to different affective and ethical responses. In the very first chapter, for example, Austen represents Emma's remarkable and loving attention to her father. Her interest in displaying her skills as matchmaker exists alongside her genuine care for Harriet. But rather than continue to summarize Austen's strategies, I will include attention to readerly dynamics in my more detailed analysis of the novel's thematic component.

In writing a novel committed to the mimetic illusion, Austen makes the mimetic and the thematic dominant over the synthetic, though as noted above, audiences can and do take pleasure in her style and other elements of her construction because they ultimately support the novel's mimetic and thematic components.[4] Furthermore, Austen constructs the progression so that the mimetic and thematic components are in a kind of feedback loop where each consistently adds something to the other. To illustrate, I focus on the scene at Box Hill, a significant turning point in the textual dynamics.

---

4. Of course, actual readers may choose to take pleasure in the style without any particular concern for its contributions to the novel's mimetic and thematic components. Such reading for style has its own pleasures and rewards, but they are different from those of reading with a primary focus on the author–audience–purpose nexus.

The main events are well known: Emma behaves badly toward Miss Bates, Mr. Knightley rebukes her, and Emma acknowledges the justice of his remarks. Both the rebuke and Emma's response to it have major ripple effects on the Mr. Knightley–Emma relationship, effects that ultimately lead to their marriage. Austen uses the excursion to Box Hill to develop other strands of the progression as well (e.g., the Frank Churchill–Jane Fairfax subplot), but the exchanges between Miss Bates and Emma and between Mr. Knightley and Emma are sufficiently rich for my purposes.

In order to liven up what has turned out to be a dull picnic, Frank Churchill addresses the company, which, in addition to Emma, includes Harriet, Mr. Knightley, Mr. Weston, Jane Fairfax, Miss Bates, and the Eltons. Frank promises that Emma will laugh heartily in response to anyone who can say "one thing very clever . . . , two things moderately clever, or three things very dull indeed." Miss Bates is the first to respond:

> "Oh! very well," exclaimed Miss Bates, "then I need not be uneasy. 'Three things very dull indeed.' That will just do for me, you know. I shall be sure to say three dull things as soon as ever I open my mouth, shan't I? (looking round with the most good-humoured dependence on every body's assent)—Do not you all think I shall?"
>
> Emma could not resist.
>
> "Ah! ma'am, but there may be a difficulty. Pardon me—but you will be limited as to number—only three at once."
>
> Miss Bates, deceived by the mock ceremony of her manner, did not immediately catch her meaning; but, when it burst on her, it could not anger, though a slight blush shewed that it could pain her.
>
> "Ah!—well—to be sure. Yes, I see what she means, (turning to Mr. Knightley,) and I will try to hold my tongue. I must make myself very disagreeable, or she would not have said such a thing to an old friend." (255–56)

I start with the mimetic illusion and how it accommodates the ideational dimensions of this passage. As a shorthand, I referred to this passage as an exchange between Emma and Miss Bates, but that shorthand is misleading because Miss Bates never addresses only Emma. She addresses her first remark to the whole group, and she begins her second the same way and then redirects it specifically to Mr. Knightley. These features of the passage contribute to its mimetic plausibility. Indeed, it is a wonderful example of Austen's ability to sustain the mimetic illusion. For example, Miss Bates's initial comment, in its good-humored self-deprecation as well as in its deferential address to the larger group, is fully consistent with the possible person Austen's audience knows her to be. In addition, Miss Bates's self-deprecation leads her to unintentionally say something very clever. At the same time, Austen's authorial audience can recognize the comment as a perfectly designed setup for the kind of mimetically consistent response Emma delivers, one in which her own class-inflected bias about Miss Bates leads her to miss the unintended cleverness. Emma's response to Miss Bates, in both its intended cleverness and its presupposition of superiority, is also consistent with some of the traits of the possible person Austen's audience knows her to be.[5]

Austen's mastery of novelistic mimesis coexists with her skill in developing the thematic component. Consider the ideational dimension. Austen constructs the scene to further thematize traits of both characters. With Emma, Austen is adding some remarkable strokes to the gradually unfolding picture of cleverness and its dangers that she has been drawing since the first chapter. That picture includes attention to the role of wealth and social position in bringing out these negatives. Rich, clever Emma has said one thing very clever, but has done so at the expense of poor, only unintentionally clever, but oh-so-kind-and-good-hearted Miss Bates. Without at all detracting from Emma's mimetic appeal, Austen uses her speech to thematize her thoughtless self-indulgence at a social inferior's expense. Similarly, with Miss Bates, Austen is making more prominent something that has been present but relatively undeveloped until the scene: what it means to occupy the kind of social space Miss Bates does, that is, on the very fringe of the privileged class. Among other things, it means that self-deprecation and finding ways to justify ill-treatment become second nature.

Now let's look at the ethical dimension. Austen's ethics of the telling relies on a great deal of shared understanding and trust between herself and her audience. She does not use the narrator to spell out Emma's ethical deficiencies, but instead invites the audience to infer at least some of those deficiencies through the narrator's description of Miss Bates's internal and bodily response and through Miss Bates's comments to Mr. Knightley. In other words, Austen relies on her audience to have a sound capacity for ethical discrimination so

---

5. In a fuller analysis, I would elaborate on the consequences for the mimetic and the thematic components of the respective synthetic roles of Miss Bates and Emma as minor character and major character. For now, I'll just say that this difference in the synthetic component means that Austen gives us a more limited view of Miss Bates than she does of Emma. As a result, Austen can show Emma behaving badly here without having her audience conclude that her behavior reflects the entirety of her character. For a provocative discussion of the synthetic consequences of the differences between major and minor characters, see Woloch.

that they can build on what she supplies and reach their own judgments about the ethics of the told. In this way, Austen and her audience establish a strong bond: They are working together to understand the nuances of the characters' actions. Furthermore, making these judgments of Emma's ethical deficiency also influences the affective layer of both the narrative and authorial audiences' responses: They become deeply sympathetic with Miss Bates and her pain, even as they feel another kind of pain about Emma's thoughtless cruelty.

But Austen wants to do more with the ethics of the told and so she turns to Mr. Knightley to deliver the fullest judgment. When Emma tries to laugh off the incident or excuse it because the ridiculous and the good are so blended in Miss Bates, Mr. Knightley counters with a much fuller description of Miss Bates and her situation:

> "She is poor; she has sunk from the comforts she was born to; and, if she live to old age, must probably sink more. Her situation should secure your compassion. It was badly done, indeed! You, whom she had known from an infant, whom she had seen grow up from a period when her notice was an honour, to have you now, in thoughtless spirits, and the pride of the moment, laugh at her, humble her—and before her niece, too—and before others, many of whom (certainly *some*,) would be entirely guided by you." (259)

This speech is further evidence of Austen's mastery of novelistic mimesis. Her initial characterization of Mr. Knightley in chapter 1 as well as her further attention to his role as ethically sound judge throughout the novel make the speech all but inevitable. But Austen also uses Mr. Knightley's mimetic component to further develop the thematic—and in so doing, she deepens other aspects of the mimetic situation. It is this interaction that I have characterized as an ongoing feedback loop between the two components.

First, although Austen has primed her audience for Mr. Knightley's judgments through her initial handling of the Emma–Miss Bates interaction, she deploys Mr. Knightley to give the full account of the gap between how Emma has treated Miss Bates and what Miss Bates deserves from her. His careful, detailed—and stylistically well-formed—contextualizing of Miss Bates's situation and his reference to Emma's own social position show both Emma and Austen's audience how and why Emma's exercise of her cleverness "was badly done indeed!" (259). In this way, Austen adds a significant dimension to her thematizing of the dangers of the best blessings of existence.

Second, Mr. Knightley's speech adds to the narrative and authorial audiences' understanding of his acute ethical perception and his willingness to act on those perceptions in relation to Emma. His action here heightens the mimetic drama of the Mr. Knightley–Emma relationship. How will she react?

Austen's handling of Mr. Knightley's concluding remarks shows that he is aware of Emma's possible reactions, even as it continues the mimetic–thematic feedback loop:

> "This is not pleasant to you, Emma—and it is very far from pleasant to me; but I must, I will,—I will tell you truths while I can; satisfied with proving myself your friend by very faithful counsel, and trusting that you will some time or other do me greater justice than you can do now." (259)

Mr. Knightley articulates an authorially endorsed thematic ethics of friendship here, one that gives more value to telling truths than to being pleasant, and one that is willing to risk temporary ill favor for greater justice over the long term. At the same time, in the very application of that ethics to their particular friendship, Mr. Knightley tempers the harsh quality of his truth-telling by expressing his trust in Emma's own sound ethical judgment. In other words, he ends his rebuke with a compliment about Emma's fundamental ethical soundness, a gesture that conveys both his affection and respect for her. As the narrative and authorial audiences take in his carefully calibrated version of "It's tough now, but we'll be good," Austen not only endorses his thematics of friendship but relies on it to create a stronger affective attachment to Mr. Knightley. That attachment in turn increases her audiences' desire for Emma and Mr. Knightley to get together, even as Mr. Knightley's final words add to their expectation of that outcome.

Austen then rounds out the scene by continuing the mimetic and thematic feedback loop but adding another twist to the mimetic component of the narrative. She shows her audiences that Mr. Knightley's trust in Emma is well founded, but keeps that knowledge from Mr. Knightley himself. Circumstance and Emma's own strong feelings prevent her from saying anything in response to Mr. Knightley, but Austen uses the narration to reveal that Emma owns her ethical deficiency:

> Never had she felt so agitated, mortified, grieved, at any circumstance in her life. She was most forcibly struck. The truth of this representation there was no denying. She felt it at her heart. How could she have been so brutal, so cruel to Miss Bates! How could she have exposed herself to such ill opinion in any one she valued! And how suffer him to leave her without saying one word of gratitude, of concurrence, of common kindness! (259)

Austen in effect shows the personal consequences for Emma of the scene's thematic lessons. More than that, Austen simultaneously heightens her audiences' affective attachment to Emma and alters their ethical judgments of her. Indeed, Emma's response to Mr. Knightley's rebuke is arguably her most impressive ethical act in the narrative. Consequently, even as Austen heightens the instability between the characters—Mr. Knightley does not know Emma's response, and she is distressed that he does not know—Austen continues to increase both the audiences' desire and expectation for their eventual union.

As for the ideological dimensions of the scene, the two most prominent ones involve class and gender. Although Clark doesn't comment directly on this scene in his perceptive commentary on class, his observations about Austen's and Emma's awareness of social gradations are very relevant here. The rhetorical perspective adds two significant elements to his observations: (1) Emma's ethical breach is very much connected to her position at the top of the class hierarchy in Highbury and to Miss Bates's marginal position in Emma's class. Emma's position, Mr. Knightley makes clear, entails a double ethical responsibility that her clever put-down has violated: First, Emma's own good fortune should make her feel and act out of compassion for the far less fortunate Miss Bates; second, Emma's social position means that others—such as Harriet—will model their behavior to Miss Bates on hers. (2) Mr. Knightley is a reliable spokesperson for Austen's views about class. She uses his discernment and his ethics of friendship to instruct both Emma and Austen's audiences about her class obligations.

To extend this illustration of how to read Austen's ideological position on class, I turn to the passage, which Clark does quote, summarizing what happens to Emma and Harriet's relationship after they are both married.

> Harriet, necessarily drawn away by her engagements with the Martins, was less and less at Hartfield; which was not to be regretted.—The intimacy between her and Emma must sink; their friendship must change into a calmer sort of goodwill; and, fortunately, what ought to be, and must be, seemed already beginning, and in the most gradual, natural manner. (332)

The narration here fluctuates so smoothly between the narrator's focalization ("Harriet . . . was less and less at Hartfield") and Emma's ("seemed already beginning") because their views are now perfectly aligned. And those views indicate that Austen, for all her nuanced analysis of human interaction, believes that at least some class distinctions are appropriate. Why must the intimacy between Emma and Harriet sink? Because she is the daughter of a tradesman and has married a farmer. While these two examples don't yield a complete view of Austen's take on class, they do indicate how rhetorical poetics would work to develop that view.

With gender, the obvious issue is that the older male schools the younger female—and that Austen asks her audience not just to approve but also to take pleasure in the process. Looking just at that prominent feature of the scene, we'd have difficulty making the case that Austen has the ideology of a protofeminist. But as with class, Austen does not put forward a single, monolithic view of gender either in *Emma* or in her work as a whole. Furthermore, in the scene itself, Austen displays an investment in more than just the gender dynamic between Mr. Knightley and Emma. In Miss Bates's response to Emma's insult and in Mr. Knightley's speech to Emma, Austen invites her audience to see that Miss Bates's vulnerability and her self-deprecation are connected to her gender, which in turn makes Emma's callous treatment of another woman all the more dismaying. Austen also invites her audiences to recognize that Emma displays her cleverness at Miss Bates's expense in part because she is showing off for Frank Churchill.

Of course, not all actual audience members will share Austen's ideological positions on class and gender, and those that don't may engage in a step 2 critique of those positions or at least consider how those differences influence their overall experiences of Austen's novels. In my case, while I greatly admire *Emma* for reasons that I hope come through in my analyses, I find myself more drawn to both *Pride and Prejudice* and *Persuasion*. And a large reason for that difference is Austen's handling of the relations between her male and female leads. Unlike Mr. Knightley and Emma, both Darcy and Elizabeth need to undergo a moral education. Unlike both Emma and Elizabeth, Anne does not need to undergo any moral education. All she needs is sufficient opportunity to act and speak in Wentworth's presence so that he can't but help recognize his folly in having hardened his heart against her.

There's a lot more to say about the thematic in *Emma* and in Austen in general, but I hope I have said enough to show that Austen's mastery of the mimetic illusion goes hand in hand with her development of an active feedback loop between the mimetic and the thematic components of the narrative. The more she develops her audiences' interest in the ideational, ethical, and ideological dimensions of the progression, the more she deepens their affective attachments to the characters. And vice versa. I submit that Austen's skill in the handling of these components, enhanced by her stylistic mastery, is one important reason why she continues to have such a large following more than two hundred years since her death.

CHAPTER 7

MTS, Fictionality, and Nonfiction

Tobias Wolff's "Old China"

JAMES PHELAN

I. FICTION, NONFICTIONAL, AND FICTIONALITY

Before I turn to my analysis of Wolff's remarkable narrative, I offer some general observations about a rhetorical approach to fiction and nonfiction—and to the broader concept of fictionality.

Just as readers have qualitatively different interests in fictions that seek to imitate the extratextual world and in those that don't, they also have qualitatively different interests in those whose global purposes rely on reference to the actual world and those whose global purposes rely on the invention of characters and events. (For ease of exposition, I will temporarily continue this discussion by referring just to fiction and nonfiction, but before it is over, I will bring in narratives that deliberately blur the line between fiction and nonfiction.) Just as the differences within the realm of fiction are tied to different kinds of relationships between the knowledge and beliefs of authorial and narrative audiences, so too are the differences between fictions and nonfictions tied to audience issues. Quite simply, because the global claim of a nonfiction narrative is that it refers to the extratextual world, actual audiences do not read with the double-consciousness they bring to fiction. Those differences have consequences for the interrelations of the mimetic, thematic, and synthetic components in each mode, and we can understand those differences more fully in light of a rhetorical approach to fictionality.

I offer six interconnected points to explicate this approach.[1]

1. Fictionality is intentionally communicated invention, projection, or other direction of an audience to imagine nonactual states or sets of events. The communication can be explicitly signaled or just implied. I parse this definition as follows:

    "Intentionally" reflects the rhetorical orientation toward a speaker's purpose. "Explicitly signaled" and "implied" distinguish fictionality from lying, which is deviant and defective nonfictionality, since it purports not to be an act of invention when it actually is—a liar intends to deceive his audience; someone using fictionality does not.

    Allowing both explicit and implicit means of communicating fictionality reflects the great range of author–audience relations. Sometimes authors explicitly mark fictionality, but sometimes they rely on audiences to recognize their shifts from nonfictionality to fictionality. In this respect, fictionality is similar to irony, which often has its most powerful effects when it relies on an unspoken understanding between author and audience: "I know that you know that I'm not being literal."

    "Invention, projection, or other direction of an audience to imagine nonactual states of affairs or sets of events" differentiates fictionality from nonfictionality, which engages directly—through reporting, interpreting, evaluating, and other activities—with actual states of affairs or sets of events.

2. Fictionality is distinct from generic fiction, for example, the novel, the short story, or the fiction film. We can profitably think of generic fictions as having developed out of humans recognizing the value of authorizing zones of discourse built on a belief in and a commitment to the possibilities of invention and imagination. But humans have also come to recognize that just about all discourse can be enhanced by integrating some fictionality into it. Thus,

3. Fictionality is pervasive throughout nonfictional discourse. Think of all the times we invent or project scenarios about what will happen if we do X or Y. Think of all the times we say "What if?" or engage in elaborate hyperbole. Fictionality is also a key tool in multiple disciplines—via thought experiments, models, hypotheses, and so on. At the same time, fictionality is often embedded in nonfictionality. If I sincerely say, "I wish

---

1. For more on this rhetorical approach to fictionality, see Walsh, the book that sparked this line of research; Nielsen, Phelan, and Walsh; and Phelan, "Local Fictionality."

that I would win the lottery," then I am not engaging in fictionality but expressing an actual desire for an imagined condition.
4. Nonfictionality is pervasive throughout fictional discourse, as is evident in such genres as the historical novel where authors often refer directly to historical people and events. But nonfictionality is pervasive throughout other global fictions as well, as a little reflection on all the realist novels set in actual places reveals. Together points 3 and 4 highlight the frequency and importance of cross-border traffic.
5. Fictionality is both a ternary and a scalar concept. It is ternary because rhetors have only three underlying options: fictionality, nonfictionality, or blurring the lines. It is scalar because once a rhetor chooses fictionality, her inventions can range from minimal to maximal departures from the actual. *Emma* has minimal departure, *1984* a greater degree of departure, and fantasy novels with invented settings and characters with superpowers move toward the maximal end of the scale. Narratives that blur the lines, such as Tim O'Brien's "The Things They Carried," will only involve minimal departures.
6. Fictionality is not an escape from the actual world but an indirect way of responding to it, and typically seeking to intervene in it. (Even engaging the imagination for the purposes of escape is a response to the actual world.) This point applies both to local fictionality within global nonfictions (thought experiments, passages of invented scenarios in memoir, etc.) and to generic fictions themselves. Indeed, this point is consistent with my more general view that humans invented narrative to come to terms with one or more aspects of our "thrownness," our finding ourselves in the world and needing to cope with our condition.

This understanding of fictionality and nonfictionality has the following consequences for the MTS model in cases of nonfiction. With the thematic component, the author of nonfiction faces the challenge of taking the raw material of actual experience and shaping it—without falsifying or distorting it—so that it acquires an ideational, ethical, and/or ideological significance that warrants the attention of others. Just how authors conduct that shaping will vary from narrative to narrative, but they can deploy the general strategies I mentioned in connection with my definition of the thematic component: the arrangement of sequences of action, explicit generalizations about the nature of the world by narrators or characters, and characters functioning as representatives of larger groups or embodiments of ideas. In my discussion of "Old China," I will discuss how Wolff uses local fictionality to thematize his actual experience.

If an author of fiction's handling of the mimetic component is tied to general models of and conventions about depicting possible people, events, places, and worlds, an author of a nonfiction's handling of the mimetic, like that of the thematic, is tied to her shaping of the raw material of actual experience.[2] Consequently, I again find it helpful to consider the mimetic and the synthetic together. As Clark and I have both noted, there is no direct mirroring or copying of the actual, so when an author begins to shape the raw material of actual experience, she will shape it in one way rather than another, and, indeed, a different author is likely to shape that same material in a different way. Any one author's choice to shape in one way rather than another will be determined by her sense of her narrative's larger purposes.

Consider, for example, the issue of how to handle a minor character in nonfiction. Just as in fiction, minor characters in nonfiction will often be less fully described than major characters. An author's choice to limit his description of a character to a few traits does not weaken the author's reference to an actual person, but it does restrict the audience's knowledge of that actual person to the information the author believes is most relevant for his purposes. Because such restriction and selection are so necessary to narrative itself, and thus, so taken for granted by authors and audiences alike, their presence won't foreground the synthetic.

So if the mimetic is grounded in referentiality, and the shaping of referentiality is the stock-in-trade of nonfiction, then how do authors of nonfiction foreground the synthetic? They employ three main strategies: They overtly comment on the choices they make to construct the narrative (meta-nonfiction); they tacitly use the resources of narrative in a way that calls attention to its construction, for example, with a baroque style or highly unusual organization of the material; or they deploy local fictionality in ways that call attention to their construction. Wolff's "Old China" provides an especially compelling example of this third strategy.

II. READING "OLD CHINA"

In Pharaoh's Army (1994; note the fictionality in the title) is Wolff's extraordinary memoir of his experiences as a US soldier in Viet Nam during the late 1960s. Told from a perspective twenty-five years after the events, Wolff offers multiple, trenchant reflections on those experiences, and he often treats his

---

2. To be sure, that shaping can be—and often is—influenced by the conventions and models that apply to fiction. But using what fiction has taught in the service of referentiality is very different from using it in the service of invention.

former self as an ethically deficient actor. The epigraph of the memoir, taken from Ford Madox Ford's *The Good Soldier*, gives some indication of its general purposes:

> You may well ask why I write. And yet my reasons are quite many. For it is not unusual in human beings who have witnessed the sack of a city or the falling to pieces of a people to set down what they have witnessed for the benefit of unknown heirs or of generations infinitely remote; or, if you please, just to get the sight out of their heads. (iv)

Wolff's strategy is to capture his experience through a diverse set of largely self-contained chapters that explore significant events and/or lead to significant reflections. In the chapter called "Close Calls," for example, he conveys his sense of what it is like to live with the awareness that one could be killed at almost any moment. "Old China" is less about the war itself than about the trajectory of his relationship with an older, more accomplished, more at-home-in-the-world Foreign Service officer, whom he had met in language school before they were both posted to Viet Nam. Wolff uses the first half of the chapter to establish the grounds of his relationship with Pete Landon, and he summarizes things this way:

> I knew he had two kid brothers back home; he treated me pretty much as if I were one of them. And if he condescended, if he gave his advice a little too freely, if he sometimes made me feel too smartly the difference in our ages, our histories and our prospects, that was all right. I knew he had my best interests at heart. (144–45)

Wolff uses the second half of the narrative to recount the events that led him to realize that Pete was far less concerned about Wolff's actual best interests than about Pete's judgments of those best interests and his power to act on those judgments. Pete comes to visit Wolff at his posting in the village of My Tho, away from the front line. After surveying Wolff's setup, Pete decides that Wolff has it too easy for his own good. Without consulting Wolff, Pete pulls some strings to get him reassigned to the front line. The order doesn't go through because Wolff is almost at the end of his tour of duty, and neither of them is happy with the other. Wolff reports Pete's last line of dialogue: "If you had even four months left I'd ram this thing through anyway. . . . For your own good." Pete leaves behind a precious china bowl that Wolff witnessed him receive as a gift from a distinguished elderly Viet Namese named Ong Loan, so Pete wires instructions to Wolff. He tells Wolff to send him the bowl on the next plane, after putting extra padding on the package. Pete's instructions end "DO NOT DELAY REPEAT DO NOT DELAY." Here is the way Wolff ends the chapter.

> That [the bowl] was ancient I knew at a glance. The blue was soft and watery, the white softly yellowed like old ivory. To see it cupped in the hand and to see it passed to another hand was to understand that it was meant for that purpose; to be passed on. Pete's bow [upon receiving it] had been cinematic but I couldn't blame him for it. That he should bow in his pleasure at so antique and beautiful a thing was only right.
>
> I put the package on the floor and pressed at it with my stockinged foot, for better control, and so as not to leave any bootprints. It was tougher than I'd expected but then of course it was tough. How else could it have lasted all those years? I gave it more and more of my weight until I was almost standing on it. Though I didn't hear the break, I felt it travel up my leg—a sudden, sad release. I picked up the package and checked to make sure I hadn't broken just the wooden base. It was the bowl. It had cracked into several pieces. I wrapped the package in some bunched sheets of *Stars and Stripes* and covered those with a layer of parcel paper. Then I took it to the air strip. I followed Pete's orders to the letter, and I did not delay.
>
> Really, now. Is the part about the bowl true? Did I do that?
>
> No. Never. I would never deliberately take something precious from a man—the pride of his collection, say, or his own pride—and put it under my foot like that, and twist my foot on it, and break it.
>
> No. Not even for his own good. (158–59)

This ending is so arresting because Wolff brilliantly combines fictionality and ambiguity, and in so doing makes all three MTS components prominent. The ambiguity highlights Wolff's synthetic construction, even as it leaves his audience unable to determine which of the last two paragraphs is his mimetically accurate report. Wolff's meticulous recounting of the experiencing-I's actions—stepping on the bowl in his stocking feet, feeling the break in his leg, making sure it was in pieces—invites his audience to accept that paragraph as nonfictional. But then his narrating-I's denial in the next paragraph is persuasive: Breaking the bowl to teach Pete a lesson for his own good would be to sink to Pete's level. Surely, Wolff must mean that he only imagined breaking the bowl but actually sent it to Pete. Yet Wolff's sardonic tone invites his audience to read the denial as ironic. Furthermore, given that Wolff has in previous chapters exposed the ethically deficient actions of the experiencing-I, his authorial audience needs to take seriously the idea that he actually did break the bowl.

Let me say a little more about how the concept of fictionality illuminates Wolff's strategy here. Without it, narrative theorists would be inclined to focus on the ambiguity about which paragraph is reliable narration and which unreliable, and about the bonding and estranging effects of our conclusions. We might couple that discussion with attention to Wolff using the technique of what Brian Richardson has identified as denarration: The first paragraph narrates that X happened and the second erases that narration, thus destabilizing what actually happened. I find such analysis worthwhile, but I believe that the concept of fictionality adds value to the analysis. While the global nonfictionality does not make either unreliability or denarration impossible, it does mean that their effects would be different than in a work of global fictionality. The question, Which paragraph represents the actual events and which the invented? has a different force here than it would if Wolff were writing fiction, because his and his audience's ultimate concerns are with what actually happened. Wolff effectively uses the determinate ambiguity about what actually happened with the bowl to add significance and force to what actually happened between him and Pete.

First, on the mimetic level, Wolff uses the ending to effectively communicate the radical alteration in his relationship with Pete. They will never again be as they were, because Wolff is no longer willing to be the kid brother, no longer willing to tolerate the condescension and remain in the role of grateful recipient of what Pete does for Wolff's own good. There's a bittersweet affective quality to this trajectory because Wolff's new insight into Pete costs him a friendship he once valued. But it is the bittersweet quality that often accompanies a loss of innocence and a gain of maturity.

On the thematic level, Wolff uses the ending, first, to highlight the ideational issue of what it means for someone to give someone else a surprise gift for that person's own good—and who gets to decide that meaning. Wolff clearly endorses the position that the recipient of the so-called gift is a far better judge of whether it's for her good than the donor. Second, Wolff uses the ambiguity about fictionality to add considerable nuance to the ethics of the told. Wolff makes a convincing case for the deficiencies of Pete's arrogant assumption that he knows what's best for Wolff. But by putting forth the ideas that the experiencing-I sank to Pete's level and that he did not, Wolff invites his audience to question whether the experiencing-I's proper ethical choice is so clear-cut. Perhaps Pete's presumption to know what's best for Wolff needs this kind of rebuke. Perhaps the experiencing-I's retaliation is an appropriate exercise of agency in a situation in which Pete has dominated all the action. The ambiguity makes it all but impossible to go beyond the "perhaps." But the need to consider the alternatives adds a significant dimension to the ethics of the told. Third, within the larger context of the memoir, the ambiguity about fictionality opens out to ideological questions about the relationship between the US and Viet Nam. Is Pete another version of the US presuming to know what's best for the kid brother country? Is the experiencing-I and his possible retaliation another version of the less powerful person in the relationship finding what de Certeau calls room for maneuver against the oppressor? I would stop short of saying that Wolff's narrative gives definitive answers to those questions, but its ability to raise them adds to its thematic and aesthetic quality.

Finally, the ambiguity about how Wolff deploys fictionality foregrounds the synthetic and, much like what happens in "Continuity of Parks," moves the ethics of the telling and the relationship between Wolff as author and his audience to the foreground. That movement is facilitated by the direct address to his audience, "Really, now. Is that last part about the bowl true? Would I do that? No, never," but the major impetus for that foregrounding comes from the ambiguity about fictionality. Wolff invites his audience to look beyond the particulars, engaging as they are, of what happened to the bowl, and to contemplate his larger effort to come to terms with his Viet Nam experience. Twenty-five years later, he is still processing this incident with Pete Landon and, indeed, so many of the other events he narrates. His rhetorical action of telling may or may not succeed in getting "the sight out of [his] head," but I venture to say that he has remarkable success in drawing his audience further in to his "memories of the lost war."

III. CONCLUSION

I want to end by thanking Clark once again for engaging so thoughtfully with the rhetorical MTS model and proposing his worthwhile alternative. Although I still aspire to have him read this response and become a fully committed rhetorical narratologist, I have, in the course of writing this piece, developed a greater appreciation for the more likely outcome: his once again saying, "Yes, but." There are two reasons for this new attitude: (1) Clark's saying "Yes, but" to my earlier work has led both to his valuable descriptive poetics and to my efforts to sharpen and extend the rhetorical version of the MTS model. I trust he will find this new version recognizable, even as I hope he appreciates how he's pushed me to fresh takes on such matters as the concept of the narrative audience, the relation between unnatural narratology and rhetorical poetics, and the feedback loop between the mimetic and the thematic in fictions built on the mimetic illusion, such as *Emma*. After this experience, I can anticipate that Clark's second "Yes, but" would lead both to a further development of his model and thus to some further revision of rhetorical poetics. (2) Wolff's "Old China." After analyzing Wolff's engagement with that aspect of his thrownness, I am given pause by my appeal to Clark to "Come home to rhetoric," with its implicit addition—"for your own good." I don't want to be narratology's version of Pete Landon, so I'll modify the injunction. "Matthew, come home to rhetoric, but only if you're absolutely convinced it's for your own good."

CHAPTER 8

Yes, but. . . .

MATTHEW CLARK

I WOULD LIKE TO EXPRESS my appreciation to James Phelan—first, for the body of engaging and enlightening work in narrative theory he has produced over the years, and second, for the grace and generosity he displays in his response to my comments on some aspects of rhetorical narratology. His own work often focuses on the ethical aspects of narrative, and in this discussion he has presented a lesson in the ethics of scholarship and criticism. I hope I can follow his example.

In my own response to Phelan's response, I would like to note a few areas where I think he and I are in fundamental agreement, to clarify some points where there could be confusion, and to explore a few areas where I think our approaches may differ.

First I should note that my discussion of the synthetic, mimetic, and thematic aspects of narrative is not intended as a comprehensive critique of rhetorical narratology. I would be the wrong person to undertake such a critique, since I am generally sympathetic to the goals and methods of rhetorical narratology. My discussion was primarily limited to just one part of rhetorical narratology, the triad of the synthetic, mimetic, and thematic: his version of this triad (MTS) and my revision of it (SMT). Any element of rhetorical narratology that I don't discuss I probably agree with. Moreover, my discussion of MTS is intended not as a critique, and certainly not as an attack, but as a proposed readjustment of terms and concepts. As I note in the introduction,

I consider my proposed changes to be friendly amendments. I believe that the changes I propose are generally compatible with the rest of rhetorical narratological theory, which, for the most part, I leave undisturbed.

According to Phelan, rhetorical narratology sees narrative "not primarily as a textual structure but as an action: somebody telling somebody else on some occasion and for some purposes that something happened" (137). I have no fundamental disagreement with this definition. I think it needs some qualifications, but I agree with all the major parts of it.[1] I agree that narrative is an action, and that narrative involves a narrator, a narration, and an audience, and I agree that there is a purpose to the narrative act. Because I agree with this definition (and with some other aspects of the theory), I am happy to say that I am generally sympathetic to the goals and methods of rhetorical narratology. Therefore, when Phelan makes his appeal—"Come home to rhetorical!" (195)—my response is, "I never left, I'm just suggesting that we rearrange some of the furniture." On the other hand, if coming home to rhetorical narratology means that I can't also do unnatural narratology, ideological narratology, or cognitive narratology, then I'm not so happy. My appeal would be "Open the doors! There's room for everyone!!"

To clarify what seems to be a misunderstanding, I do not believe that narratives are simply textual structures or textual compositions. I agree that a narrative is an action—a transaction between a narrator and an audience for a purpose. It may be that Phelan has misunderstood my position here because my definitions of the synthetic, mimetic, and thematic aspects do not mention narrators and audiences and their responses and interests. All of these seem to me sufficiently implied by the general definition of narrative, and that implication carries over to the particular definitions of the triad, but I recognize that my omission of the terms in my particular definitions could lead to confusion, and I am happy to clarify the point here.

My interest in narrators and audiences and their purposes, responses, and interests is evident throughout my discussion. For example, when I introduce Phelan's definition of narrative, I note that Phelan's definition "makes narrative—both the telling and the hearing of narrative—a human activity, and thus corrects some of the excesses of various kinds of formalism, including structuralism and deconstruction, which sometimes seem to suspend narrative in some disembodied Platonic realm" (14). My discussion of particular texts also moves beyond textual structure. Here is a passage from my discussion of Beckett's *How it Is*: "Beckett's text insistently foregrounds the verbal

---

1. As I note in the introduction, Phelan's definition would have to be adjusted to fit traditional narratives, such as myths, oral epics, or jokes, which don't usually have single narrators or audiences or occasions of performance.

synthetic. . . . But the reader who stays at the level of the verbal synthetic will miss the point of the story" (74). And a little later, when I discuss the general feeling of sensory disgust that pervades *1984*, I note that "the narrator's own emotion is evident" (88). Even when my point is the synthetic aspect of narrative, the author and the audience are still in the picture—thus, when I compare the opening of *Little Dorrit* to the opening of *Ragtime*: "Both styles, then, are overtly synthetic, but in different ways for different ends. Dickens is interested in bringing the reader into a vivid sensory experience of a particular moment, but he does most of the work himself, while the reader watches the performance; Doctorow is interested in drawing a more general picture of a period, and he leaves most of the connections to be made by the reader" (30–31). These and other passages show that there is really no disagreement here—at most a difference of emphasis.

As I understand the mimetic and the thematic aspects, neither one is simply a verbal structure, and my definitions and my practice don't take them to be simply verbal structures. (Nor is the synthetic aspect simply a verbal structure, as I will try to explain below.) Consider, by analogy, a painting such as Picasso's *Guernica*. There is a sense in which this painting is just paint, but that sense would be terribly inadequate. The painting is also mimetic—it is a representation, in several ways: It represents things in the world, such as people and horses, and it also represents a particular historical event, the attack on Guernica in the Spanish Civil War. It is also thematic—it expresses a judgment about that attack. Neither the mimetic nor the thematic can be reduced to the synthetic, though neither would exist without the synthetic. In narrative also the mimetic and the thematic depend on the synthetic, but they are not therefore simply synthetic in themselves. My approach is not reductionist.

A particular achievement of rhetorical narratology is the theorizing of the unreliable narrator, "the communication by an author to an audience that a narrator's telling is in some way off-kilter" (140). In one simple form, a narrating character takes a moral position the author can assume no one in the audience—or at least no one in his preferred audience—will share. Thus the author and the reader agree with each other against the narrating character. Examples of unreliable narrators abound, but I will mention just one, from the first chapter of Philip K. Dick's *Confessions of a Crap Artist*. The narrator of this part of the story is Jack Isidore, the crap artist of the title. At this point in the story, Dick has already shown the reader that Jack is full of crap—intellectual crap and also moral crap. At the end of the chapter, we find out that Jack has a job regrooving old tires—that is, he takes tires with no tread left and with a hot implement retraces the grooves so they look as if the tires still have tread:

> The job doesn't pay much, but it's sort of fun, figuring out the old tread pattern—sometimes you can scarcely see it. In fact, sometimes only an expert, a trained technician like myself, can see it and trace it. And you have to trace perfectly, because if you leave the old tread pattern, there's a huge gouge mark that even an idiot can recognize as not having been made by the original machine. When I get done regrooving a tire, it doesn't look hand-done by any means. It looks exactly like the way it would look if a machine had done it, and, for a regroover, that's the most satisfying feeling in the world. (8)

Of course Dick expects that the reader will disapprove of Jack's line of work. On the other hand, Jack's pride in craftsmanship in other situations would be laudable. The reader is left with a complex response: Dick, I think, is asking the reader not just to disapprove of Jack, but to examine moral principles that we may approve in general but that allow Jack to take pride in an activity we condemn. This complexity of reaction carries through the whole novel, which is deeply concerned with the kinds of ethical responses rhetorical narratology has done so much to identify. It's true that my revision of MST didn't treat unreliable narrators—because I didn't feel that revision was needed.

Granted these fundamental points of agreement, I can identify three primary points of difference between MTS and SMT. First, SMT encourages attention to the synthetic aspect of realistic narratives. Second, SMT takes mimesis to be all kinds of representation, whereas MTS restricts mimesis to realistic representation. And third, the thematic component in MTS refers to the "authorial shaping of readerly interests and responses to the ideational, ideological, and ethical dimensions of narrative" (146); SMT certainly recognizes authorial shaping, but it also pays attention to unconscious and unintended meanings. My discussion of these points will necessarily involve some overlap, since the aspects of narrative are interconnected and simultaneous, and the discussion will also touch on several secondary points, including audiences and the mimetic illusion. I will try not to repeat at any length arguments I have made in the earlier part of this discussion, and I do not attempt to answer every point in Phelan's response.

The synthetic aspect. In the MTS model, a narrative that foregrounds the synthetic tends to do so at the expense of the mimetic (Herman et al. 113). In the SMT model, however, there is no conflict between the synthetic and the mimetic aspects; all narratives can be considered from the synthetic aspect and all narratives can be considered from the mimetic aspect. The two aspects merge, somewhat in the way that the views through the red and green lenses in 3-D glasses merge and give an image in depth. (The addition of the thematic aspect adds another dimension of depth.)

In chapter 1, I have given examples that show the importance of the synthetic aspect in realistic narrative. I will add just one more here, a passage (abbreviated) from the beginning of Frank McCourt's *Angela's Ashes*:

> When I look back on my childhood I wonder how I survived at all. It was, of course, a miserable childhood: the happy childhood is hardly worth your while. Worse than the ordinary miserable childhood is the miserable Irish childhood, and worse yet is the miserable Irish Catholic childhood.
>
> . . . .
>
> Above all—we were wet.
>
> Out in the Atlantic Ocean great sheets of rain gathered to drift slowly up the River Shannon and settle forever in Limerick. The rain dampened the city from the Feast of the Circumcision to New Year's Eve. It created a cacophony of hacking coughs, bronchial rattles, asthmatic wheezes, consumptive croaks. It turned noses into fountains, lungs into bacterial sponges. It provoked cures galore; to ease the catarrh you boiled onions in milk blackened with pepper; for the congested passages you made a paste of boiled flour and nettles, wrapped it in a rag, and slapped it, sizzling, on the chest. . . . .
>
> The rain drove us into the church—our refuge, our strength, our only dry place. At Mass, Benediction, novenas, we huddled in great damp clumps, dozing through priest drone, while steam rose again from our clothes to mingle with the sweetness of incense, flowers and candles.
>
> Limerick gained a reputation for piety, but we knew it was only the rain.
>
> (11–12)

This (nonfiction) passage is thoroughly mimetic and thoroughly synthetic at the same time.[2] A reading that responds to this passage just as mimesis will miss half the fun.

Style is probably the easiest kind of synthesis to notice and analyze, but synthesis in the SMT model includes many devices at all levels of composition; I have discussed a number of these in chapter 1. In general, we know a good deal more about grammatical and rhetorical figures and their possible uses and meanings than we do about the use and meaning of the larger forms of synthesis, most of which even lack names. One of the goals of SMT is the identification, analysis, and interpretation of synthetic figures at all levels of composition in all kinds of narratives.

Thus the synthetic aspect of narrative is not simply a matter of verbal structures. Plot structures, for example, or the temporal arrangement of a nar-

---

2. I have discussed this passage at some length in Clark, *Matter* 135–37.

rative, operate above the level of words. Consider once again Dick's *Confessions of a Crap Artist*. The first chapter of the novel is narrated by the crap artist of the title, Jack Isidore, as is the second chapter. The third chapter, however, is told by a heterodiegetic narrator, and the fourth is told by Jack's sister Fay. Of the twenty chapters in the novel, Jack narrates eight, Fay narrates three, and the heterodiegetic narrator narrates nine. (I pass over questions of focalization.) The hand of the author is evident, as he decides how best to organize the telling of his story.

The mimetic aspect. Phelan's revised definition of the mimetic component refers to "the actual world," "the cause-effect logic of the extratextual world," "characters functioning as possible people or being representations of actual people," and "space and time following the known laws of physics" (146). The mimetic component seems to be firmly on the side of the real or at least the realistic.

The MTS model makes a definite division between "mimetic" narratives and "antimimetic" or "unnatural" narratives. Mimetic and unnatural narratives belong to different "domains" or "components" of the model, as we can see in the following passage from Phelan's response: "For Clark, the unnatural belongs in the domain of the mimetic because it is one kind of representation. For me, the unnatural belongs in the domain of the synthetic because it flaunts its rejection of imitation, and because I think that move leads to a qualitatively different reading experience than the one we have with texts that embrace imitation" (148–49).

In the SMT model, however, there are no domains and no components. The synthetic, mimetic, and thematic are aspects, that is, ways of looking at a narrative, and every narrative can be looked at in any of the three aspects. As I argue in the introduction, it is definitely not the case, for instance, that the unnatural or metafictional matches simply with the synthetic. The synthetic is an aspect of all kinds of narratives—realistic, unnatural, metafictional, nonfictional—just as the mimetic and the thematic are aspects of all kinds of narratives.

In the SMT model, there is no conflict between the synthetic and the mimetic: Every narrative embraces imitation, but the modes of imitation vary. This is not the place to develop any extensive account of the modes of imitation, but a few examples will suggest the complexities involved. We can begin with nonfiction told in a primarily referential manner—for example, historical narrative, such as Doris Kearns Goodwin's *Team of Rivals*; many autobiographies and biographies are similarly referential. These narratives are not "real," but they attempt to map representation closely to reality.[3] Some nonfictional

---

3. Of course, these referential nonfictions can still be considered from the synthetic aspect; it would be interesting and instructive to analyze Goodwin's *Team of Rivals* with the terms developed in chapter 1.

narratives, while still referring to reality, also foreground the synthetic, as we see in the passage from *Angela's Ashes* quoted above. Another mode could include fictions closely related to some real event. An example might be Robert Graves's *They Hanged My Saintly Billy*, a true-crime novel presented in documentary form, as if it were an investigator's account. A related mode would include fictional narratives that include the description of historical events, as in many historical novels and novels firmly situated in historical contexts, such as *Vanity Fair* or *War and Peace* or *The Red Badge of Courage*.

If nonfiction maps representation onto the real, realistic fiction maps realism onto the representation of the real—realism is the imitation of an imitation. This kind of realism narrates plausible actions in pseudo-referential language. But there are many other modes of fiction. Gertrude Stein's story "Melanctha," for instance, narrates plausible characters and actions in language that certainly is meant to call attention to itself; many other modernist fictions are written in some version of this mode. And realistic fiction includes a range of plausibility. Could Miss Havisham exist in the real world? I don't know, but I am quite sure she could not exist in *Pride and Prejudice*.

Some science fiction stories—such as Andy Weir's *The Martian*—are told as if they were realistic narratives sent back from the future, with no violations of what we now think of as the laws of nature. Other science fiction stories are written in a pseudo-referential style but use unnatural devices, such as time travel or travel through hyperspace, which have become conventions of the genre. And some (such as Edgar Rice Burroughs's Martian tales) are freely fantastic. Fantasy covers a lot of ground. Sometimes a fantastic world (such as Ursula Le Guin's Earthsea) is presented as the only world that exists. Other stories start in something like our reality and travel to Wonderland and back.

Phelan's distinction between mimetic and antimimetic narratives correlates with what he feels are two different reading experiences. I would suggest that there are many different reading experiences; each mode in the list above has its own experience. The MTS model makes a single cut, with mimetic narratives on one side and antimimetic narratives on the other; the SMT model argues that representation is multidimensional and requires multidimensional analysis.

The mimetic component in the MTS model is connected to a number of related concepts—double-consciousness, the narrative and authorial audiences, and the mimetic illusion. These concepts can be useful, but I think they need to be refined and perhaps qualified. In the introduction and in chapter 2, I have outlined a few questions I have about these concepts; here I present a few further speculations and questions. These points are not central to the project of this book, except insofar as they relate to the nature of the mimetic.

Perhaps I push these concepts harder than was intended, but if they are going to do their work, their powers should be clear.

Audiences and double-consciousness. The MTS model identifies several audiences of fictional narrative: the flesh-and-blood audience, the authorial audience, the narratee, the narrative audience, and the ideal narrative audience. Here I will discuss only the authorial audience, which knows that the characters are artificial constructs, and the narrative audience, which responds to fictional characters as if they were real people; these two audiences together produce a kind of double-consciousness.[4] The MTS model of audiences does not conflict with anything in the SMT model; on the other hand, SMT does not require this division of the reader into hypothetical audiences.

The MTS theory of multiple audiences attempts to account for the ontological and epistemological problems of fictional characters and our responses to them, but it does so by creating new entities with their own ontological difficulties. If these entities are understood as metaphors, they may be useful, as in Phelan's discussion of ghosts in fiction, but they can cause problems if they begin to take on a reality of their own.[5] In any case, there may be simpler or more direct ways to achieve the same goals.

The idea of the authorial audience as the author's ideal audience has helped me to understand and state my own reactions to Stephen Hunter's thriller *Point of Impact*. Hunter is a very skilled writer, and there are many aspects of this novel that I quite like, but my political and ethical positions are very distant from those of Hunter's authorial audience. Hunter's authorial audience has a very broad interpretation of the Second Amendment, and it believes that all evils spring from East Coast intellectuals who read the *New York Review*. (I am caricaturing his views slightly, but only slightly.) Hunter also teases his audience's reaction to violence in a way that I find disturbing. Hunter is very aware that not all of his flesh-and-blood readers will agree with the positions his authorial audience holds, and he works hard to persuade them to join his authorial audience. Rhetorical narratology is very well suited to explain the persuasive and dynamic aspects of Hunter's narration, and this model has helped me understand my own reluctance to enter his authorial audience. On the other hand, it may be simpler just to say that this particular flesh-and-blood reader lacks sympathy for some of the ethical and political opinions expressed in this thriller.

---

4. The idea of "double-consciousness" in rhetorical narratology seems unrelated to double-consciousness as identified by W. E. B. Du Bois.

5. David Herman warns about the dangers of "losing sight of the heuristic status of these models and reifying or hypostatizing the entities they encompass" (Herman et al. 152).

Once we begin to posit audiences, I'm not sure where we should stop. I find in myself a complex constellation of audiences, each of which could be located in a hypothetical audience: (1) The narrative audience, which enters the story and which is not aware of (or at least pays no attention to) the synthetic and thematic aspects. (2) The author's ideal audience. This audience shares "the knowledge, values, prejudices, fears, and experiences" the author expects, and it will notice only those synthetic elements that the author wants it to see. (3) The audience that does not initially share the values the author expects, but over the course of the reading can be persuaded to do so. (4) The audience that can be aware of all the synthetic and thematic elements, including those not foregrounded by the author. (5) The suspicious audience, which watches to see where the text deconstructs itself. (6) The audience that is reading for the first time and only notices first-reading effects. (7) The audience that is reading for the second time and notices second-reading effects. (8) The editorial audience, which makes corrections as it reads. (I am capable of correcting a typo while I weep.) Nor, I think, is this list complete. But such a menagerie of audiences seems excessive. Where in principle should we stop? Is it possible to avoid all of these audiences and simply acknowledge the complexity of readers' responses?

The narrative audience, as Phelan explains it, enters the world of the narrative and reacts to the characters as if they were real. Phelan imagines that this audience in effect puts on a cloak of invisibility, and so it sees and hears everything without being seen or heard itself. But it is not clear exactly what the narrative audience sees and hears. In book 1 of the *Iliad*, when Achilles is about to draw his sword to kill Agamemnon, Athena comes down from heaven to restrain him; Achilles sees her, but the rest of the army doesn't. Does the narrative audience see what Achilles sees or what the army sees?

In Vladimir Nabokov's *Bend Sinister*, objects sometimes take on human characteristics. Krug, the hero, enters his apartment, takes off his overcoat, and hangs up his hat: "His wide-brimmed black hat, no longer feeling at home, fell off the peg and was left lying there." In the hallway, "a rubber ball the size of a large orange was asleep on the floor" (30). A few days later, Krug takes his son away to stay with friends in the country, and the next morning he awakes: "'We met yesterday,' said the room. 'I am the spare bedroom in the Maximovs' dacha'" (76). And a few pages later: "David's toothbrush gave him a smile of recognition" (79). Does the narrative audience take these descriptions at face value or as representations of Krug's mental state? Can the narrative audience make such a distinction? Is it possible that some of the effect comes from a blurring of such distinctions?

According to Rabinowitz, the novel as a form "is generally an imitation of some nonfictional form (usually history, including biography and autobiography)," and "the narrative audience believes the narrator is a real, existing historian." He suggests that "one way to determine the characteristics of the narrative audience is to ask 'What sort of person would be implied if this work of fiction were real?' or, even better, 'What sort of person would I have to pretend to be—what would I have to know and believe—if I wanted to take this work of fiction as real?'" (Rabinowitz, "Truth" 127–28, 134). I must admit that I do not know how to read *Bend Sinister* as if the narrator were a real historian.

The MTS model, as formulated by Rabinowitz and Phelan, relies heavily on the idea of pretense, but I am not sure this term means just what they want. I take pretense to involve action without belief (as Odysseus pretends to be a beggar), but the narrative reader's response in the MTS model is belief without action. Perhaps we need a new term to describe the specific response to fictions, which involves engagement without either action or belief. Questions about belief in fiction I think can be considerably clarified by attention to possible worlds theory and cognitive linguistics. Here rhetorical narratology would benefit from an opening to cognitive narratology.[6]

The mimetic illusion. There are, I think, several different experiences that could be called "mimetic illusion." According to Ford Madox Ford:

> [The novelist] aspires—and for centuries has aspired—so to construct his stories and so to manage their surfaces that the carried-away and rapt reader shall really think himself to be in Brussels on the first of Waterloo days or in Grand Central Station waiting for the Knickerbocker Express to come in from Boston though actually he may be sitting in a cane chair lounge on a beach of Bermuda in December. (*The English Novel* 79)

Ford seems to be describing a realism so convincing that the reader takes it for reality—the world of the story replaces the real world. This effect, in Ford's account, is specific to a particular genre, the modern realistic novel; presumably epics and fantasies don't create this illusion.[7]

Roger Gard's brief account also ties the illusion to realism: "The creation of realistic fiction depends on the reader's being only momentarily and fleetingly conscious of the artifices and conventions that sustain the illusion" (144).

Paul Goodman offers an account of a general aesthetic illusion:

---

6. See, for example, Fauconnier; Pavel; Ronen; and Ryan.

7. Ford suggests that the illusion is a characteristic of modern realistic fiction, but it is quite similar to what ancient rhetoricians called "enargeia," that is, vividness.

> Unlike most sensations, however, the art work is perceived in isolation. It is not at once taken as a quality of some substance in a situation. We give it our attention, and it fills our attention, more and more excluding, as the experience grows, any awareness of our surroundings in the theatre or that we are reading a book. This isolation is, I think, the simple truth in the advice to "maintain the illusion"; it is not that the art experience is illusory but that this part of our reality is heightened and the rest temporarily excluded. (3–4)

Goodman does not link this kind of illusion to any particular form of art or any particular genre of narrative: An epic or a fantasy could surely create this effect. Goodman's illusion is a kind of attention rather than a kind of belief.

The MTS model, so far as I can find, does not offer an explicit definition of the mimetic illusion, but it does indirectly suggest what it is and how it operates. "Realistic fiction," according to Phelan, "seeks to create the illusion that everything is mimetic and nothing synthetic, or, in other words, that the characters act as they do by their own choice rather than at the behest of the author" (Phelan, *Living* 20). The mimetic illusion is tied to the mimetic component and to the narrative audience, since it is the narrative audience that takes the story to be real. "The art of realistic fiction consists of conveying the illusion that the characters are acting autonomously" (Herman et al. 113). In these and other passages, the illusion is tied to realistic fiction.

Other comments, however, suggest that the illusion is not restricted to realistic fictions. The narrative audience "accepts the basic facts of the storyworld regardless of whether they conform to those of the actual world" (Herman et al. 6–7); furthermore, "rhetorical theory does not view the concept of the narrative audience as exclusive to realistic narratives" (154). Here the theory seems to be arguing against itself.

The mimetic illusion can be broken if the reader is too much aware of the hand of the author, if the reader becomes too much aware of the synthetic: "The mimetic and synthetic components are often (though not always) on a seesaw. When a progression increases our interest in one, it tends to decrease our interest in the other" (Herman et al. 113; see also Gard, above). As Phelan notes about an incident in *Emma*:

> Austen invents the incident of a burglary in the hen house at Hartfield to motivate Mr. Woodhouse's change of mind: With Mr. Knightley at Hartfield, he will feel safer. In arranging the incident, Austen flirts with breaking the mimetic illusion—she seems to rely on a robber ex machina—but by this point in the progression, her narrative and authorial audiences so strongly desire the marriage that the invention does not break the illusion. (178)

Since the narrative audience just sits within the story, it should not question the incident; it should simply see that the henhouse was robbed. I imagine it would put up with anything the author does. What matters here is flesh-and-blood readers: Some will let this contrivance pass, others may not. Clearly the flesh-and-blood Phelan has registered this little contrivance, but he doesn't mind. The whole plot of *Emma* is full of contrivances. Take, for instance, the conversation between Emma and Harriet (volume 3, chapter 3) when Emma mistakenly thinks that Harriet is in love with Frank Churchill. This conversation works only because neither Emma nor Harriet uses a proper name. The conversation is cleverly contrived, and it is easy to see the hand of the author manipulating the characters, as she makes sure that neither uses a proper name. It is easy to find contrivances in *Emma,* and in *Pride and Prejudice*—and probably in every interesting plot ever conceived. Some contrivances work, some don't. As a general rule, a contrivance works when it is consistent with the rest of the storyworld, especially including the psychology of the characters. Readers don't object to contrivance; they object to clumsy contrivance.

The mimetic illusion is also related to the reader's emotional response to fictional characters and situations. According to Phelan, "the mimetic component of narrative is responsible for our emotional responses to it" (Phelan, *Living* 8); "responses to the mimetic component include our evolving judgements and emotions, our desires, hopes, expectations, satisfactions, and disappointments" (Herman et al. 7). Evidently we can feel emotions for characters only to the extent that we believe they are real, only to the extent that we enter the narrative audiences. Attention to the aesthetic qualities of a narrative breaks the reader's participation in the narrative audience. Thus, according to Rabinowitz, the reader's awareness of "the novel as art . . . tends to diminish our direct emotional engagement in it" (Rabinowitz, "Truth" 132).

I find this account contrary to experience—my own and, I believe, common experience. For example, John Cheever's story "The Swimmer" is both a masterpiece of unnatural temporality and a deeply moving story of a life gone wrong, as the passage of one afternoon somehow is simultaneous with the passage of a season and the passage of a life. I do not see how any audience, including the narrative audience, could take this story for history. The artifice of the telling is blatant, and it is this artifice that creates the emotional response. One might further mention Gertrude Stein's "Melanctha," John Barth's "Menelaid," Anthony Burgess's *A Clockwork Orange,* Samuel Beckett's *How It Is,* China Mieville's *The City and the City,* Kazuo Ishiguro's *The Unconsoled,* and so on and so on; in all of these the synthetic is foregrounded and the synthetic contributes to the reader's emotional response. In practice, rhetorical narratologists acknowledge the emotional power of these narratives, but they need a theory consistent with their practice.

The thematic aspect. My problem with the thematic component in the MTS model is that it's too small. Phelan's problem with the thematic aspect in the SMT model is that it's too big. Phelan argues that the thematic aspect in SMT encroaches on the synthetic and the mimetic; I argue, on the other hand, that the thematic component in MTS leaves out interesting and important parts of narrative meaning. Phelan argues that the conception of the thematic in the SMT model includes kinds of meaning that don't rise the level of the thematic: "Given Clark's definition, his claim that 'every sentence in a narrative has meaning—indeed, every word has meaning' implies that every word and every sentence in a narrative is an aspect of its thematic component. . . . While everyone would agree that [words and sentences] have meaning, focusing on this truism obscures the significant differences in the functions of these words and sentences" (172).

I grant Phelan's point here: My first formulation of the thematic is too inclusive. As I continued the discussion, I tried to pull back somewhat, noting that the meaning of the whole is gradually formed from the words and sentences as they are experienced by the reader. And later I clarified that meaning is built up gradually, sentence by sentence, in the course of reading. Some narrative acts will stand out; others will fade into the background, though these, too, contribute to the gradual construction of meaning. Still, my initial formulation was misleading, and I am happy to qualify it in the light of Phelan's comment.

But this qualification still leaves a fairly broad understanding of the thematic. Specifically, I want to include kinds of narrative meaning not (I think) usually included in the thematic. I believe that narratives are typically rich in meanings, far beyond the paraphrasable arguments often identified as themes. I want to include meanings not consciously intended by the author; meanings expressed indirectly—for instance, through the structure of the composition; marginal or secondary meanings; and the reading experience as a kind of meaning.

Phelan argues that topics "don't become properly part of the thematic until authors communicate their stances on them via explicit statements or the narrative progression" (176). At first Phelan seems to be linking the thematic to explicit statements by the narrator; he gives as an example a comment by the narrator of *Emma*: "Seldom, very seldom, does complete truth belong to any human disclosure; seldom can it happen that something is not a little disguised or a little mistaken." Of course, narrators do sometimes make such explicit comments, but much of the meaning of a narrative is indirect, and an interpretive model must also take this kind of meaning into account. Phelan grants that "the narrative progression" can make a topic part of the thematic. I am not sure exactly what he means here, and how far this qualification extends. He may mean something like what I call structural meaning. But other comments suggest that Phelan takes the conscious intent of the author as essential. He argues, for instance, that "Clark . . . with his ultimate focus on textual composition, unmoors construction, representation, and signification from how they're used by authors in order to accomplish purposes in relation to audiences" (143).[8] The thematic in the SMT model certainly includes meanings intended by the author—as well as unintended meanings. The MTS model, however, seems to exclude unintended meanings and purposes. We will see that Phelan perhaps builds an escape hatch, but it is hard to understand his objection to the SMT definition of the thematic unless he intends to exclude meanings not intended by the author.

Intent is, of course, a sticky point in literary theory. Rhetorical narratology takes the position that authorial intent is a real thing and that it can be taken into account in interpretation. I agree, but I don't think that's the whole story. Speakers and writers are not always aware of the meanings their stories convey, and a theory of meaning in literature has to take into account the times when we can't tell an author's motivation, or when it doesn't matter.[9] I have argued, for example, that Orwell presents an essentializing view of the feminine when he describes Julia's use of cosmetics. I am not at all sure that he meant to convey this view—but there it is. (Perhaps it is relevant that critics generally ignore the passage.) I suspect that this kind of essentializing was simply taken for granted in Orwell's world, an unconscious aspect of ideology—as many aspects of ideology are unconscious. Part of the job of criticism is the archaeology of the ideological unconscious. This passage is probably marginal or at least secondary to the primary thematic point of the novel, but it should not be left out of account. My understanding of the thematic thus is consistent with one of the goals of feminist criticism, which attempts to "scrutinize details that nonfeminist criticism might find trivial or peripheral," as Robyn Warhol says (Herman et al. 12). Warhol's point can be generalized to cover various kinds of peripheral and perhaps unintended meanings.

---

8. I have already pointed out that the SMT model is not ultimately a textualist approach, and I will not further argue the point here.

9. "Everyone knows today that human beings do not always, or perhaps even habitually, act from motives of which they are fully conscious or which they are willing to avow; and to exclude insight into unconscious or unavowed motives is surely a way of going about one's work with one eye willfully shut" (Carr 48).

Phelan is of course aware of the difficulties involved in establishing conscious intent: "The aim of the rhetorical approach is not to determine the conscious intention of the actual author (although, if available, that may be one piece of relevant information) but rather to discern the system of intentionality that explains why the text has this particular shape rather than some other one" (Herman et al. 32). Phelan's position here is consistent with Ralph Rader's comment, "I stress that what I refer to as intention is something immanent in the work—its formal principle as a work—and available only by hypothesis, though there is no reason why we should not take an author's statements about his intention as relevant to or corroborative of a hypothesis about immanent intention" (Rader, "Emergence" 95–96). Phelan's theory of immanent textual intent—which seems to unmoor intention from the consciousness of the author and to shift it to the text itself—is one way of acknowledging some of the difficulties in determining the intent of the flesh-and-blood author. If this is Phelan's position, I am not sure where he disagrees with my understanding of unconscious narrative meaning.

Thematic interpretation in the SMT model doesn't insist that all meanings are equal, but it does allow every word and sentence and every narrative structure to make a claim to thematic value. Thus, in my discussion of the *Iliad* and the *Odyssey*, I argue that the patterning of the word *gaster*—"stomach" or "belly"—contributes to the thematic aspect of the epics. A reading that pays some attention to *gaster*, I claim, is a better reading than one that doesn't. Can we know that the author or authors of the epics intended to make this pattern? One could argue that the patterning is accidental, or that it is the unconscious result of mimetic consistency. We simply don't know, but in any case the patterning contributes to the meaning of the epics.

Meaning can be conveyed in many ways. When it is conveyed by words, we often talk about verbal meaning; I suggest that when it is conveyed by structures, we can talk about structural meaning. Phelan argues that the term "structural meaning" mistakes "a means of conveying the thematic for the thematic itself," and therefore it should be located "in the domain of the synthetic" rather than in the thematic (174–75). He notes that in my discussion of *1984*, I use the parallel scenes at the Chestnut Tree Café as an example of both structural meaning and the synthetic category of repeated events. According to Phelan, "the scenes belong in the domain of the synthetic because Orwell is not making any thematic point about parallel structure but instead is using the parallel to make thematic points about the power of the totalitarian state" (175). He attributes what he calls "the problem" not to carelessness but to "such an expansive view of the thematic that it seems almost natural for it to encroach upon the synthetic" (175).

Once again we see the difference between the components of the MTS model and the aspects of the SMT model. The SMT model does not have domains. These particular parallel scenes can be considered from the synthetic aspect, from the mimetic aspect, and from the thematic aspect. Whenever we notice some synthetic feature of a narrative, we should ask what it means; otherwise the synthetic elements remain simply textual structures. The thematic aspect does not encroach on the synthetic: The synthetic and the thematic are complementary ways of thinking about what Orwell is doing. The repetition of these scenes in *1984* is meaningful, and if that meaning isn't part of the thematic aspect, I don't know where to put it.

The important point here is that meanings in narrative are often conveyed by structures in the narrative or indeed by the structure of the narrative. A part of my project is to identify what I have called narrative figures, and then to try to understand how these narrative figures can be used to convey meaning. Meanings come in various types, and not all types are easily paraphrased in the form of propositions, but all types, including stylistic structures, can rise to thematic significance. In my opinion, Austen's use of tricolon, and especially the extended tricolon, rises to thematic significance, as do the forms of repetition in Ford Madox Ford's *The Good Soldier* and the short sentences in Doctorow's *Ragtime*.

The thematic element of literature often tends toward the cognitive or the intellectual, and the definition of the thematic in the MTS model follows that tendency: The thematic is "that component of a narrative text concerned with making statements, taking ideological positions, teaching readers truths" (Phelan, *Living* 219). There is, however, no strict dichotomy between thought and feeling; as Jerome Bruner notes, "people 'perfink'—perceive, think, and feel at once" (Bruner 69). This principle is especially true in art. Thus, the SMT model attempts to form a model of the thematic that extends beyond the thinking and includes perceiving and feeling—the experience of reading.

Phelan remarks that "meaning as the experience of reading" is "at best a fuzzy category" (174). Rhetorical narratology, however, includes the idea of experience, though not as part of the thematic component. Phelan and Rabinowitz note that "rhetorical theory's interest in the 'purpose(s)' of narrative" tends to shift the "analytical focus from the 'meaning' (typically the thematic component) of narrative to the experience of narrative" (Herman et al. 141). I am doing nothing new in wanting to think about experience; the only innovation is taking experience to be a kind of meaning.

I suppose there are stories that are interesting just as intellectual puzzles, but usually if we don't feel a story, even a story that foregrounds the synthetic, we probably won't like it very much or for very long. Puzzles get used up in a way that stories don't. And, following Bruner, I don't want to divide the feeling off from the perceiving and the thinking. I don't want to locate the perceiving, the feeling, and the thinking in different components. I can feel the synthetic, just as I can perceive the thematic, or think the mimetic. In the SMT model, all of these are simultaneous, all are linked, and all blend together.

The thematic aspect of the SMT model is indeed quite broad. It includes explicit statements by the author or narrator, but it also includes meanings outside the awareness of the author, meanings expressed indirectly or through the structure of the narration, as well as a recognition that the ideational part of the narrative experience is bound up with perceptions and feelings.

None of the changes I have proposed conflicts with the fundamental principles of rhetorical narratology. In particular, these changes are compatible with the principle that a narrative is a transaction between a storyteller and an audience. The model outlined here recognizes the value of identifying the synthetic, mimetic, and thematic as elements of narrative. The changes proposed are intended, however, to open rhetorical narratology to other approaches—including unnatural, feminist, and cognitive narratologies. The SMT model can be applied to the interpretation of particular narratives, and it also points the way to a program for further research within rhetorical narratology, including analysis of synthetic devices in realistic narratives; of narrative world-making in all of its complex forms; and of the contribution made to the thematic aspect of narrative by all kinds and levels of meaning. I don't know that I have come home to rhetorical narratology—I believe I never left—but with these changes I have tried to open some doors and windows.

BIBLIOGRAPHY

Abrams, M. H. *The Mirror and the Lamp: Romantic Theory and the Critical Tradition.* Oxford: Oxford University Press, 1953.

Adams, Hazard. *Critical Theory since Plato.* New York: Harcourt Brace Janovich, 1971.

Ahl, Frederick, and Hanna M. Roisman. *The Odyssey Re-formed.* Ithaca, NY: Cornell University Press, 1996.

Alber, Jan. *Unnatural Narrative: Impossible Worlds in Fiction and Drama.* Lincoln: University of Nebraska Press, 2016.

———. "Unnatural Spaces and Narrative Worlds." In Alber et al., *Poetics of Unnatural Narrative*, 45–66.

Alber, Jan, Henrik Skov Nielsen, and Brian Richardson, eds. *A Poetics of Unnatural Narrative.* Columbus: The Ohio State University Press, 2013.

Alber, Jan, and Rüdiger Heinze, eds. *Unnatural Narratives—Unnatural Narratology.* Berlin: De Gruyter, 2011.

Altman, Rick. *A Theory of Narrative.* New York: Columbia University Press, 2008.

Amis, Martin, *Time's Arrow.* New York: Vintage, 1991.

Anderson, William. *Dante the Maker.* London: Hutchinson & Co, 1983.

Aristotle. *Poetics.* Translated by S. H. Butcher. Introduction by Francis Fergusson. New York: Hill and Wang, 1961.

Auerbach, Erich. *Mimesis: The Representation of Reality in Western Literature.* New York: Doubleday, 1957 [1946].

Austen, Jane. *Emma.* Norton Critical Ed., edited by George Justice. 4th ed. New York: W. W. Norton & Company, 2012 [1816].

———. *Persuasion.* Edited with an Introduction and notes by Gillian Beer. London: Penguin Books, 2003 [1818].

Austin, J. L. *How to Do Things with Words.* Cambridge, MA: Harvard University Press, 1975.

Austin, Norman. *Archery at the Dark of the Moon: Poetic Problems in Homer's Odyssey.* Berkeley: University of California Press, 1975.

Babb, Howard S. *Jane Austen's Novels: The Fabric of Dialogue.* Columbus: The Ohio State University Press, 1962.

Bachelard, Gaston. *The Poetics of Space.* Boston: Beacon Press, 1969 [1958].

Bal, Meike. *Narratology: Introduction to the Theory of Narrative.* Toronto: University of Toronto Press, 1985.

Barth, John. *Lost in the Funhouse.* New York: Bantam Books, 1978.

Basset, Samuel. *The Poetry of Homer.* Berkeley: University of California Press, 1938.

Beckett, Samuel. *How It Is.* New York: Grove Press, 1964.

Booth, Wayne C. *The Rhetoric of Fiction.* 2nd ed. Chicago: University of Chicago Press, 1983.

Boyd, John D. *The Function of Mimesis and Its Decline.* Cambridge, MA: Harvard University Press, 1968.

Bridgeman, Teresa. "Time and Space." In Herman, *Cambridge Companion to Narrative,* 52–65.

Brontë, Emily. *Wuthering Heights.* Guelph, Ontario: Broadview Press, 2007 [1847].

Browning, Robert. *Poems of Robert Browning.* Edited by Donald Smalley. Boston: Houghton Mifflin Company, 1956.

Bruner, Jerome. *Actual Minds, Possible Worlds.* Cambridge, MA: Harvard University Press, 1986.

Burgess, Anthony. *A Clockwork Orange.* New York: W. W. Norton and Company, 1986 [1962].

Burrows, J. F. *Jane Austen's* Emma. Sydney: Sydney University Press, 1968.

Buxton, Richard. "Similes and Other Likenesses." 1968. In Robert Fowler, *Cambridge Companion to Homer,* 139–55.

Byrne, Sandie. *Jane Austen's Possessions and Dispossessions: The Significance of Objects.* New York: Palgrave Macmillan, 2014.

Calder, Jenni. *Chronicles of Conscience: A Study of George Orwell and Arthur Koestler.* Pittsburg: University of Pittsburg Press, 1968.

Calvino, Italo. *If on a winter's night a traveler.* Translated by William Weaver. New York: Harcourt Brace Jovanovich, 1981.

Carr, E. H. *What Is History?* Harmondsworth: Penguin Books, 1964.

Clark, Matthew. "Chryses' Supplication: Speech-Act and Mythological Allusion." *Classical Antiquity* 17, no. 1 (April 1998): 5–24.

———. "The Cognitive Turn." *Narrative Inquiry* 22, no. 2 (2012): 405–10.

———. "The Concept of Plot and the Plot of the Iliad." *Phoenix* 55, no. 1/2 (Spring–Summer 2001): 1–8.

———. "Fighting Words: How Heroes Argue." *Arethusa* 35, no. 1 (2002): 99–115.

———. "Formulas, Metre and Type-Scenes." In Robert Fowler, *Cambridge Companion to Homer,* 117–38.

———. *A Matter of Style: On Writing and Technique.* Toronto: Oxford University Press, 2002.

———. *Narrative Structures and the Language of the Self.* Columbus: The Ohio State University Press, 2010.

Clarke, Austin. "If Only, Only If . . ." From *Nine Men Who Laughed.* Markham, Ontario: Penguin Books, 1986.

Clarke, Michael. "Manhood and Heroism." In Robert Fowler, *Cambridge Companion to Homer,* 74–90.

Coetzee, J. M. *Foe.* London: Penguin Books, 1986.

Cohen, Beth. *The Distaff Side: Representing the Female in Homer's* Odyssey. Oxford: Oxford University Press, 1995.

Cohn, Dorrit. "Metalepsis and Mise en Abyme." Translated by Lewis Gleich. *Narrative* 20 (2012): 105–14.

Coleridge, Samuel Taylor. *The Table Talk.* Edited by T. Ashe. London: George Bell and Sons, 1888.

Connor, W. Robert. *Thucydides.* Princeton, NJ: Princeton University Press, 1984.

Conrad, Joseph. *The Secret Agent*. London: Penguin Books, 2012 [1907].

Cook, Erwin. *The Odyssey in Athens: Myths of Cultural Origins*. Ithaca, NY: Cornell University Press, 1995.

Copeland, Edward. "Money." In Copeland and McMaster, *Cambridge Companion to Jane Austen*, 131–48.

Copeland, Edward, and Juliet McMaster. *The Cambridge Companion to Jane Austen*. Cambridge: Cambridge University Press, 1997.

Cortázar, Julio. *Blow-Up and Other Stories*. Translated by Paul Blackburn. New York: Pantheon, 1985 [1967].

Craig, Sheryl. *Jane Austen and the State of the Nation*. New York: Palgrave Macmillan, 2015.

Crane, R. S. "The Concept of Plot and the Plot of *Tom Jones*." In *Critics and Criticism*, 62–93. Chicago: University of Chicago Press, 1957.

Crick, Bernard. "The Reception of *Nineteen Eighty-Four*." In Gertrude Clarke Whittal Poetry and Literature Fund, *George Orwell*, 97–103.

Crotty, Kevin. *The Poetics of Supplication*. Ithaca, NY: Cornell University Press, 1994.

Curtius, Ernst Robert. *European Literature and the Latin Middle Ages*. Translated by Willard R. Trask. Princeton, NJ: Princeton University Press, 1973.

Dangerfield, George. *The Strange Death of Liberal England*. New York: Capricorn Books, 1961.

Davidson, Jenny. *Reading Style: A Life in Sentences*. New York: Columbia University Press, 2014.

Dick, Philip K. *The Confessions of a Crap Artist*. New York: Random House, 1992.

Dickens, Charles. *Little Dorrit*. Harmondsworth: Penguin Books, 1967 [1857].

———. *The Mystery of Edwin Drood*. London: Penguin Books, 1985 [1870].

Doctorow, E. L. *Ragtime*. New York: Random House, 2007.

Doležel, Lubomír. *Heterocosmica: Fiction and Possible Worlds*. Baltimore: Johns Hopkins University Press, 1998.

Donaghue, Denis. "*Nineteen Eighty-Four*: Politics and Fable." In Gertrude Clarke Whitall Poetry and Literature Fund, *George Orwell*, 57–69.

Dougherty, Carol. *The Raft of Odysseus: The Ethnographic Imagination of Homer's Odyssey*. Oxford: Oxford University Press, 2001.

Douglas, Mary. *Thinking in Circles*. New Haven, CT: Yale University Press, 2010.

Duckworth, Alistair M. *The Improvement of the Estate: A Study of Jane Austen's Novels*. Baltimore: Johns Hopkins University Press, 1994.

Duffy, Joseph M. Jr. "*Emma*: The Awakening from Innocence." *ELH* 21, no. 1 (March 1954): 39–53.

Eagleton, Terry. *Ideology: An Introduction*. London: Verso, 1991.

———. *Literary Theory: An Introduction*. Oxford: Basil Blackwell, 1983.

Eliot, George. *Adam Bede*. London: Penguin Books, 1985 [1859].

Falkner, Thomas M. "Containing Tragedy: Rhetoric and Self-Representation in Sophocles' *Philoctetes*." *Classical Antiquity* 17, no. 1 (April 1998): 25–58.

Fauconnier, Giles. *Mental Spaces*. Cambridge: Cambridge University Press, 1994.

Faulkner, William. *Three Famous Short Novels: Spotted Horses, Old Man, The Bear*. New York: Random House, 1961.

———. *The Wild Palms*. New York: New American Library, 1948.

———. *The Wild Palms*. New York: Random House, 1966 [1939].

Felson, Nancy. *Regarding Penelope: From Character to Poetics*. Princeton, NJ: Princeton University Press, 1994.

Finley, Sir Moses. *The World of Odysseus*. New York: New York Review Books, 2002.

Flaubert, Gustav. *Madame Bovary.* Translated by Lydia Davis. New York: Penguin Books, 2011.
Fletcher, Angus. *Allegory: The Theory of a Symbolic Mode.* Ithaca, NY: Cornell University Press, 1964.
Foley, John Miles. *Immanent Art: From Structure to Meaning in Traditional Oral Epic.* Bloomington: Indiana University Press, 1991.
Ford, Ford Madox. *The English Novel from the Earliest Days to the Death of Joseph Conrad.* Manchester: Carcanet Press, 1997 [1930].
———. *The Good Soldier: A Tale of Passion.* New York: Penguin, 2007 [1915].
Forster, E. M. *Aspects of the Novel.* New York: Harcourt, Brace & World, 1927.
Fowler, Alastair. *Kinds of Literature: An Introduction to the Theory of Genres.* Cambridge, MA: Harvard University Press, 1982.
Fowler, Robert, ed. *The Cambridge Companion to Homer.* Cambridge: Cambridge University Press, 2004.
Fowler, Roger. *The Language of George Orwell.* London: Macmillan Press, 1995.
Frye, Northrop. *The Anatomy of Criticism: Four Essays.* New York: Atheneum, 1967.
Gallagher, Catherine. "The Rise of Fictionality." In *The Novel,* edited by Franco Moretti, 336–63. Princeton, NJ: Princeton University Press, 2006.
Gard, Roger. *Jane Austen's Novels: The Art of Clarity.* New Haven, CT: Yale University Press, 1992.
Genette, Gérard. *Narrative Discourse: An Essay on Method.* Translated by Jane E. Lewin. Ithaca, NY: Cornell University Press, 1980.
Gertrude Clarke Whittall Poetry and Literature Fund. *George Orwell & "Nineteen Eighty-Four."* Washington, DC: Superintendent of Documents, US Government Printing Office, 1985.
Gervais, Bertrand. "Reading Tensions: Of Sterne, Klee, and the Secret Police." *New Literary History* 26, no. 4 (Autumn 1995): 855–84.
Gleason, Abbot, Jack Goldsmith, and Martha Nussbaum, eds. *On "Nineteen Eighty-Four": Orwell and Our Future.* Princeton, NJ: Princeton University Press, 2005.
Golden, Leon. *Aristotle on Tragic and Comic Mimesis.* Atlanta: Scholars Press, 1992.
Gombrich, Ernest. *Art and Illusion.* New York: Pantheon Books, 1960.
Gomel, Elana. *Narrative Space and Time: Representing Impossible Topologies in Literature.* New York: Routledge, 2014.
Goodman, Nelson. *Languages of Art.* Indianapolis: Hackett Publishing Company, 1976.
———. *Ways of Worldmaking.* Hassocks, UK: The Harvester Press, 1978.
Goodman, Paul. *The Structure of Literature.* Chicago: University of Chicago Press, 1968 [1954].
Graff, Gerald. *Literature against Itself: Literary Ideas in Modern Society.* Chicago: Chicago University Press, 1979.
Grass, Günter. *The Tin Drum.* New York: Pantheon Books, 1962.
Graves, Robert. *They Hanged My Saintly Billy.* London: Xanadu Publications, 1989 [1957].
Green, Clarence. *The Neo-Classic Theory of Tragedy in England during the Eighteenth Century.* Cambridge, MA: Harvard University Press, 1934.
Grice, Paul. *Studies in the Way of Words.* Cambridge, MA: Harvard University Press, 1989.
Griffin, Jasper. *Homer on Life and Death.* Oxford: Clarendon Press, 1980.
Handler, Richard, and Daniel Segal. *Jane Austen and the Fiction of Culture: An Essay on the Narration of Social Realities.* Updated ed. Lanham, MD: Rowman and Littlefield, 1990.
Hardy, Thomas. *The Return of the Native.* London: Macmillan, 1974.
Harvey, W. J. "The Plot of *Emma.*" In Lodge, *Jane Austen: "Emma,"* 232–47.

Heidegger, Martin. *Being and Time*. Translated by Joan Stambaugh. Albany: SUNY Press, 2010 [1927].

Heinze, Ruediger. "Violations of Mimetic Epistemology in First-Person Narrative Fiction." *Narrative* 16, no. 3 (2008): 279–97.

———. "The Whirligig of Time: Towards a Poetics of Unnatural Temporality." In Alber et al., *Poetics of Unnatural Narrative*, 31–44.

Heitman, Richard. *Taking Her Seriously: Penelope and the Plot of Homer's "Odyssey."* Ann Arbor: University of Michigan Press, 2005.

Heller, Joseph. *Catch-22*. 50th anniversary ed. New York: Simon and Schuster, 2011 [1961].

Herman, David, ed. *The Cambridge Companion to Narrative*. Cambridge: Cambridge University Press, 2007.

———. *Story Logic: Problems and Possibilities of Narrative*. Lincoln: University of Nebraska Press, 2002.

Herman, David, James Phelan, Peter J. Rabinowitz, Brian Richardson, and Robyn Warhol. *Narrative Theory: Core Concepts and Critical Debates*. Columbus: The Ohio State University Press, 2012.

Highet, Gilbert. *The Anatomy of Satire*. Princeton, NJ: Princeton University Press, 1962.

Hockett, Charles. "The Problem of Universals in Language." In *Universals of Language*, edited by Joseph H. Greenberg. Cambridge, MA: MIT Press, 1961, 1–29.

Homer. *The Iliad of Homer*. Translated by Richmond Lattimore. Chicago: University of Chicago Press, 1961.

———. *The Odyssey of Homer*. Translated by Richmond Lattimore. New York: HarperCollins, 1991.

Honig, Edwin. *Dark Conceit: The Making of Allegory*. Providence: Brown University Press, 1972.

Horkheimer, Max, and Theodor W. Adorno. *Dialectic of Enlightenment*. New York: Continuum, 1996 [1944].

Howe, Irving, ed. *"1984" Revisited: Totalitarianism in Our Century*. New York: Harper and Row, 1983.

Hunter, Richard. *The Measure of Homer*. Cambridge: Cambridge University Press, 2018.

Isherwood, Christopher. *Goodbye to Berlin*. London: The Hogarth Press, 1969.

Jakobson, Roman. "The Dominant." In *Readings in Russian Poetics: Formalist and Structuralist Views*, edited by Ladislav Matejka and Krystyna Pomorska, 82–87. Cambridge, MA: MIT Press, 1978.

James, Henry. *The American*. Oxford: Oxford University Press, 1999.

———. *The Turn of the Screw: A Case Study in Contemporary Criticism*. Edited by Peter Beidler. Boston: Bedford-St. Martin's, 2010.

———. *The Wings of the Dove*. New York: New American Library, 1964 [1902].

Johnson, Gary. *The Vitality of Allegory: Figural Narrative in Modern and Contemporary Fiction*. Columbus: The Ohio State University Press, 2012.

Johnson, Samuel. "Preface to Shakespeare." In *Johnson on Shakespeare*, edited by Walter Raleigh. London: Oxford University Press, 1925, 9–63.

Johnson, Samuel. *The History of Rasselas, Prince of Abissinia*. London: Oxford University Press, 1971.

Johnson, W. R. *Darkness Visible: A Study of Vergil's "Aeneid."* Berkeley: University of California Press, 1976.

Katz, Marilyn A. *Penelope's Renown: Meaning and Indeterminacy in the Odyssey*. Princeton, NJ: Princeton University Press, 1991.

Kearns, Emily. "The Gods in the Homeric Epics." In Robert Fowler, *The Cambridge Companion to Homer*, 59–73.
Kermode, Frank. "Secrets and Narrative Sequence." In Mitchell, *On Narrative*, 79–97.
Kesey, Ken. *One Flew over the Cuckoo's Nest*. New York: New American Library, 1962.
Kittay, Eva Feder. *Metaphor: Its Cognitive Force and Linguistic Structure*. Oxford: Clarendon Press, 1987.
Kövecses, Zoltán. *Metaphor: A Practical Introduction*. Oxford: Oxford University Press, 2002.
Kroeber, Karl. *Styles in Fictional Structure: The Art of Jane Austen, Charlotte Brontë, George Eliot*. Princeton, NJ: Princeton University Press, 1971.
Lakoff, George, and Mark Johnson. *Metaphors We Live By*. Chicago: Chicago University Press, 1980.
Lamberton, Robert. *Homer the Theologian: Neoplatonist Allegorical Reading and the Growth of the Epic Tradition*. Berkeley: University of California Press, 1989.
——. *Proclus the Successor on Poetics and the Homeric Poems: Essays 5 and 6 of His Commentary on the Republic of Plato*. Atlanta: Society of Biblical Literature, 2012.
Lamberton, Robert, and John J. Keaney, eds. *Homer's Ancient Readers: The Hermeneutics of Greek Epic's Earliest Exegetes*. Princeton, NJ: Princeton University Press, 1992.
Lanham, Richard. *Tristram Shandy: The Games of Pleasure*. Berkeley: University of California Press, 1973.
Le Guin, Ursula K. *The Dispossessed*. New York: Avon Books, 1974.
——. *The Word for World Is Forest*. New York: Berkley Publishing Corporation, 1972.
Levaniouk, Olga. *Eve of the Festival: Making Myth in Odyssey 19*. Washington, DC: Center for Hellenic Studies, 2011.
Levin, Richard. *New Readings vs. Old Plays: Recent Trends in the Reinterpretation of English Renaissance Drama*. Chicago: University of Chicago Press, 1979.
Lewis, C. S. *Out of the Silent Planet*. New York: Collier Books, 1962.
Lodge, David, ed. *Jane Austen: "Emma": A Casebook*. London: Macmillan & Company, 1968.
Loomis, Roger Sherman. *The Development of Arthurian Romance*. New York: W. W. Norton & Company, 1963.
Louden, Bruce. *The Odyssey: Structure, Narration, and Meaning*. Baltimore: Johns Hopkins University Press, 1999.
Lowe, N. J. *The Classical Plot and the Invention of Western Narrative*. Cambridge: Cambridge University Press, 2000.
Lowrey, Malcolm. *Under the Volcano*. New York: Reynal & Hitchcock, 1947.
MacDonald, George. *Phantases and Lilith*. Grand Rapids, Michigan: Wm. B. Erdmans, 1968 [1858].
Mäkelä, Maria. "Realism and the Unnatural." In Alber et al., *Poetics of Unnatural Narrative*, 142–66.
Mann, Thomas. *Confessions of Felix Krull, Confidence Man*. Translated by Denver Lindley. London: Secker & Warburg, 1955.
McCourt, Frank. *Angela's Ashes*. New York: Simon & Schuster, 1996.
McCoy, Horace. *Kiss Tomorrow Goodbye*. New York: Random House, 1948.
McEwan, Ian. *Atonement*. New York: Knopf, 2001.
McHale, Brian. "The Unnaturalness of Narrative Poetry." In Alber et al., *Poetics of Unnatural Narrative*, 199–222.
McMaster, Juliet. "Class." In Copeland and McMaster, *Cambridge Companion to Jane Austen*, 115–30.

Melberg, Arne. *Theories of Mimesis.* Cambridge: Cambridge University Press, 1995.

Meyers, Jeffrey. "*Nineteen Eighty-Four:* A Novel of the 1930s." In Gertrude Clarke Whittall Poetry and Literature Fund, *George Orwell,* 79–89.

Miller, Mark Crispin. "The Fate of *1984.*" In Howe, *"1984" Revisited,* 19–46.

Milton, John. *Paradise Lost.* 2nd ed. Edited by Scott Elledge. New York: W. W. Norton, 1975.

Mitchell, W. J. T., ed. *On Narrative.* Chicago: University of Chicago Press, 1981.

Morris, Ian. "The Use and Abuse of Homer." *Classical Antiquity* 5, no. 1 (April 1986): 81–138.

Morris, Pam. *Realism.* London: Routledge, 2003.

Morrison, Toni. *Beloved.* New York: Knopf, 1987.

———. *Jazz.* New York: Vintage Books, 2004.

Muellner, Leonard. *The Anger of Achilles: Mênis in Greek Epic.* Ithaca, NY: Cornell University Press, 1996.

Muir, Edwin. *The Structure of the Novel.* New York: Harcourt, Brace & World, 1957.

Mulvihill, Robert, ed. *Reflections on America, 1984: An Orwell Symposium.* Athens: University of Georgia Press, 1986.

Munro, Alice. "Prue." In *The McGraw-Hill Book of Fiction,* edited by Robert DiYanni and Kraft Rompf, 787–90. New York: McGraw-Hill, 1995 [1982].

Murnaghan, Sheila. *Disguise and Recognition in the Odyssey.* Princeton, NJ: Princeton University Press, 1987.

Nabokov, Vladimir. *Bend Sinister.* Harmondsworth: Penguin Books, 1964.

Nagy, Gregory. *The Best of the Achaeans: Concept of the Hero in Archaic Greek Poetry.* Baltimore: Johns Hopkins University Press, 1979.

Nell, Victor. *Lost in a Book: The Psychology of Reading for Pleasure.* New Haven, CT: Yale University Press, 1988.

Nielsen, Henrik Skov, James Phelan, and Richard Walsh. "Ten Theses about Fictionality." *Narrative* 23, no. 1 (2015): 61–73.

O'Brien, Flann. *The Third Policeman.* London: Pan Books Ltd., 1967.

Orwell, George. *1984.* Edited by Irving Howe. New York: Harcourt Brace Jovanovich, 1982 [1949].

Osborne, Robin. "Homer's Society." In Robert Fowler, *Cambridge Companion to Homer,* 206–19.

Page, Denys. *The Homeric Odyssey.* Oxford: Clarendon Press, 1955.

Page, Norman. *The Language of Jane Austen.* Oxford: Blackwell, 1972.

Palaephatus. *On Unbelievable Tales.* Translation, introduction, and commentary by Jacob Stern. Wauconda, IL: Bolchazy-Carducci Publishers, 1996.

Parker, Mark. "The End of Emma: Drawing the Boundaries of Class in Austen." *The Journal of English and Germanic Philology* 91, no. 3 (July 1992): 344–59.

Parry, Milman. *The Making of Homeric Verse: The Collected Papers of Milman Parry.* Edited by Adam Parry. Oxford: Clarendon Press, 1971.

Pavel, Thomas G. *Fictional Worlds.* Cambridge, MA: Harvard University Press, 1986.

Phelan, James, ed. "Authors, Resources, Audiences: Toward a Rhetorical Poetics of Narrative." Special Issue, *Style* 52, nos. 1–2 (2018).

———. *Experiencing Fiction: Judgments, Progressions, and the Rhetorical Theory of Narrative.* Columbus: The Ohio State University Press, 2007.

———. "Fictionality, Audiences, and Character: A Rhetorical Alternative to Catherine Gallagher's 'The Rise of Fictionality.'" *Poetics Today* 39, no. 1 (2018): 113–29.

———. "Local Fictionality in Global Nonfiction: Roz Chast's *Can't We Talk about Something More Pleasant?*" *Enthymema* 16 (December 2016). http://riviste.unimi.it/index.php/enthymema/article/view/7473.

———. *Living to Tell about It: A Rhetoric and Ethics of Character Narration*. Ithaca, NY: Cornell University Press, 2005.

———. *Narrative as Rhetoric: Technique, Audiences, Ethics, Ideology*. Columbus: The Ohio State University Press, 1996.

———. *Reading People, Reading Plots: Character, Progression, and the Interpretation of Narrative*. Chicago: University of Chicago Press, 1989.

———. *Somebody Telling Someone Else: A Rhetorical Poetics of Narrative*. Columbus: The Ohio State University Press, 2017.

———. *Worlds from Words: A Theory of Language in Fiction*. Chicago: University of Chicago Press, 1981.

Pifer, Ellen. *Nabokov and the Novel*. Cambridge, MA: Harvard University Press, 1980.

Plato. *Republic*. Translated by Robin Waterfield. Oxford: Oxford University Press, 2008.

Potolsky, Matthew. *Mimesis*. New York: Routledge, 2006.

Power, Michael. *Transportation and Homeric Epic*. Unpublished doctoral diss., Australian Nation University, 2006.

Quilligan, Maureen. *The Language of Allegory: Defining the Genre*. Ithaca, NY: Cornell University Press, 1979.

Rabinowitz, Peter J. *Before Reading: Narrative Conventions and the Politics of Interpretation*. Ithaca, NY: Cornell University Press, 1987.

———. "Truth in Fiction: A Reexamination of Audiences." *Critical Inquiry* 4, no. 1 (Autumn 1977): 121–41.

Rader, Ralph W. "The Dramatic Monologue and Related Lyric Forms." *Critical Inquiry* 3, no. 1 (Autumn 1976): 131–51.

———. *Fact, Fiction, and Form: Selected Essays of Ralph W. Rader*. Edited by James Phelan and David H. Richter. Columbus: The Ohio State University Press, 2011.

Richardson, Brian. "Beyond Story and Discourse: Narrative Time in Postmodern and Nonmimetic Fiction." In *Narrative Dynamics: Essays on Time, Plot, Closure, and Frames*, edited by Brian Richardson, 47–63. Columbus: The Ohio State University Press, 2002.

———. "The Other Reader's Response: On Multiple, Divided, and Oppositional Audiences." *Criticism* 39, no. 1 (Winter 1997): 31–53.

———. *Unnatural Narrative: Theory, History, Practice*. Columbus: The Ohio State University Press, 2015.

———. *Unnatural Voices: Extreme Narration in Modern and Contemporary Fiction*. Columbus: The Ohio State University Press, 2006.

Richter, David. *Fable's End: Completeness and Closure in Rhetorical Fiction*. Chicago: University of Chicago Press, 1974.

Ricoeur, Paul. *The Rule of Metaphor: Multi-Disciplinary Studies of the Creation of Meaning in Language*. Toronto: University of Toronto Press, 1977.

Rimmon-Kenan, Shlomith. *Narrative Fiction: Contemporary Poetics*. London: Methuen, 1983.

Robinson, R. *Plato's Earlier Dialectic*. Oxford: Oxford University Press, 1953.

Ronen, Ruth. *Possible Worlds in Literary Theory*. Cambridge: Cambridge University Press, 1994.

Rose, Peter W. *Sons of the Gods, Children of Earth: Ideology and Literary Form in Ancient Greece*. Ithaca, NY: Cornell University Press, 1992.

Rowling, J. K. *Harry Potter and the Philosopher's Stone*. London: Bloomsbury, 1997.

Ryan, Marie-Laure. *Possible Worlds, Artificial Intelligence, and Narrative Theory*. Bloomington: Indiana University Press, 1991.

Sacks, Sheldon. *Fiction and the Shape of Belief*. Chicago: University of Chicago Press, 1980 [1964].

———. "Golden Birds and Dying Generations." *Comparative Literature Studies* 6, no. 3 (September 1969): 274–91.

Scholes, Robert. "The Fictional Criticism of the Future." *Triquarterly* 34 (Fall 1975): 233–47.

———. *Textual Power*. New Haven, CT: Yale University Press, 1985.

Scholes, Robert, and Robert Kellogg. *The Nature of Narrative*. Oxford: Oxford University Press, 1966.

Segal, Charles. *Singers, Heroes, and Gods in the* Odyssey. Ithaca, NY: Cornell University Press, 1994.

Shannon, Edgar F. Jr. "*Emma*: Character and Construction." In Lodge, *Jane Austen: "Emma,"* 130–47.

Shaw, Harry. *Narrating Reality: Austen, Scott, Eliot*. Ithaca, NY: Cornell University Press, 1999.

Shen, Dan. "Defense and Challenge: Reflections on the Relation between Story and Discourse." *Narrative* 10, no. 3 (October 2002): 222–43.

Slatkin, Laura. *The Power of Thetis: Allusion and Interpretation in the Iliad*. Berkeley: University of California Press, 1991.

Spenser, Edmund. *The Faerie Queene*. New York: Penguin, 1979 [1590].

Stein, Gertrude. *Three Lives*. New York: Penguin Books, 1990.

Stendhal. *Le Rouge et le Noir*. Laussane: Éditions Rencontre, 1968.

Stokes, Myra. *The Language of Jane Austen: A Study of Some Aspects of Her Vocabulary*. London: Macmillan, 1991.

Sucksmith, Harvey Peter. *The Narrative Art of Charles Dickens: The Rhetoric of Sympathy and Irony in his Novels*. Oxford: Clarendon Press, 1970.

Sutherland, James R. *On English Prose*. Toronto: University of Toronto Press, 1957.

Taylor, A. J. P. *Bismarck: The Man and the Statesman*. London: New English Library, 1965 [1955].

Thalmann, William G. *The Swineherd and the Bow: Representations of Class in the* Odyssey. Ithaca, NY: Cornell University Press, 1998.

Thomas, Francis-Noël, and Mark Turner. *Clear and Simple as the Truth: Writing Classic Prose*. Princeton, NJ: Princeton University Press, 1994.

Trollope, Anthony. *Framley Parsonage*. London: Penguin Books, 2004 [1861].

Tuve, Rosemund. *Allegorical Imagery: Some Mediaeval Books and Their Posterity*. Princeton, NJ: Princeton University Press, 1966.

Twain, Mark. *Adventures of Huckleberry Finn*. London: Penguin Books, 2014.

Vendler, Helen. *The Art of Shakespeare's Sonnets*. Cambridge, MA: Harvard University Press, 1997.

Volpe, Edmond L. *A Reader's Guide to William Faulkner*. New York: Farrar, Straus and Giroux, 1964.

Walsh, Richard. *The Rhetoric of Fictionality: Narrative Theory and the Idea of Fiction*. Columbus: The Ohio State University Press, 2007.

Watt, Ian. *The Rise of the Novel: Studies in Defoe, Richardson and Fielding*. Harmondsworth: Penguin, 1963 [1957].

Weil, Simone. *The Iliad; or, The Poem of Force*. Translated by Mary McCarthy. Wallingford, PA: Pendle Hill, 1962.

Whitman, Cedric. *Homer and the Heroic Tradition*. New York: W. W. Norton & Company, 1958.

Wilde, Oscar. "The Decay of Lying." In Adams, *Critical Theory*, 673–86.

Willcock, M. M. "Mythological Paradeigma in the *Iliad*." *Classical Quarterly* 14 (1964): 141–54.

Wilson, Edmund. "The Ambiguity of Henry James." *Hound and Horn* (April–May 1934): 385–406.

Wiltshire, John. "*Mansfield Park, Emma, Persuasion.*" In Copeland and McMaster, *Cambridge Companion to Jane Austen*, 58–83.

Wimsatt, Willam K. Jr., and Cleanth Brooks. *Literary Criticism: A Short History.* New York: Vintage Books, 1967.

Wolfe, Tom. *The Right Stuff.* New York: Bantam Books, 1980.

Wolff, Tobias. *In Pharaoh's Army: Memories of the Lost War.* New York: Vintage Books, 1994.

Woloch, Alex. *The One vs. the Many: Minor Characters and the Space of the Protagonist in the Novel.* Princeton, NJ: Princeton University Press, 2003.

Woolf, Virginia. *Mrs. Dalloway.* New York: Alfred A. Knopf, 1993 [1925].

INDEX

actual audience ("flesh-and-blood reader"), 16, 66, 152–57, 163, 204; of Jane Austen, 185; in nonfiction, 187; in *Time's Arrow*, 166; and unnaturalness, 165. *See also* audience

Adams, Hazard, 53n1, 57n5

Adorno, Theodor, 112–14

Adventures of Huckleberry Finn, The (Mark Twain), 2–5, 16, 68, 97, 134; objects described in, 75–76; synthetic in, 8–9

Aeschylus: *Agamemnon*, 110; *Persians*, 62

aesthetics, 15, 139–40, 206–8; in *The Adventures of Huckleberry Finn*, 23n8; aesthetic judgments, 2n4; in *Emma*, 47, 156; as a function of communication, 149; in "Old China," 193–94; and realistic representations, 54

affective response, 4–6, 66, 139, 144–45, 153–55, 177, 208; in *Emma*, 179, 183–85; to tragedy, 62–63

Ahl, Frederick, 134n47

Alber, Jan, 7, 70n22, 166

allegory, 98–99, 109–14, 149; allegoresis, 109; relationship to the thematic, 98–99, 177; as a scalar quality, 110

allusion, 97–98, 102

Altman, Rick, 109n9

Amis, Martin (*Time's Arrow*), 165–66

anadiplosis, 29

anaphora, 27, 28n12, 29, 29n13

Anderson, William, 110n10

Animal Farm (George Orwell), 149, 177

antinomic narration, 166

antistrophe, 29n13

apologue, 98–99, 109

aposiopesis, 42

Aristotle, 31, 55, 61–63

Asimov, Isaac, 72, 86

asyndeton, 29–30

Atonement (Ian McEwan), 141n6, 142–43, 149

audience: in *The Adventures of Huckleberry Finn*, 3–5, 8–9; and allegory, 177; in *Beloved*, 163–65; in "Continuity of Parks," 166–68; and double-consciousness, 204–6; in *Emma*, 155–58, 179–85; and ghost stories, 158–65; and the mimetic illusion, 65–67, 152–58; in *1984*, 168–70; in "Old China," 187–94; and progression, 178; proliferation of terms for, 205; and the purposes of, 14–15; in *Time's Arrow*, 166; in *The Turn of the Screw*, 158–62; and unreliability, 140; in *Wuthering Heights*, 162–63. *See also* actual audience; authorial audience; mimetic illusion; narratee; narrative audience

Auerbach, Erich, 12n16, 77, 109n9

Austen, Jane: *Persuasion*, 184; *Pride and Prejudice*, 10, 33, 38, 72, 184, 203. *See also* *Emma*

Austin, J. L., 107

Austin, Norman, 114n16

author, 7, 16n21, 176–78; and direction of readerly interest, 149; in the feedback loop, 16, 137–38; and the mimetic, 146–47, 207; and narrative resources,

137, 143–44; of nonfiction, 189–90; as a source of foregrounding, 12–13; and the synthetic, 148; tension with authorial audience, 86, 158; and the thematic, 5, 10–11, 95–96, 102, 109, 171, 209–11; in traditional narratives, 14; vs. implied author, 16. *See also* audience; authorial audience; unreliability

authorial audience, 16–17, 66, 152–65, 167–70, 177–78, 182–83, 192, 204; in *Beloved*, 163–65; in "Continuity of Parks," 167–68; and the critic's fallibility, 158n2; definition of, 16; in *Emma*, 154, 156–57, 178, 182–83; in *1984*, 169–70; in "Old China," 192; in *Othello*, 154; in relation to narrative and actual audiences, 16, 153–58; in *The Turn of the Screw*, 159–63; in *Wuthering Heights*, 163

Babb, Howard S., 40n25, 45n28, 47

Bachelard, Gaston, 70n22

Bal, Mieke, 70n22

Balzac, Honoré de, 58

Barth, John ("Menelaiad"), 149, 208

Basset, Samuel, 66n18

Beckett, Samuel (*How It Is*), 66, 154, 198–99, 208; "opaque" narrative style in, 20; space in, 73–74

beginning, 16, 36, 61–63, 178; of *Agnes Grey*, 44–45; of *Angela's Ashes*, 201; of *Emma*, 79, 103; of the *Iliad*, 35–36, 121; of *Little Dorrit*, 25–29; of *The Mystery of Edwin Drood*, 68–69; of *1984*, 33, 87; of *Phantastes*, 78; of *Ragtime*, 29–31; of *The Return of the Native*, 107; of *Roderick Hudson*, 36; of *The Secret Agent*, 33–34

Bellow, Saul (*Seize the Day*), 71

Beloved (Toni Morrison), 150, 162–65; authorial audience in, 163–65

Boyd, John D., 53n1

Bridgeman, Teresa, 70n22

Brontë, Anne: *Agnes Grey*, 44, 115–16; *The Tenant of Wildfell Hall*, 115–16

Brooks, Cleanth, 109n9

Browning, Robert ("My Last Duchess"), 16n24, 22–24

Bruner, Jerome, 212–13

Burgess, Anthony (*A Clockwork Orange*), 38–39, 47, 208

Burroughs, Edgar Rice, 203

Burrows, J. F., 59–60

Byrne, Sandie, 77n27

Cain, James M. (*The Postman Always Rings Twice*), 97–98, 110

Calder, Jenni, 86n36

Camoens (*Os Lusíadas*), 120

Carr, E. H., 210n9

character, 2, 11–12, 53–54, 80–85, 136, 142–45, 177, 204; and action, 61; in *The Adventures of Huckleberry Finn*, 3–4, 9, 23; in *The American*, 81–82, 84; in *Beloved*, 164–65; in *Bismarck*, 82–84; character sets, 38; in *Emma*, 47–52, 79, 103–4, 116, 153, 155–57, 179–85; in *Framley Parsonage*, 37; in *How It Is*, 73–74; and the mimetic, 64–65; in *1984*, 36, 86–93; in nonfiction, 190; in *Out of the Silent Planet*, 85; in realistic fiction, 7; in *The Return of the Native*, 107; and the thematic, 95–102, 115; in *Time's Arrow*, 166. *See also* mimetic; synthetic; thematic

Chariton, 22

Cheever, John ("The Swimmer"), 208

Clark, Matthew: "Chryses' Supplication," 121n26; "The Cognitive Turn," 80n31; "The Concept," 80n30, 121n26; *A Matter of Style*, 35n16, 80n31, 201n2; *Narrative Structures and the Language of the Self*, 38n21, 72n26

Clarke, Austin, 97

Coetzee, J. M. (*Foe*), 66–67

cognitive narratology, 2, 13, 198

cognitive response, 55n3, 61–63, 107, 139, 178, 212. *See also* intellectual response

Cohen, Beth, 134n47

coherence, 143

Cohn, Dorrit, 167

Coleridge, Samuel Taylor, 20

comprehensiveness, 142–44, 151–52, 176

congeries, 28n12, 29–30

Connor, W. Robert, 37

Conrad, Joseph (*The Secret Agent*), 33–34

Cook, Erwin, 114n16, 132, 133n44

Copeland, Edward, 77n27

correspondence, 142–44, 151–78

Cortázar, Julio ("Continuity of Parks"), 165–68
Craig, Sheryl, 116n20
Crane, R. S., 1n1
Crick, Bernard, 87n40
Crotty, Kevin, 129n38
Curtius, Ernst Robert, 109n9

Dangerfield, George, 62n10
Davidson, Jenny, 40n25
de Certeau, Michel, 194
denarration, 193
descriptive poetics of narrative, 137
Dick, Philip K. (*Confessions of a Crap Artist*), 199–200, 202
Dickens, Charles: *Great Expectations*, 71; *Little Dorrit*, 25–28, 30–31, 36, 199; *The Mystery of Edwin Drood*, 68–69; rhetorical devices used by, 26–28
Divine Comedy, The (Dante Alighieri), 7, 47, 110–11
Doctorow, E. L. (*Ragtime*), 29–31, 37, 199, 212
Doležel, Lubomír, 12n16, 64n14, 64n15
dominant: in allegory, 177; in "Continuity of Parks," 168; in *Emma*, 156, 179; in *1984*, 169; in "Old China," 194; in Roman Jakobson's work, 149; in *Time's Arrow*, 165–66; in *The Turn of the Screw*, 161
Don Quixote (Miguel de Cervantes), 6
Donaghue, Denis, 87n38
double-consciousness, 65, 153–58, 204–6; compared to W. E. B. Du Bois's usage, 204n4; in "Continuity of Parks," 167; and fictionality, 187. *See also* actual audience; authorial audience; narrative audience
Dougherty, Carol, 134n47
Douglas, Mary, 35n17
Dracula (Bram Stoker), 66
Duckworth, Alistair M., 119n22
Duffy, Joseph M. Jr., 47n32

Eagleton, Terry, 21n5, 114–16
Eliot, George: *Adam Bede*, 57, 97, 115; *Silar Marner*, 36
Emma (Jane Austen), 59–60, 79, 81n32, 86, 149, 194; affective responses to, 179, 183–85; authorial audience in, 182; double-consciousness in, 153–57; ethics in, 179, 181–83; fictionality in, 189; ideology in, 116–19, 183–84; mimetic in, 59–60, 179–81, 207–9; narrated space in, 72; narrated time in, 71; narrative audience in, 66, 182; narrative progression in, 47–52; objects described in, 76–77; synthetic in, 40–52, 155–57; thematic in, 55n3, 103–4, 116–19, 173–77, 179–85; "transparent" narrative style in, 20

ending, 16, 36, 178; of "Continuity of Parks," 166–67; of the *Iliad*, 35, 130; of *Little Dorrit*, 27; of "Old China," 191–94; of *1984*, 108, 169–70; of *The Return of the Native*, 107–8

epistrophe, 28n12
epizeuxis, 28n12

ethics, 146, 176, 199–200; in *The Adventures of Huckleberry Finn*, 4–5, 9; in *Emma*, 179, 181–85; in "Old China," 193–94; in *Othello*, 154; of the telling vs. of the told, 176; and the thematic, 176

Faerie Queene, The (Edmund Spenser), 177
Falkner, Thomas M., 1n3, 12n16
Farmer, Philip José, 73
Fauconnier, Giles, 206n6
Faulkner, William: *The Hamlet*, 37–38; *The Sound and the Fury*, 142; *The Wild Palms*, 37–38
feedback loop, 16
Felson, Nancy, 134n47
fictionality: and cross-border traffic with nonfictionality, 189; definition of, 188; local fictionality, 189–95; and the mimetic, 190; in nonfictional discourse, 188, 190–95; in "Old China," 191–94; as a ternary and scalar quality, 189
Finney, Jack (*From Time to Time* and *Time and Again*), 72
Fletcher, Angus, 109n9, 111n12
Foley, John Miles, 32n14
Ford, Ford Madox: *The English Novel*, 206; *The Good Soldier*, 191, 212
foregrounding: and the author, 12–13; of synthetic vs. mimetic, 12, 21–22, 53
Fowler, Alistair, 109n9
Fowler, Roger, 86n36, 87n41

Frye, Northrop, 109n9

Gallagher, Catherine, 144–45
Gard, Roger, 7n14, 21, 65n17, 116n20, 206
Gaskell, Elizabeth (*Mary Barton* and *North and South*), 115
Genette, Gérard, 70n22
genre, 98–99; as narrative resource, 137; nonfiction, 189; novel, 144–45; realistic fiction, 7–8, 12, 21–25, 54, 60, 65–66, 74, 93, 95, 153, 169, 203, 206–7; science fiction, 72–74, 203; tragedy, 61–62; unnatural narrative, 6–7, 21, 54, 64–67, 84–85, 90, 143, 148, 159–68, 202–3, 208
Gervais, Bertrand, 1n3
ghost, 158–65; in *Beloved*, 163–65; as mimetic or antimimetic, 161–63; in *The Turn of the Screw*, 159–62; in *Wuthering Heights*, 162–63
Glasgow, Ellen (*The Romantic Comedians*), 71n23
Gleason, Abbot, 86n36
Golden, Leon, 53n1, 55n3, 63n12
Golding, William (*The Lord of the Flies*), 106
Goldsmith, Jack, 86n36
Gombrich, Ernest, 53n1
Gomel, Elana, 70n21
Goodman, Nelson, 53n1
Goodman, Paul, 206–7
Goodwin, Doris Kearns (*Team of Rivals*), 202
gradatio, 28n12
Graff, Gerald, 100
Graves, Robert (*They Hanged My Saintly Billy*), 203
Great Gatsby, The (F. Scott Fitzgerald), 38
Green, Clarence, 65
Griffin, Jasper, 77n29
Gulliver's Travels (Jonathan Swift), 98

Handler, Richard, 116n20
Hardy, Thomas (*The Return of the Native*), 38, 71–72, 107–8
Harvey, W. J., 47n31
Heidegger, Martin ("thrownness"), 139, 176, 189, 195

Heinlein, Robert: "All You Zombies," 72; *The Door into Summer*, 72; *Methuselah's Children*, 86; *Revolt in 2100*, 86n37; *Starman Jones*, 36; *Time for the Stars*, 72; *Tunnel in the Sky*, 36, 106
Heinze, Rüdiger, 1n3, 70n22
Heitman, Richard, 134n47
Heller, Joseph (*Catch-22*), 33
Herman, David, 63–64, 64n14, 106, 147, 204n5
history, 15n18, 22, 66, 69, 71–72, 82n33, 83, 115–16, 206, 208; of mimesis, 54–64
Homer: See *Odyssey*; *Iliad*
Honig, Edwin, 109n9
Horkheimer, Max, 112–14
Howe, Irving, 86n36, 87n38, 92n45
Hunter, Richard, 57n6
Hunter, Stephen (*Point of Impact*), 204
Huxley, Aldous, 86n37
hypothesis testing: criteria for, 141–43. See also cohesion; comprehensiveness; correspondence

ideation, 2, 95, 102, 148, 171, 176–81, 185, 189, 191, 200, 213. See also thematic
ideology, 2, 13, 24, 115, 176; in *Emma*, 116–19, 181–85; in the *Iliad*, 122–23; in *1984*, 177–78; in "Old China," 194; and the thematic, 114–19
If on a winter's night a traveler (Italo Calvino), 149
Iliad (Homer), 66n18, 80n30, 97; and class, 114n15; and ideology, 122–23; *mênis* as theme, 120–23, 172; and the narrative audience, 205; narrative figures in, 32, 35; objects in, 77; thematic in, 119–34, 172, 211; time and space in, 70–72
implied author, 16. See also author
intellectual response, 63, 139–40, 212. See also cognitive response; ideation
"Invisibility Cloak," narrative audience as wearing one, 157, 168
Invisible Man (Ralph Ellison), 142
Isherwood, Christopher (*Goodbye to Berlin*), 57n5
Ishiguro, Kazuo (*The Unconsoled*), 208
isocolon, 44
Iversen, Stefan, 7

James, Henry, 69; *The American*, 81–82, 84; "The Beast in the Jungle," 174; *Roderick Hudson*, 36; *The Turn of the Screw*, 159–62; *The Wings of the Dove*, 10, 36

Johnson, Gary, 177n2

Johnson, Mark, 107n6

Johnson, Samuel, 55, 65

Johnson, W. R., 111n11

Kant, Immanuel, 2n4

Katz, Marilyn A., 134n47

Keaney, John J., 111n12

Kearns, Emily, 134n47

Kellogg, Robert, 109–10

Kermode, Frank, 12n17

Kesey, Ken (*One Flew Over the Cuckoo's Nest*), 36, 110

Kipling, Rudyard (*Captains Courageous*), 115

Kittay, Eva Feder, 107n6

Kövecses, Karl, 107n6

Kroeber, Karl, 21, 40, 59n7, 65

Lakoff, George, 107n6

Lamberton, Robert, 110n10, 111n12, 112

Lanham, Richard, 19

Le Guin, Ursula, 203

Lessing, Gotthold (*Laocoon*), 57n6

Levaniouk, Olga, 114n16

Levin, Richard, 100–102, 115; the thematic leap, 101

Lewis, C. S., 109; *Out of the Silent Planet*, 85, 93

litotes, 42

Loomis, Roger Sherman, 109n8

Lord of the Rings, The (J. R. R. Tolkien), 6, 38, 47, 68

Louden, Bruce, 35n17

Lowe, N. J., 80n30

Lowry, Malcolm (*Under the Volcano*), 71

Lysias, 22

MacDonald, George (*Phantastes*), 78

Madame Bovary (Gustave Flaubert), 6, 37

Malory, Sir Thomas, 22

Mann, Thomas (*Buddenbrooks*), 71

Marquez, Gabríel Gárcia (*One Hundred Years of Solitude*), 71

McCourt, Frank (*Angela's Ashes*), 201, 204

McHale, Brian, 23

McMaster, Juliet, 116n20

Melgerg, Arne, 53n1

metalepsis, 167; and the foregrounding of the synthetic, 7

Meyers, Jeffrey, 87n38

middle, 16, 61, 63, 178; of *The Adventures of Huckleberry Finn*, 5; of *Beloved*, 164

Mieville, China (*The City and the City*), 208

Miller, Mark Crispin, 87n39

Milton, John (*Paradise Lost*), 120

mimetic, 53–93, 202–9, and passim; and action, 78–80; in *Beloved*, 149–50, 163–65; and character, 80–85; Clark's definition, 12–13; as "component" vs. "aspect," 136; in "Continuity of Parks," 167; critique of Phelan's definition, 6, 12, 64–65, 69, 202; as deception, 65; descriptive mimesis, 56–61; in *Emma*, 155–56, 179–81; and invention, 62–63; and narrated time and space, 69–74; narrative mimesis, 61–63; in *1984*, 86–93, 168–70; Phelan's definition, 53, 146; pictorial mimesis, 54–56; as related to plausibility, 67–69; and science fiction, 72–73, 84–85, 203; in *Time's Arrow*, 166; in *The Turn of the Screw*, 159–62; vs. antimimetic and nonmimetic, 6–7, 66; as world-building, 63–64; in *Wuthering Heights*, 162–63

mimetic illusion, 6–8, 22, 65–67, 148, 151–52, 167–68, 206–9; in "Continuity of Parks," 167–68; in *Emma*, 155–57, 178–82; in "My Last Duchess," 22–24; in *The Turn of the Screw*, 161

Morris, Pam, 53n1, 65

Morrison, Toni (*Jazz*), 35n16. See also *Beloved*

MTS model, 1–2; as "components" vs. "aspects," 11; defined, 2, 146–48; directly compared to SMT model, 11–14, 53–54, 95–96, 99, 102, 125, 138, 141, 200, 203–4, 209–12; relation to Authors, Resources, Audience model, 137. See also SMT model

Muir, Edwin, 71n24

Muellner, Leonard, 120–21, 121n25, 126n33

Mulvihill, Robert, 86n36
Munro, Alice ("Prue"), 149
Murnaghan, Sheila, 114n16

Nabokov, Vladimir: *Bend Sinister,* 205; *Pale Fire,* 111n12; *Pnin,* 36; and self-consciousness, 67n19
Nagy, Gregory, 32n14, 115n18, 127n35, 130–31
narratee, 16, 204; in *The Adventures of Huckleberry Finn,* 3
narrative: definition of, 14, 198
narrative audience, 7n13, 16–17, 145n11, 153–58, 187, 204–7; in "Continuity of Parks," 167–68; in *Emma,* 155–57, 182; and ghosts, 159–65; and the mimetic illusion, 24, 65–66, 204–8; in *1984,* 89, 169; and nonfiction, 153–54; in *Time's Arrow,* 166
narrative figures, 31–39, 212; anticipations, 36–37; architecture, 38–39; character sets, 38; in *Emma,* 40–52; ending with a beginning, 36, 48, 52, 97, 107, 152; juxtaposition, 37–38; links, 33–35; repeated events, 33; repeated language, 32–33; repeated narration, 33; ring composition, 35–36
narrative progression, 15–16, 173–76, 178, 210; compared to plot, 178; in *Emma,* 178–85; textual vs. readerly dynamics, 178; in *Wuthering Heights,* 162–63
Narrative Theory: Core Concepts and Critical Debates (David Herman, et al.), 1, 2n4, 3, 6, 12n16, 14, 15n19, 16, 16n21, 21–22, 40, 63, 65, 95, 200, 204, 207–8, 210–12
Nell, Victor, 65n16
Nielsen, Henrik Skov, 7, 188
Nivens, Larry (*Ringworld*), 73
Nussbaum, Martha, 86n36

O'Brien, Flann (*The Third Policeman*), 60
O'Brien, Tim ("The Things They Carried"), 189
Odyssey (Homer), 17, 66n18, 172; as allegory, 111–14; and descriptive mimesis, 57–58; narrative figures in, 32, 35; objects in, 77; and plausibility, 68; thematic in, 96–97, 119–21, 126–27, 130–34, 211; time and space in, 70–72
"Old China" (Tobias Wolff), 149, 187, 189–95; ambiguity in, 192; ethics in, 193–94; synthetic in, 192; unreliability in, 193

Orwell, George (*Animal Farm*), 95. See also *1984*
Othello (William Shakespeare), 154

Page, Norman, 40, 40n25, 130
Palaephatus, 111
palilogia, 26, 29n13
Panini, 31
Parker, Mark, 116n20
Parry, Milman, 32
Pastis, Stephen, 67n19
Pavel, Thomas, 64n14, 206n6
Petrarch (*Africa*), 120
Phelan, James: *Experiencing Fiction,* 1, 5n7, 6n11, 7, 15, 178; *Living to Tell About It,* 1, 2, 5–7, 10, 15–17, 21, 53, 65–67, 80, 95, 114, 140, 207–8, 212; *Reading People, Reading Plots,* 1, 7n13, 16n23, 16n24, 23, 65–68, 86, 95, 99, 100n3, 102, 136, 169, 174, 178; *Somebody Telling Somebody Else,* 1, 15, 137, 140, 166n6, 178; *Narrative as Rhetoric,* 1, 114n17, 153, 164; target essay in *Style,* 158n2; *Worlds from Words,* 152n1
Picasso, Pablo, 199
Pifer, Ellen, 6n9
Pilgrim's Progress, The (John Bunyan), 177
Plato (*Republic*), 54–57, 61
Pliny the Elder (*Natural History*), 54
pluralism, 139n2
polyptoton, 41
polysyndeton, 28n12, 29–30, 29n13
Potolsky, Matthew, 53n1, 65n17
Power, Michael, 67n18
Pynchon, Thomas (*The Crying of Lot 49*), 111n12

Quilligan, Maureen, 109n9, 111n12

Rabinowitz, Peter J., 3, 38n22, 153; *Before Reading,* 153; "Truth in Fiction," 16n20, 153, 206, 208
Rader, Ralph W., 155, 211; "The Dramatic Monologue," 23n7, 23n8; *Fact, Fiction, and Form,* 155
Rasselas (Samuel Johnson), 98–99, 110
reader: *See* audience; readerly interests

readerly interests, 1–2, 53–54, 65, 136–38, 142, 144–48, 176, 187, 198

Red Badge of Courage, The (Stephen Crane), 203

rhetorical poetics, 136; and audience, 138–39; Clark's review of Phelan and Rabinowitz's model, 14–17, 198–99; compared with a text-centric approach, 137–44, 161, 171, 179; and fictionality, 187–94; and multilayered nature of narrative communication, 139–41

Richardson, Brian, 6n10, 7, 12n16, 16n22, 21n6, 21, 24, 63, 166, 193

Richter, David, 98–99, 109

Ricoeur, Paul, 12n16, 107n6

Rimmon-Kenan, Shlomith, 70n22

Roisman, Hanna M., 134n47

Ronen, Ruth, 64n14, 206n6

Rose, Peter, 114n15, 123, 134n47

Rowling, J. K., 157

Ryan, Marie-Laure, 64n14, 206n6

Sacks, Sheldon, 98–99, 104n4, 109; "walking concept," 177

Scholes, Robert, 99, 109–10

Segal, Daniel, 116n20, 133n45

Shannon, Edgar F. Jr., 47n32

Shaw, Harry, 20n1, 21n4, 68–69, 69n20, 75

Shen, Dan, 1n3

Slatkin, Laura, 32n14, 114n16

Smith, Cordwainer, 72

SMT model: as "aspects" vs. "components," 11; defined, 11–14; directly compared to MTS model, 11–14, 53–54, 95–96, 99, 102, 125, 138, 141, 200, 203–4, 209–12, goals of, 201. *See also* MTS model

Solzhenitsyn, Alexander (*One Day in the Life of Ivan Denisovich*), 71

Stapledon, Olaf, 86n37

Stein, Gertrude ("Melanctha"), 203, 208

Stendhal (*Le Rouge et le Noir*), 56

Stevenson, Robert Louis (*Kidnapped*), 110

Stokes, Myra, 40n25

structural meaning, 174–75, 209–11

stubbornness, 164–65

style, 25, 97, 129, 143, 152, 152n1, 156, 159–60, 190, 199–201, 203; in *Emma*, 20, 40–46, 50n34, 179; in *How It Is*, 20; in *Little Dorrit*, 25–28, 30–31; in *1984*, 28–29; in *Ragtime*, 29–31; "transparent" vs. "opaque," 19–22. *See also* narrative figures

Sucksmith, Harvey Peter, 25n10

Sutherland, James R., 20

synecdoche, 28n12

synthetic, 19–52, 200–202, and passim; in *Beloved*, 163–65; as "component" vs. "aspect," 136; in "Continuity of Parks," 167; Clark's definition, 11–12; in *Emma*, 40–52, 155–57; in *Little Dorrit*, 25–28; as narrative infrastructure, 19; in "Old China," 191–92; Phelan's definition, 148, 155; in *Time's Arrow*, 166; in *The Turn of the Screw*, 159–62

Tasso, Torquato (*Gerusalemme Liberata*), 120

Taylor, A. J. P., 80, 82–84

Thackeray, William (*Vanity Fair*), 37, 203

Thalmann, William G., 134n47

thematic, 95–134, 209–13, and passim; and allegory, 109–14; Clark's definition, 13, 209; as "component" vs. "aspect," 136; critiques of thematic reading, 99–102; in *Emma*, 103–4, 173–75, 179–85; and ideology, 114–19; in the *Iliad* and the *Odyssey*, 120–34; and intentionality, 95; and intertextuality, 134; and narrative meaning, 96–98; in *1984*, 104–6, 177–78, 210–12; and nonpropositional meaning, 106–8; Phelan's definition, 148; in relation to narrative structures, 97

Thomas, Francis-Noël, 22

Tom Jones (Henry Fielding), 98

Tomashevsky, Boris, 21

tragedy, 61–63

transparent narration, 19–21

tricolon, 27, 40–44

Trollope, Anthony (*Framley Parsonage*), 35–36, 71n23, 84

Turner, Mark, 22

Tuve, Rosemund, 109n9

Twain, Mark: *The Adventures of Tom Sawyer*, 134; *Life on the Mississippi*, 9n15; *Pudd'nhead Wilson*, 115. *See also The Adventures of Huckleberry Finn*

Ulysses (James Joyce), 7, 71

unnatural narratology, 2, 7, 13, 144, 148; integration into rhetorical poetics, 165, 198

unreliability, 140, 199–200; in *The Adventures of Huckleberry Finn,* 9; rhetorical definition of, 140; in *Time's Arrow,* 166n6; in *Wuthering Heights,* 162

variatio, 28n12

Vendler, Helen, 100

Verne, Jules, 86n37

Virgil (*The Aeneid*), 70, 111n11, 120, 134

Volpe, Edmond, 37

Walsh, Richard, 188

War and Peace (Leo Tolstoy), 203

Warhol, Robyn, 22, 40, 145, 210

Watt, Ian, 21

Weil, Simone, 128–29

Weir, Andy (*The Martian*), 203

Whitman, Cedric, 32n14, 35n17

Whittal, Gertrude Clark, 86n36

Willcock, M. M., 130n39

Wilson, Edmund, 160

Wiltshire, John, 60

Wimsatt, William K. Jr., 109n9

Wolff, Tobias: "Close Calls," 191; *In Pharaoh's Army,* 190. *See also* "Old China"

Woloch, Alex, 181

Woolf, Virginia (*Mrs. Dalloway*), 37, 71

Wuthering Heights (Emily Brontë), 162–63

Zamyatin, Yevgeny (*We*), 86n37

THEORY AND INTERPRETATION OF NARRATIVE
JAMES PHELAN, PETER J. RABINOWITZ, AND KATRA BYRAM, SERIES EDITORS

Because the series editors believe that the most significant work in narrative studies today contributes both to our knowledge of specific narratives and to our understanding of narrative in general, studies in the series typically offer interpretations of individual narratives and address significant theoretical issues underlying those interpretations. The series does not privilege one critical perspective but is open to work from any strong theoretical position.

Debating Rhetorical Narratology: On the Synthetic, Mimetic, and Thematic Aspects of Narrative by Matthew Clark and James Phelan

Environment and Narrative: New Directions in Econarratology edited by Erin James and Eric Morel

Unnatural Narratology: Extensions, Revisions, and Challenges edited by Jan Alber and Brian Richardson

A Poetics of Plot for the Twenty-First Century: Theorizing Unruly Narratives by Brian Richardson

Playing at Narratology: Digital Media as Narrative Theory by Daniel Punday

Making Conversation in Modernist Fiction by Elizabeth Alsop

Narratology and Ideology: Negotiating Context, Form, and Theory in Postcolonial Narratives edited by Divya Dwivedi, Henrik Skov Nielsen, and Richard Walsh

Novelization: From Film to Novel by Jan Baetens

Reading Conrad by J. Hillis Miller, Edited by John G. Peters and Jakob Lothe

Narrative, Race, and Ethnicity in the United States edited by James J. Donahue, Jennifer Ann Ho, and Shaun Morgan

Somebody Telling Somebody Else: A Rhetorical Poetics of Narrative by James Phelan

Media of Serial Narrative edited by Frank Kelleter

Suture and Narrative: Deep Intersubjectivity in Fiction and Film by George Butte

The Writer in the Well: On Misreading and Rewriting Literature by Gary Weissman

Narrating Space / Spatializing Narrative: Where Narrative Theory and Geography Meet by Marie-Laure Ryan, Kenneth Foote, and Maoz Azaryahu

Narrative Sequence in Contemporary Narratology edited by Raphaël Baroni and Françoise Revaz

The Submerged Plot and the Mother's Pleasure from Jane Austen to Arundhati Roy by Kelly A. Marsh

Narrative Theory Unbound: Queer and Feminist Interventions edited by Robyn Warhol and Susan S. Lanser

Unnatural Narrative: Theory, History, and Practice by Brian Richardson

Ethics and the Dynamic Observer Narrator: Reckoning with Past and Present in German Literature by Katra A. Byram

Narrative Paths: African Travel in Modern Fiction and Nonfiction by Kai Mikkonen

The Reader as Peeping Tom: Nonreciprocal Gazing in Narrative Fiction and Film by Jeremy Hawthorn

Thomas Hardy's Brains: Psychology, Neurology, and Hardy's Imagination by Suzanne Keen

The Return of the Omniscient Narrator: Authorship and Authority in Twenty-First Century Fiction by Paul Dawson

Feminist Narrative Ethics: Tacit Persuasion in Modernist Form by Katherine Saunders Nash

Real Mysteries: Narrative and the Unknowable by H. Porter Abbott

A Poetics of Unnatural Narrative edited by Jan Alber, Henrik Skov Nielsen, and Brian Richardson

Narrative Discourse: Authors and Narrators in Literature, Film, and Art by Patrick Colm Hogan

An Aesthetics of Narrative Performance: Transnational Theater, Literature, and Film in Contemporary Germany by Claudia Breger

Literary Identification from Charlotte Brontë to Tsitsi Dangarembga by Laura Green

Narrative Theory: Core Concepts and Critical Debates by David Herman, James Phelan and Peter J. Rabinowitz, Brian Richardson, and Robyn Warhol

After Testimony: The Ethics and Aesthetics of Holocaust Narrative for the Future edited by Jakob Lothe, Susan Rubin Suleiman, and James Phelan

The Vitality of Allegory: Figural Narrative in Modern and Contemporary Fiction by Gary Johnson

Narrative Middles: Navigating the Nineteenth-Century British Novel edited by Caroline Levine and Mario Ortiz-Robles

Fact, Fiction, and Form: Selected Essays by Ralph W. Rader. Edited by James Phelan and David H. Richter.

The Real, the True, and the Told: Postmodern Historical Narrative and the Ethics of Representation by Eric L. Berlatsky

Franz Kafka: Narration, Rhetoric, and Reading edited by Jakob Lothe, Beatrice Sandberg, and Ronald Speirs

Social Minds in the Novel by Alan Palmer

Narrative Structures and the Language of the Self by Matthew Clark

Imagining Minds: The Neuro-Aesthetics of Austen, Eliot, and Hardy by Kay Young

Postclassical Narratology: Approaches and Analyses edited by Jan Alber and Monika Fludernik

Techniques for Living: Fiction and Theory in the Work of Christine Brooke-Rose by Karen R. Lawrence

Towards the Ethics of Form in Fiction: Narratives of Cultural Remission by Leona Toker

Tabloid, Inc.: Crimes, Newspapers, Narratives by V. Penelope Pelizzon and Nancy M. West

Narrative Means, Lyric Ends: Temporality in the Nineteenth-Century British Long Poem by Monique R. Morgan

Understanding Nationalism: On Narrative, Cognitive Science, and Identity by Patrick Colm Hogan

Joseph Conrad: Voice, Sequence, History, Genre edited by Jakob Lothe, Jeremy Hawthorn, James Phelan

The Rhetoric of Fictionality: Narrative Theory and the Idea of Fiction by Richard Walsh

Experiencing Fiction: Judgments, Progressions, and the Rhetorical Theory of Narrative by James Phelan

Unnatural Voices: Extreme Narration in Modern and Contemporary Fiction by Brian Richardson

Narrative Causalities by Emma Kafalenos

Why We Read Fiction: Theory of Mind and the Novel by Lisa Zunshine

I Know That You Know That I Know: Narrating Subjects from Moll Flanders *to* Marnie by George Butte

Bloodscripts: Writing the Violent Subject by Elana Gomel

Surprised by Shame: Dostoevsky's Liars and Narrative Exposure by Deborah A. Martinsen

Having a Good Cry: Effeminate Feelings and Pop-Culture Forms by Robyn R. Warhol

Politics, Persuasion, and Pragmatism: A Rhetoric of Feminist Utopian Fiction by Ellen Peel

Telling Tales: Gender and Narrative Form in Victorian Literature and Culture by Elizabeth Langland

Narrative Dynamics: Essays on Time, Plot, Closure, and Frames edited by Brian Richardson

Breaking the Frame: Metalepsis and the Construction of the Subject by Debra Malina

Invisible Author: Last Essays by Christine Brooke-Rose

Ordinary Pleasures: Couples, Conversation, and Comedy by Kay Young

Narratologies: New Perspectives on Narrative Analysis edited by David Herman

Before Reading: Narrative Conventions and the Politics of Interpretation by Peter J. Rabinowitz

Matters of Fact: Reading Nonfiction over the Edge by Daniel W. Lehman

The Progress of Romance: Literary Historiography and the Gothic Novel by David H. Richter

A Glance Beyond Doubt: Narration, Representation, Subjectivity by Shlomith Rimmon-Kenan

Narrative as Rhetoric: Technique, Audiences, Ethics, Ideology by James Phelan

Misreading Jane Eyre: *A Postformalist Paradigm* by Jerome Beaty

Psychological Politics of the American Dream: The Commodification of Subjectivity in Twentieth-Century American Literature by Lois Tyson

Understanding Narrative edited by James Phelan and Peter J. Rabinowitz

Framing Anna Karenina: Tolstoy, the Woman Question, and the Victorian Novel by Amy Mandelker

Gendered Interventions: Narrative Discourse in the Victorian Novel by Robyn R. Warhol

Reading People, Reading Plots: Character, Progression, and the Interpretation of Narrative by James Phelan

www.ingramcontent.com/pod-product-compliance
Lightning Source LLC
Chambersburg PA
CBHW030110010526
44116CB00005B/179